contents

iv   **Preface**
by Michael DeMarco, M.A.

CHAPTERS

1   **The Material Culture of the Martial Arts: Exhibiting Okinawan Karate — Exhibit Hall of Okinawan Karate**
by Anne Manyak, M.A. and Jim Silvan, B.A.

13   **Exploring Our Roots: Historical & Cultural Foundations of Ideology of Karate-do**
by Carrie Wingate, Ph.D.

44   **The Makiwara as a Tool for Learning**
by John R. Stebbins

52   **Three Distinctive Techniques of Pwang Gai Noon-ryu**
by Mary Bolz, B.S.

63   **The World Within Karate and Kinjo Hiroshi**
by Patrick McCarthy

76   **The Karate of Miyagi Chojun**
by John Porta and Jack McCabe

88   **The Sources of Power in Karate**
by Kazumasa Yokoyama

101   **The Okinawan Sai – A Kobudo Weapon for Self-defense**
by Mary Bolz, B.S.

116   **Control of Center: The Technical, Strategic, and Spiritual Foundations of Ko-ryu Karatedo**
by Robert E. Wolfe, II, B.A.

141   **An Interview with Brian Frost on Testing Through Tameshiwari**
by John C. Taylor, B.A.

151   **Supplementary Weight Training for Miyagi Chojun's Goju-ryu Karate**
by John Porta & Jack McCabe, B.A.

169   **An Interview with Uehara Seikichi on Motobu-ryu Udun-di Bujutsu**
by Richard B. Florence, M.A.

198   **Karate Techniques: Applied Physiology and Biomechanics**
by Ronald Freund, M.D.

203   **The Distinguishing Traits of Mas Oyama and Kyokushin Karate**
by Michael J. Lorden

230   **Without Spirit Budo is But an Empty Shell**
by Jon Bluming

244   **Index**

preface

What would you like to obtain from your research and practice of an Okinawan martial art? For an academic, it would be to obtain historical and cultural facts and details. For a practitioner, it would be to gain expertise in the combative skills. If you're interested in both, this first of a three-volume anthology is assembled for your convenience to facilitate your endeavors. These volumes assemble a wealth of material originally published during the two decades when the *Journal of Asian Martial Arts* was in print.

Hundreds of pages and photographs present the richness of Okinawan martial traditions, from the original combatives to those influenced by Chinese and mainland Japanese martial art styles. The variety of topics shown in the table of contents indicate the depth and breath in the chapters, along with the authors who are well-known for their meticulous research and practical skills in specific arts.

These three volumes dive deep into the history and culture of Okinawan martial arts. You'll find coverage of the actual artifacts—the material culture related to weaponry and training methods. Instructions from the masters details both open-hand techniques as well as with weapons. The chapters offer insights into the lives of many masters over the past few centuries, giving the *raison d'être* for these unique fighting arts—their reason for being.

Many streams of arts have contributed to the martial traditions found on the small island: Naha-*te*, Shuri-*te*, Fukien White Crane, Shorin, Goju, Motobu, Shotokan, Isshin, Kyokushin, Pwang Gai Noon, Shito, Uechi, and the list continues. . .

Along with the various styles come the associated training methods, such as conditioning exercises with weights and creatively designed apparatus, such as the punching post (*makiwara*), or stone lever and stone padlock-shaped weights. Some become battle-hardened by active and passive breaking of objects (*tameshiwari*), including wooden boards, baseball bats, rocks, and ice. The extensive use of weaponry is found in many Okinawan styles, often associated with their farming and fishing occupations.

Such a blend of history and culture make the Okinawan fighting traditions a fascinating field of study. Besides being such vital sources of information, these three volumes will prove enjoyable reading and permanent at-hand reference sources in your library.

Michael A. DeMarco, Publisher
Santa Fe, New Mexico
December 2016

Okinawan Martial Traditions Vol. 1

te, tode, karate, karatedo, kobudo

沖縄手

An Anthology of Articles from the *Journal of Asian Martial Arts*

Compiled by Michael A. DeMarco, M.A.

Disclaimer
Please note that the authors and publisher of this book are not responsible in any manner whatsoever for any injury that may result from practicing the techniques and/or following the instructions given within. Since the physical activities described herein may be too strenuous in nature for some readers to engage in safely, it is essential that a physician be consulted prior to training.

All Rights Reserved
No part of this publication, including illustrations, may be reproduced or utilized in any form or by any means, electronic or mechanical, including photocopying, recording, or by any information storage and retrieval system (beyond that copying permitted by sections 107 and 108 of the US Copyright Law and except by reviewers for the public press), without written permission from Via Media Publishing Company.

Warning: Any unauthorized act in relation to a copyright work may result in both a civil claim for damages and criminal prosecution.

Copyright © 2016 by Via Media Publishing Company
941 Calle Mejia #822, Santa Fe, NM 87501 USA

All articles in this anthology were originally published in the *Journal of Asian Martial Arts*. Listed according to the table of contents for this anthology:

Manyak, A. & Jim Silvan, J. (1992). Vol. 1 No. 4, pp. 100-111
Wingate, C. (1993). Vol. 2 No. 3, pp. 10-35
Stebbins, J. (1993). Vol. 2 No. 3, pp. 94-101
Bolz, M. (1993). Vol. 2 No. 3, pp. 82-93
McCarthy, P. (1994). Vol. 3 No. 2, pp. 90-99
Porta, J. & McCabe, J. (1996). Vol. 5 No. 2, pp. 62-71
Yokoyama, K. (1994). Vol. 3 No. 3, pp. 72-83
Bolz, M. (1995). Vol. 4 No. 1, pp. 84-99
Wolfe, R. (1995). Vol. 4 No. 3, pp. 76-99
Taylor, J. (1996). Vol. 5 No. 1, pp. 78-85
Porta, J. & McCabe, J. (1996). Vol. 5 No. 2, pp. 60-73
Florence, R. (1996). Vol. 5 No. 3, pp. 66-89
Freund, R. (1996). Vol. 5 No. 3, pp. 40-43
Lorden, M. (1997). Vol. 6 No. 3, pp. 60-79
Bluming, J. (1998). Vol. 7 No. 2, pp. 74-85

Book and cover design by Via Media Publishing Company
Edited by Michael A. DeMarco, M.A.

Cover illustration
Artistic interpretation of Master Matsumura Sokon (cir. 1800-1892), who greatly influenced the thoughts and practices of the martial arts on Okinawa.
© Illustration by Feodor Tamarsky • www.tamarskygallery.com

ISBN: 978-1893765405

www.viamediapublishing.com

chapter 1

The Material Culture of the Martial Arts: Exhibiting Okinawan Karate
— Exhibit Hall of Okinawan Karate —

by Anne Manyak, M.A. and Jim Silvan, B.A.

1) Painting of the God of Martial Arts taken from the *Bubishi*. *All photos courtesy of Jim Silvan.*

"The painting aids in setting the tone of the museum— one of reverence and respect for the multifaceted heritage and history of the martial arts."

Introduction

The martial arts are consistently characterized as a performance art. Although this portrayal is accurate, a material aspect of the art exists which can be displayed, such as associated artifacts and documented lore. By collecting and displaying the material aspects of the martial arts, a context is provided for examining the historical development as well as the variety of these arts. The material culture of the martial arts also provides a means for analyzing and separating legend from fact.

The Exhibit Hall of Okinawan Karate, established and operated by karate *sensei* (teacher) and martial arts historian Hokama Tetsuhiro,[1] brings together an ample collection of Okinawan martial arts paraphernalia: weapons, lineage charts, photographs, and art work (photo #1). This chapter presents a brief summary of the history of Okinawan martial arts, features an overview of Hokama's collection, and illustrates the ways the material aspects of the martial arts reflect its history. Specific attention will be given to analysis of the artifacts and folklore of the Okinawan martial arts tradition.

Background and History

In both size and population, Okinawa is the largest island of the Ryukyu Archipelago. The archipelago consists of 105 islands, many of which are no larger than rocks and several of which are still uninhabited (Pearson, 1969: 17). Okinawa, or as it is referred to in nineteenth century writings, the Great Loochoo, is sixty miles long and two to sixteen miles wide. It is rather astonishing that so small an island could be the birthplace of such a popular and widespread art form, as karate. In large part, this is due to the strategic location of Okinawa and the multitude of surrounding influences.

Located between the Pacific Ocean and the South China Seas, Okinawa has long been a trading post for the surrounding Asiatic cultures. As a result, it is a melting pot of a variety of cultures, customs, and arts. Thus, Okinawa is characterized by diversity and a distinctiveness that arises from the blending of many different cultures. The development, history, and styles of Okinawan karate, no less, reflect this larger national pattern.

The Okinawan martial arts have a long and rich history. Originally developed within family lineages as a secretive avocation passed down from generation to generation, the art eventually broadened and diversified into a complex and comprehensive system. Given that the art originated within a family context, has been passed on from sensei to student, and is dynamic and diverse, tracing historical origins is difficult.

Okinawan karate is comprised of a wide variety of Asiatic fighting forms: Japanese, Thai, Malay, Burmese, and Philippine. The most notable and easily traced influence, however, is Chinese. Communication between China and Okinawa was opened during the Ming Dynasty (1368-1644), during which time Chinese *kempo* (fighting art) was introduced to Okinawan culture. Although an indigenous Okinawan "empty-handed form of self-defense" called *te* (*tee*)[2] was likely to have been evolving long before the introduction of Chinese kempo, this Chinese influence provided the impetus for a more extensive development of a distinct and sophisticated Okinawan style (Silvan, in press).

Although it is difficult to trace and verify, it is believed that another indigenous Okinawan martial art, *kobujutsu*, or the method of fighting with weapons, was developing at the same time as *te*. However, in 1609, the Japanese invaded and conquered Okinawa. Although the veracity of folk tradition is inconclusive because no written documentation exists, Okinawan verbal lore maintains that the Japanese placed a ban on all indigenous fighting weaponry. Some accounts suggest that not only was a ban placed on weaponry, but also on the practice of any form of indigenous martial arts. Supposedly, Japanese occupiers confiscated all weapons and halted the manufacture and import of weapons including even ceremonial swords (Draeger and Smith, 1990: 58).

Okinawan martial arts practitioners, however, were well aware of the considerable disadvantages they faced against armed Japanese adversaries. In order not to attract the attention of Japanese invaders, yet to increase their effectiveness in self-defense, Okinawans incorporated the use of inconspicuous farm tools into their fighting practice. In addition to using farm tools as weapons, Okinawans also developed distinct fighting weapons, usually from available materials but unrelated to farming apparatus. Although te and kobujutsu developed separately and were practiced as distinct martial art forms in the past, today the two traditions are practiced together.

In the 1700s, Sakugawa Kanga (1733-1815) who is attributed the honor of "Father of Okinawan Karate," synthesized te and Chinese kempo to form the Shuri-te system (Kim, 1974: 20-25). The Shuri-te style was the first formalized Okinawan karate system and, therefore, the system that defined Okinawan karate as a distinctive martial art. Along with the founding of the Shuri-te system several other major and distinct Okinawan styles developed independently, such as Naha-te and Tomari-te. In addition to these, many other lesser known but nevertheless important family styles developed, all with numerous and diverse katas.

Hokama Tetsuhiro and The Exhibit Hall of Okinawan Karate

Hokama Tetsuhiro has an impressive family background in the martial arts. Both his great uncle and grandfather were practitioners and innovators of Okinawan karate. Hokama began his training in high school and has continued to pursued it. He is a seventh-degree blackbelt in the Goju-ryu system and also has expertise with martial art weaponry, especially the *bo*. His primary occupation is that of a high school computer science teacher. As a dedicated student of the martial arts, however, Hokama has established in Okinawa five *dojos* (training halls) which are under the association name Okinawan Goju-ryu Kenshi-kai. Along with his accomplishments in karate he has a keen passion for studying the history of Okinawan karate about which he has written several books including *History of Okinawa Karatedo* (1984) and *Okinawan Ancient Martial Arts Tools* (1989).³

Given Hokama's strong martial arts background, it is not surprising that throughout his life he has been collecting martial arts paraphernalia, much of which has been donated by other enthusiasts. In addition, Hokama has traveled extensively throughout China, collecting artifacts and lore and also putting together disparate pieces of information. Initially, Hokama used his first dojo as a place to display his collection and as a training studio. Overcrowding soon became a problem and he transformed the dojo into a permanent museum, which has two rooms to house his more than three hundred artifacts. The largest room (approximately 14,000 square feet) displays the majority of his collection; the second room (approximately two hundred square feet) provides space for the "overflow" of artifacts.

As an outgrowth of Hokama's interests, he has established a study group of karate blackbelts in order to exchange information about the history, philosophy, and technique of Okinawan karate. The study group consists of many blackbelts representing the various combative styles of Okinawan martial arts. Hokama's museum, study group, and his commitment to the historical study of Okinawan martial arts is largely responsible for our current understanding of the discipline.

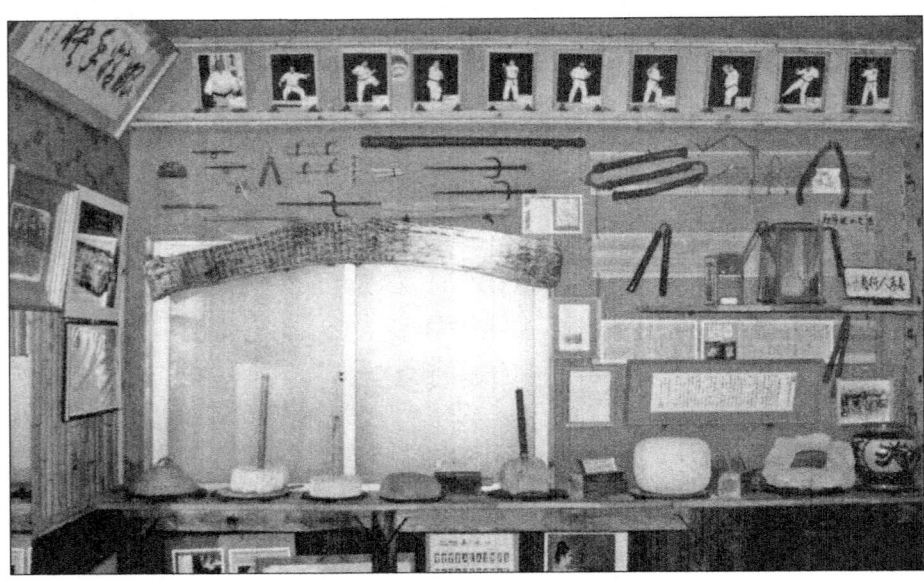

2) Overview of displays in Hokama's museum.
Notice the three-tiered arrangement of artifacts.

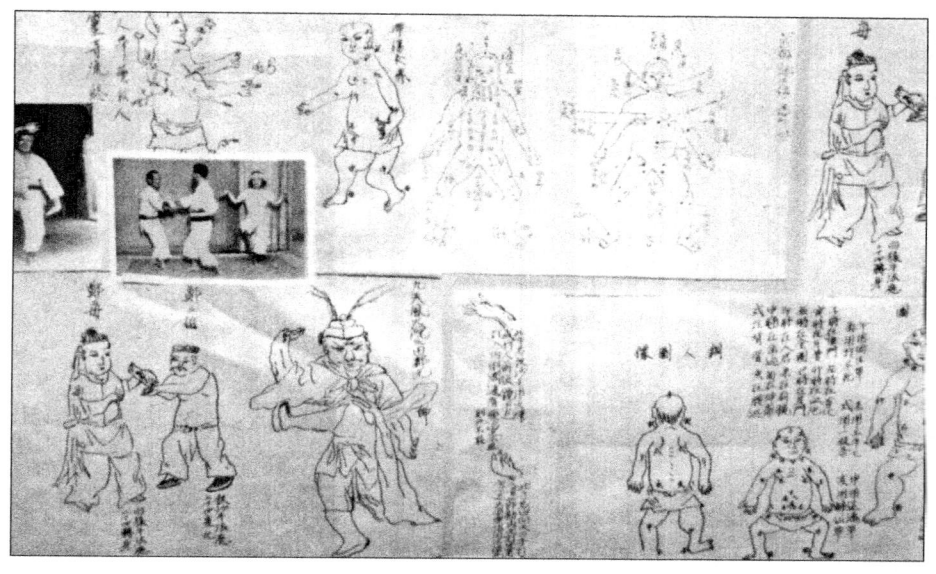

3) Illustrations of pressure points taken from the *Bubishi*.

The Collection

The tradition and history of the Okinawan martial arts is reflected in the material artifacts and lore displayed in Hokama's museum of karate. Material displays of the martial arts lend themselves to further speculation and inquiries into the historic development and lore of Okinawan martial arts. The museum is organized in a three-tiered fashion: the upper level displays photographs of karate masters and significant documents; the central level primarily exhibits weaponry; and the lower tier concentrates on various training aids and strengthening devices (photo 2).

When one enters the museum, the first item he notices is the large, impressive painting at the end of the room (photo 1 on page 1). It is painted on stone and depicts the God of the Martial Arts of the ancient Chinese martial arts fighting manual, *The Bubishi*. The painting aids in setting the tone of the museum—one of reverence and respect for the multifaceted heritage and history of the martial arts. Also replicated from the classic manual are drawings of various postures and pressure points (photo 3).

Perhaps the most striking aspect of the collection and that which is most open to interpretation is the weaponry. As mentioned above, many Okinawan weapons are believed to have their origins in early agricultural tools. Connections between modern day weapons, such as the *nunchaku, kai, tunfa, bo, suruchin,* and *sai* and conventional farm tools are readily discerned in Hokama's displays.

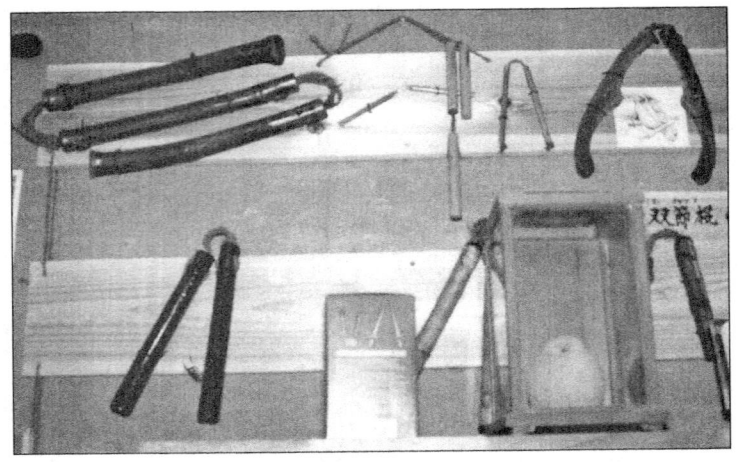

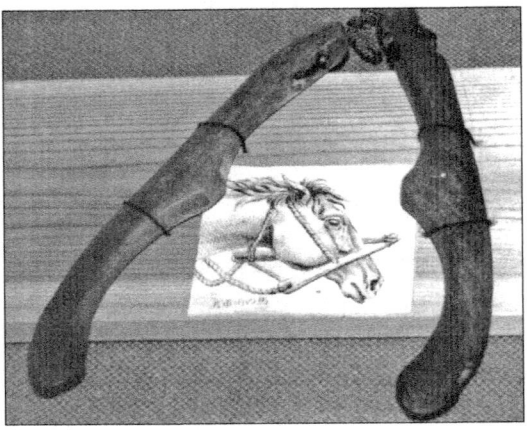

4-5) In the nunchaku display, an illustration shows a similarity to a horse's harness, indicating a possible origin for the weapon.

Popularized by Bruce Lee movies, the *nunchaku* (*kwagi*) is probably the most famous martial arts weapon. It is double-sided, made of hardwood, and hinged together end to end by silk cords or rope. Although lore suggests several origins for the nunchaku, such as an agricultural flailing tool used as a manual threshing device in rice fields (Draeger and Smith, 1990) or as a part to a traditional weaving machine, Hokama identifies as its origin a horse's harness (photos 4 and 5). The original shape has undergone years of modification and streamlining to attain its modem form. Because only an oral history of the nanchaku exists, it is unknown if the weapon originated in Okinawa or if the Okinawans had previous knowledge of the weapon from Southeast Asia or China. The weapon is used primarily for flinging and striking an opponent's pressure points.

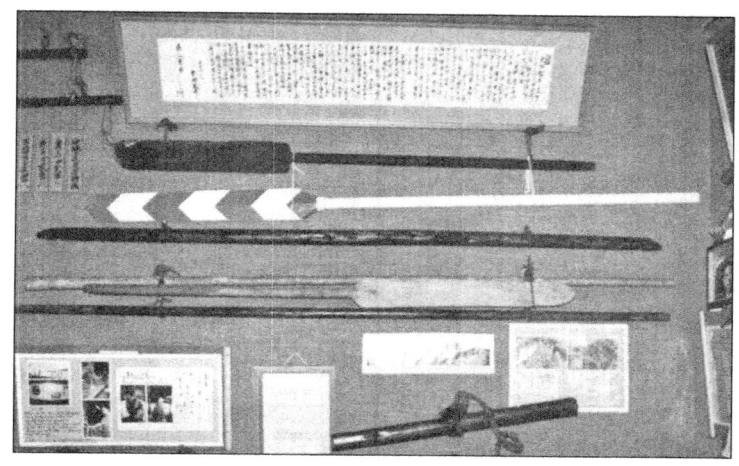

6) Kai display.
Also shown are several bos replica
of Matsumura Shokon's letter to students.

7-8) An alternative use of the kai as a prop
in traditional Okinawan dance (*odori*).

The *kai* (*ekku*) is a long, narrow piece of wood with a flattened end which is used primarily for detaining an opponent through blocking, striking, jabbing, and/or swinging. Its similarity to the common boat oar is readily apparent (photo 6). Since traditional Okinawa was characterized by fishing villages, boat oars would have been plentiful and their manufacture certainly outside the control of the Japanese. Like many of the martial arts weaponry, the kai is used in various ways, such as in traditional Okinawan dance (*odori*) (photos 7 and 8).

In the same photograph as the kai, directly above it, is pictured a replica of Matsumura Sokon's (1796-1893) letter to martial arts students. Matsumura was a very famous Okinawan karate practitioner and instructor who trained under Sakugawa Kanga. Matsumura is credited with being the founding father of the Shorin-ryu system. His letter encourages students to persist in training and to hone their mental and physical abilities to peak performance. The letter remains a source of inspiration for martial arts students today.

The *tunfa* (*tunkwa*) is a short tapering bar with an affixed "cylindrical grip projecting at right angles from the shaft" (Draeger and Smith, 1990: 67). The weapon is used in pairs, one for each hand (photo 9). The origin of the tunfa is believed to be the turning shaft from a traditional rice grinding mill. It is used by swinging or spinning the longer end while holding the short handle. It can be used for flinging, blocking, and seizing techniques. The weapon has made its impact on modern Western law enforcement as the precursor to the PR-24.

The *bo* is one of the oldest of all martial arts fighting weapons. It is basically a long stick or staff made of wood and is used primarily for blocking (photos 6, 9 and 10). Given its simplicity, the bo was likely to have been the most available weapon since any number of items could serve its purposes. Contrary to modern conceptions of the bo, it is not always six feet in length. As the art grew more sophisticated and the bo more standardized, the length was determined by the height of its practitioner. It is only in very recent times that the length of the bo has been standardized at six feet for purposes of mass production.

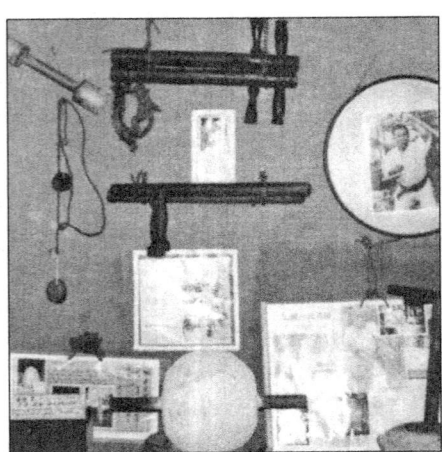

9) Tunfa display. Also, several training devices. 10) Hokama's weapon instructor, Matayoshi Shinpo, demonstrating the ancient art of *bojutsu* (bo technique).

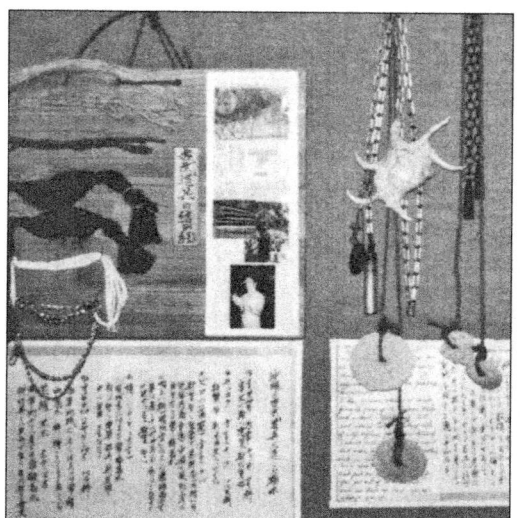
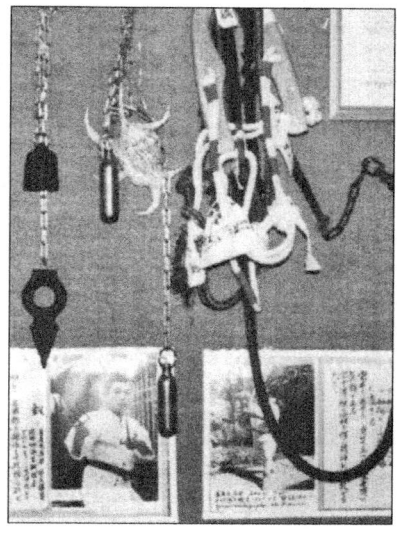

11-a-b) Suruchin display.

Various swinging objects, or *suruchin*, are also utilized in Okinawan martial arts. For example, as shown in photograph 11a-b, on the left side, several early forms are made from available organic materials, such as root, bark, horse-tail, hair, and silk, which were used for whipping and grappling. At the bottom of the photo, a metal chain is shown which has only recently been incorporated into swinging weaponry. The items in the center of the photograph are common swinging weapons made of available resources.

The *sai* is a lethal-looking, three-pronged metal weapon which is used for purposes of defense, especially when one is fighting an opponent armed with the bo or blade. Tracing the origin of the sai is particularly difficult. It has been suggested that, like the previously mentioned weapons, the sai was originally a pitchfork or an instrument used for pulling fishing nets out of the sea. Others, however, suggest it developed strictly for fighting purposes with no agricultural origins. Given that the sai is made only of solid iron, relatively recent origins are suggested though some argue its origins can be traced back to ancient Indonesian traditions (Draeger and Smith, 1990: 65). Clearly, more systematic studies are needed in this area.

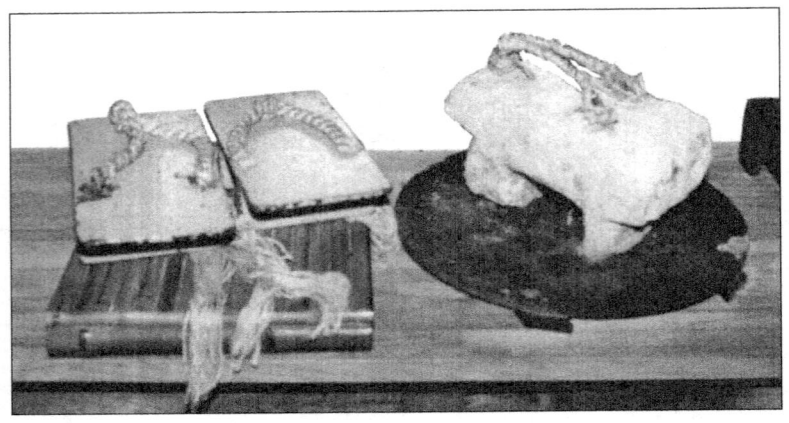

12) Geta displayed.

In addition to weapons, Hokama also has various training and strengthening devices which can be seen on the lower tiers of the displays. Iron clogs (photo 12) or *geta* are used to strengthen the muscles of the legs, abdomen, and back through kicking exercises. *Sushi* or stone padlocks are used to develop the muscles of the forearms, upper arms, and wrists and are the predecessors to modem dumbbells. Also included in Hokama's museum are *kami* (jars filled with sand which are for gripping), *sunabako* (stone bowls or buckets filled with rock for punching and hand techniques), *chishi* (for upper body techniques), and *ishibukro* (rocks wrapped in net for throwing, catching, and gripping). (See Higaonna, 1985, for demonstrations).

Left: Hokama demonstrating the use of the *sunabako* (sandbox filled with beans, sand, or rocks. A karateka thrusts his open hands into it in order to strengthen them.
Right: The *makiage kiga* or wrist roller was an early training device used to strengthen a karateka's wrists and forearms.

A common training device for practitioners of Goju-ryu karate is the *ishisashi* (stone padlock). Used during kata practice, the ishisashi is used to strengthen the entire upper torso. Hokama Sensei is pictured using the ishisashi during the practice of Sanchin Kata.

A precursor to the barbell, the *sashiishi* (natural stone weight) is simply a stone with a stick through it. It is used to develop upper body strength.

Discussion

The martial arts are an important and integral component of Okinawan culture. However, interest in the martial arts is, more often than not, generated by those outside of the Asian cultures and removed from the practice. Within the culture, the art is taken for granted and a prevailing apathy about the rich tradition exists. This attitude was clearly demonstrated when Hokama persistently offered his collection to a prefecture (state) museum and the offer was repeatedly declined. We can only be grateful that Hokama persevered in his endeavor and established his martial arts museum. It is within this historical context that a greater understanding of the history of the martial arts can be developed, systematic studies facilitated, and cultural enthusiasm generated.

Notes

[1] The convention in traditional Japan is for the surname (family) to precede the given (birth) name.
[2] Many karate terms are in Japanese. When possible, the indigenous Okinawan spelling will be provided in parentheses.
[3] These titles are English translations.

Bibliography

Draeger, D. and Smith, R. W. (1990). *Comprehensive Asian fighting arts*. Tokyo: Kodansha International.

Higaonna, M. (1985). *Traditional Karate-do: Okinawan Goju Ryu*. Tokyo: Japan Publications Trading Co., Ltd.

Hokama, T. (1984). *History of Okinawa karatedo*. Okinawa: Minami Publishing Company.

Hokama, T. (1989). *Okinawan ancient martial arts tools*. Okinawa: Shinpo Shupan Publishing Company.

Kim, R. (1974). *The weaponless warriors: An informal history of Okinawan Karate*. California: Ohara Publications, Inc.

Pearson, R. (1969). *Archaeology of the Ryukyu Islands: A regional chronology from 3000 BCE to the historic period*. Hawaii: University of Hawaii Press.

Silvan, J. (in press). *Okinawan karate: Its teachers and their styles*. NY: Vantage Press.

chapter 2

Exploring Our Roots: Historial and Cultural Foundations of Ideology of Karatedo
by Carrie Wingate, Ph.D.

Japan Karate Association Champions Tanaka Masahiko and Gerald Evans face-off at the World Cup. Ideology and practice are often at odds in modern karate. Many question whether competition has a place in the traditions of budo.
Photos courtesy of C. Wingate.

Introduction

In any human social endeavor, there is a distinction between ideology and practice. The ideology of a social group is the body of ideas that defines and gives meaning to it. These ideas can be found in the doctrine, myth, ritual, and symbolism adopted by the group's members. The ideology of a social group and the actual practices of the group and its members sometimes seem contradictory. Ideologies frequently distort social realities in order to maintain the viability of particular groups or processes.

We are often fascinated by the differences between ideology as the official self-interpretation of an entire social group and the actuality of its workings and the behavior of its members. As Berger (1963) notes, those who adopt and follow certain ideologies that seem to outsiders to be at odds with actuality are not liars or hypocrites. Nor are they victims of conspiracy. Rather, they are sincere believers in their own propaganda. If we wish to understand these social processes, our challenge is to uncover the self-delusions that emerge from the inconsistency between ideology and behavior. In doing so, we can deepen our understanding of ourselves as social beings and of society as something greater than the sum of its individual members.

Berger (1963) emphasizes that, having exposed ideological myths, we can advance either with cynicism or with compassion. A constructive or compassionate approach requires that we try to understand and create the conditions required for reconciling ideology and practice. Konzak (1980) argues that sport is especially well-suited to this kind of constructive and compassionate approach.

Wertz (1977) points out that, increasingly, individuals are participating in sports for reasons of self-exploration and self-development. He presents a cogent analysis of the potential contributions of the principles of Zen and yoga to self-discovery in sport. In light of such recent trends, several authors have argued that Oriental martial arts are particularly good choices for those who seek self-discovery through physical activity (e.g., Becker, 1982; Fuller, 1988; Kauz, 1977; Thirer and Grabiner, 1980).

This suggestion is supported by adherents of the martial arts, who have long claimed that practice of these arts provides significant benefit not only in the areas of self-defense and physical fitness, but also in terms of psychological adjustment, mental health, self-development, and spiritual advancement. Indeed, according to many masters of the traditional arts, these non-physical benefits are the ultimate purpose of such training (Funakoshi, 1973, 1988; Kauz, 1977; Stein, 1988; Ueshiba, 1984).

Ueshiba Morihei, founder of aikido, explained the purpose of the *budo*, or martial arts, as follows:

> True budo calls for bringing the inner energy of the universe in order, protecting the peace of the world and molding, as well as preserving, everything in nature in its right form. – Ueshiba, 1984: 9

Munenori Yagyu, in his seventeenth century treatise *The Household Transmission of the Art of Fighting*, tells us:

> the goal of training in the martial arts is to overcome six kinds of disease: the desire for victory, the desire for technical cunning, the desire to show off, the desire to psychologically overwhelm the opponent, the desire to remain passive in order to wait for an opening, and the desire to become free of these diseases. – Ueshiba, 1984: 8

In almost every traditional Shotokan karate *dojo* (training hall) in the world, the words of Funakoshi Gichin, revered as the Father of Karatedo, are displayed: "The ultimate aim of the art of karate lies not in victory or defeat, but in the perfection of the character of its participants."

Like other established forms of human endeavor, the martial arts have an ideology that defines their identity and purpose. And as in other social processes, there is often inconsistency between this ideology and actual practice. Konzak (1980) suggests that martial arts are more ideologically defined than most physical activities because of their cultural and historical roots in the Orient. In fact, the belief that martial arts are not "just sports" is a major component of their ideology (Kauz, 1977; Konzak, 1980; Random, 1977).

Oriental martial arts are now practiced throughout the world. Individuals participate in these arts for recreation, for health benefits, for sport competition, and for self-defense. In any of these aspects, there are many other activities that provide similar experiences. Yet the martial arts remain unique. This uniqueness is expressed in an ideology reflecting centuries of cultural and historical evolution, rooted particularly in the Japanese concepts of Zen, budo, and bushido.

A thorough understanding of the roots of the martial arts, based in Eastern culture in general and its martial traditions in particular, is necessary if we wish to understand and assess their ideology. Karate, a primarily weaponless art of Okinawa and Japan, is one of the most popular of the martial arts exported from the Orient. This chapter will describe the historical and cultural roots of karate, the philosophical and spiritual precepts that define its ideology, and, based on this ideology, the benefits of training as claimed in the martial arts literature and tradition.

KARATE AS A MARTIAL ART: HISTORICAL AND CULTURAL BACKGROUND

Karate and Karatedo

Though karate was first introduced to Japan during the 1920s, its traditions in Okinawa are centuries old. Like many Japanese and Okinawan arts, its roots can be traced to ancient China.

The art introduced to Japan in the 1920s as karate was known for several centuries in Okinawa as *te* or, later, *tode*. *Te* simply means "hand"; *tode*, "Chinese hand." Karate was adopted as the name for the Okinawan martial art around 1875 (Lovret, 1988). At that time, the characters used to write the word karate were the same as those for *tode* ("Chinese hand"); only the pronunciation differed. These characters are still used in a few Okinawan styles of karate (McCarthy, 1987).

手	*te*	=	hand
唐手	*to te*	=	Chinese hand
空手	*kara te*	=	empty hand

When Funakoshi introduced karate to Japan, he changed the first character of the word to one with the same pronunciation, but meaning "empty." Thus karate became "empty hand" rather than "Chinese hand." This has been the predominant name for the art since the 1920s; Funakoshi (1973, 1988) explains the reason for the change, including historical, sociological, and philosophical arguments, and concludes:

> Just as an empty valley can carry a resounding voice, so must the person who follows the Way of Karate make himself void or empty by ridding himself of all self-centeredness and greed. Make yourself empty within, but upright without. This is the real meaning of the "empty" in karate ... Karate alone explicitly states the basis of all martial arts. Form equals emptiness; emptiness equals form. The use of the character in karate is indeed based on this principle. – Funakoshi, 1988: 24-25

While the issue of whether to call this art "Chinese hand" or "empty hand" might seem trivial, it inspired a storm of controversy in Okinawa and Japan during the 1920s and 1930s. Some of the fervor had to do more with cultural identity and sociopolitical issues among the Japanese and Okinawan peoples than with philosophical arguments about the ultimate meaning of the martial arts, but in successfully adopting the "empty hand" version of karate, Funakoshi paved the way for the adoption of this martial art into Japanese culture. More importantly, the name change marks a philosophical turning point for the art of karate. Only with this change and its introduction into Japan did karate become *karatedo* (the Way of karate), part of the tradition of budo.

In Japanese, the word commonly expressed in English as "martial arts" is *budo*, which literally translates as "the Way of stopping conflict." This term is used as distinct from *bujutsu*, which means "military science." According to Lovret (1988), *budo* is a martial art practiced for self-development while *bujutsu* is a martial science practiced for combat. The essential element of the difference is *do*, which means "Way" or "path." In Zen Buddhism, a major influence on the development of martial tradition in Japan, a Way is a path or way of life which is practiced for its own sake and which brings about self-knowledge and spiritual enlightenment. (The concepts of Zen and budo will be discussed in greater detail in later sections of this chapter).

When Funakoshi introduced karatedo to Japan, he introduced much more than an Okinawan fighting art. By calling his art karatedo, rather than simply karate, he claimed a spiritual and philosophical foundation for karate training. As a *do*-form, karate was transformed from an art of fighting into a Way, a discipline whose practice led to self-development and enlightenment and which could rightfully claim a place among the traditional Japanese budo.

Bushido: The Samurai Creed

The concept most intimately tied to the warrior culture of Japan is that of *bushido*, the Way of the warrior. The ideology of bushido developed during the Tokugawa Shogunate (1603-1878); the first known use of the word was in 1685 (Ratti and Westbrook, 1973). It was during this relatively peaceful Edo period that *bushido*, the Way of the warrior class or samurai, began to develop into a coherent ethical system designed to produce principled citizens as well as effective soldiers.

Centuries of constant warfare had given the Japanese culture a pervasive martial spirit. This was personified by the samurai, the professional warrior class that arose during the eleventh century and continued to flourish and gain political power well into the seventeenth. Practice of the martial arts during this period was combat oriented, and the development of virtues such as courage, self-discipline, and loyalty was seen as necessary to the effective functioning of the warrior. The martial arts were not viewed as vehicles for self-development or enlightenment; rather, the principles and methods of Zen and other disciplines were incorporated into martial training because they would improve the functioning of warriors as warriors (Pieter, 1989; Ratti and Westbrook, 1973).

A present-day samurai on parade in Kyoto.

The principles of bushido have their origin in the *kyuba no michi*, or Way of the bow and the horse, that began to appear in the eleventh century. Derived from Shinto, Buddhist, and Confucian precepts, the Way includes ancestor worship, duty, obedience to sovereign and lord, righteousness of heart and spirit, patience, acceptance of fate, and especially, a correct attitude toward death. Over time, the kyuba no michi was refined and expanded to include more specific guidelines for behavior. In the early Edo Period, Tokugawa Ieyesu began to codify these guidelines into regulations for his warrior class. Apart from its influence on the samurai, bushido has been central to the development of the spirit and culture of the Japanese people as a whole (Nitobe, 1969; Pieter, 1989; Random, 1978; Ratti and Westbrook, 1973).

The victory of Tokugawa Ieyesu at the Battle of Sekigahara in 1600 put an end to the civil wars that had torn the country apart, and occupied the samurai, for several centuries. With the enforced peace that followed the subsequent establishment of the Tokugawa Shogunate in 1603, the samurai way of life was irrevocably altered. During the Edo period, the samurai continued to hold an elite status, and military virtues still dominated the ethos of Japanese life. The arts of combat continued to be developed and refined: even in peacetime a standing army of over 400,000 was maintained. With no wars to fight, however, the samurai's accustomed ways of life became untenable.

The samurai, now military officials, administrators, and farmers, found themselves relatively idle. New values began to develop, strongly encouraged by the government and clergy, who saw this class of idle and largely uneducated warriors as a danger to the nation.

Rielly (1975) describes the ethical norms of bushido, pointing out that these developed in part as a code to curtail the excesses of a warrior class given carte blanche in feudal Japanese society.

> The set of norms which bushido comprises seems to have remained consistent throughout a period of several centuries, even though some details may have been altered... They include frugality, stoicism, honor, benevolence, obedience, a sense of duty, a war-like spirit, loyalty, courage, a sense of morality, self-discipline, decorum, sobriety, honesty, practical ethics, and the study of war and administration.
> – Rielly, 1985: 64

Eventually, the samurai began to adopt many of the cultural attitudes of the traditional nobility. A new emphasis was placed on learning and the cultivation of artistic and spiritual pursuits. During the pre-Tokugawa period, only the children of the highest-ranking samurai received any education, and anti-intellectualism was prominent among the ranks of the warrior class. With the social and military changes of the Edo period, however, education became necessary to the samurai's functioning and was as a sign of civility and status.

In addition to the usual military specialties, young samurai were obliged to study the Chinese classics, music, religion, calligraphy, etiquette, mathematics, medicine, and astronomy (Ratti and Westbrook, 1973). During this period, there arose among the samurai a principle expressed as *bunburyodo*: the Ways of the pen and the sword are one. This principle, emphasizing the need for a balance of both martial and literary skills, was discussed by the great swordsman Musashi (1974) in his famous treatise *Go Rin No Sho* (*Book of Five Rings*), written in the seventeenth century.

During the Tokugawa shogunate, the principles of bushido became a highly codified set of guidelines for the behavior of the samurai. As the samurai were transformed from fierce warriors to learned administrators, the ethical system and values of bushido paved the way for other developments as well. While bushido continued to dominate Japanese cultural values (as it does to this day), enforced peace during the Edo period and the flourishing of Zen Buddhism opened the way for pursuing the martial arts as intentional vehicles for self-development and enlightenment rather than simply ways of war. Spiritual development became valued as a virtue in itself rather than merely as a way of controlling the warrior class or improving its effectiveness. Several written works were produced in the early years of the Edo period encouraging this emphasis (e.g., Musashi, 1974; Takuan, 1986; Wilson, 1984). This change in attitudes was a major factor in the development of budo.

Budo

It was during the Tokugawa Shogunate that aspects of *bujutsu* (military sciences) and the emerging *bushido* (the code of the warrior) were developed into *budo*, the Way of stopping conflict. As previously noted, budo is the practice of a martial art for the sake of self-development rather than for combat (*bujutsu*).

Classical budo first emerged in Japan at the beginning of the Tokugawa period, with the development of *kendo* (the Way of the sword) from *kenjutsu* (the techniques of the sword). Other martial disciplines became *do* forms, and new martial arts developed during this period as well (Pieter, 1989). Though most classical *do* forms evolved from classical bujutsu, there are important differences between the two.

The orientation toward actual combat in bujutsu is central to the art.

Discipline and virtue follow combat in importance and only insofar as they contribute to the warrior's success as a warrior. Budo, on the other hand, are spiritual disciplines. D. T. Suzuki, in his introduction to *Zen in the Art of Archery* (Herrigel, 1953), explains this:

> One of the most significant features we notice in the practice of archery, and in fact of all the arts as they are studied in Japan... is that they are not intended for utilitarian purposes only or for purely aesthetic enjoyments, but are meant to train the mind; indeed, to bring it into contact with the ultimate reality. – Herrigel, 1953, Introduction: 1

Likewise, Draeger describes the budo:

> All of these disciplines are complicated, intricate challenges in the pursuit of a better way of life and are based on the firm conviction that no man is as complete a human being [now] as he can be after sufficient experience with the "do." – Draeger, 1973: 25

It must be emphasized that the unarmed budo, such as judo, aikido, and especially karatedo, are taught not as combat systems, but as self-defense. The distinction is critical. Practitioners of these arts are not learning to fight; they are learning to defend themselves against attack. Ultimately, in these philosophical systems, self-defense entails avoiding conflict altogether. The ideal budo master is one who has never used his skill. This is hardly the case for a master of bujutsu.

Another essential difference between bujutsu and budo lies in their practitioners. As combat forms, bujutsu were developed and practiced by warriors. Budo, especially the more recent disciplines, are intended for study by anyone. In fact, one of the aspects that distinguish contemporary budo such as karate, judo, and aikido from sports is that the former may be practiced and developed throughout life, without regard to age, gender, or strength. Rank is based, not on physical prowess, but on mastery of technique, development of character, and deepening understanding of the principles involved in the art.

While Zen and other religious practices in Japan had a notable influence on bujutsu only insofar as they contributed to the ability of the warrior to do his job, spiritual aspects are central to the meaning of budo. Concepts of nature and original energy, of the five elements, of spirit and the void, and of conscious development of power may have been included in some esoteric forms of bujutsu, but in budo they were pivotal in the development of both technique and awareness. It is the emphasis on such concepts in the budo that has led some writers to approach the martial arts as occult phenomena (e.g., Barclay, 1973; Layton, 1989).

The principles of budo are deeply rooted in Japanese religious practices, including Shinto, Confucianism, Daoism, and especially Zen Buddhism. Several volumes have been devoted specifically to the relationship between Zen and the martial arts (Deshimaru, 1982; Herrigel, 1953; Hyams, 1979), and most books about the martial arts devote some space to Zen (Harrison, 1955; Hassell, 1980; Kauz, 1977; Payne, 1981; Random, 1977; Scott and Pappas, 1985; Stein, 1988).

"Budo may be practiced without regard to age, gender, or strength."

Zen and the Martial Arts

The introduction of Zen to Japan around the thirteenth century coincided with the rise of the samurai and the establishment of feudalism (Random, 1977; Ratti and Westbrook, 1973). While it is difficult to describe what Zen is, it is easy to say what it is not: Zen is not a religion or a system of ideas. Zen has no dogma or ritual. It offers nothing: no paradise, no salvation, no earthly or heavenly reward.

Zen explains nothing because explanation is objectification, removing us from the experience of the moment. Ultimate understanding exists within us; we need only remove the obstacles to our perception. Awareness of this understanding is called *satori* and is available to all. Different schools of Zen have different methods for experiencing satori; in general, one practices by emptying the mind of conscious thought and practicing correct breathing and self-discipline.

Deshimaru (1982) describes the elements of Zen that are important to the *budoka*, or martial artist: pacification of the emotions, tranquil compliance with the inevitable, self-control, intimate understanding of death, and detachment from the material. In addition, he emphasizes that Zen is a way of life: "You have to practice until you die" (p. 14).

In practicing Zen, one learns to direct the mind toward right action by not thinking. Being aware in the present, without attachment to past or future, one becomes aware of one's true nature and thus of the true nature of the Buddha and ultimate reality. Zen is an experience; its only goal is the treading of the path itself.

Zen teaches that mind and body are one.
Physical hardship forges the spirit; spiritual practice perfects technique.

Zen, like budo, emphasizes self-discipline, breathing, and correct attitude as a way of aligning oneself with universal energy and thus experiencing harmony. Zen is not meditation, but unconsciousness, the absence of thought. Zen does not seek a special state of illumination, but an ongoing inner unity. Thus, one does not achieve enlightenment, but lives in such a way as to become aware of one's own enlightenment.

Zen is process, not product, and can be applied to every aspect of our daily lives. Those who practice Zen do not isolate themselves from the everyday world; they cultivate Zen in it.

These aspects of Zen were central to the development of budo. Experience is seen as the ultimate teacher, and students are trained in a non-verbal, highly intuitive manner. Hardship is necessary to develop self-discipline, to break our attachments to material things, to end our reliance on conscious thought, and to forge the spirit. Above all, budo training is of the whole person and is meant to influence the whole life. One carries one's training out into the world and applies it in all things.

In Zen, as in other Japanese spiritual disciplines, the mind and body are not separate entities. We speak of them as two because of the limitations of both our language and our understanding of reality. The concepts of physical, mental, and spiritual training are heuristics that allow us to communicate aspects of the human experience, but they fail to capture the essential truths of ultimate reality.

As this is reflected in both Zen practice and in budo, we cannot train the body without training the mind and the spirit. All are one. This is why physical hardship is necessary to forge the spirit and why spiritual practices are essential for perfecting physical techniques. This is also why martial artists advance in rank according to their holistic development and not their physical ability. Thus, the Japan Karate Association describes its highest ranks in terms of mastering "a high level of karate both in technique and in soul." The highest rank attainable is that of tenth *dan* or level, and consists of those who have mastered completely the secret of karate and entered into a transcendental level!" (Japan Karate Association, 1988).

HISTORICAL ASPECTS OF OKINAWAN KARATE

Okinawan Karate

Most historical accounts agree that Okinawan tode was a combination of an indigenous Okinawan fighting art (*te*) heavily influenced by techniques of Chinese boxing (*quanfa*). Many of the great Okinawan masters studied in China, and obvious similarities exist between Okinawan karate techniques and the fighting arts of China, especially those of Fujian Province (Kim, 1974; McCarthy, 1987; Nakaya, 1986, Scott and Pappas, 1985).

Weapons bans, imposed on the Okinawans at various points in their history, encouraged the refinement of empty-hand techniques. *Kobudo*, or traditional weapon ways, also developed in response to these bans. Kobudo employs weapons derived from farming and fishing tools and is part of most karate training in Okinawan *ryu* (styles).

While the karate introduced to Japan in the 1920s was presented as a *do* form and in fact quickly became a sport as well, in Okinawa the art developed in deadly earnest as self-defense against armed and unarmed assailants and was usually practiced in secret. During Japanese occupation of the island in the sixteenth and seventeenth centuries, karate and kobudo were often used against samurai armed with swords. There is little evidence in Okinawan te or early karate of the philosophical and spiritual emphasis found later in the Japanese version of this art; however, some aspects of the samurai creed of bushido can be seen.

Little has been written about the historical development of Okinawan karate, and even less is available in English. Its practice as a secret art and the lack of a strong literary tradition in Okinawa combine to make reliable information difficult to obtain. It seems clear, however, that Okinawan te was taught as a form of self-defense and that personal characteristics of self-discipline, self-control, etiquette, and respect for others were emphasized in training (Kim, 1974). The *Bubishi*, the only extant historical writing about Okinawan te, has never been published in translation, but its contents include chapters on etiquette, herbal medicine, resuscitation of opponents, and pharmacology (McCarthy, 1987).

Kim (1974), in his collection of stories about the great Okinawan karate masters, tells of many instances in which these masters manifested the values of bushido. In addition, their teachings evidently included the tenets that te was to be used only for self-defense (not to attack or for show), that one proficient in te should seek to avoid conflict if at all possible and refrain from inflicting harm on one's opponents, and that such training carried with it an obligation to protect others and serve the cause of justice. Mental and spiritual aspects of training seem to have been emphasized in te as well.

By the time of Matsumura Sokon (1796-1893) and Itosu Yasutsune (1830-1915), two of the great nineteenth century *meijin* (masters), karate training explicitly included the ideals of character development. In 1901, Itosu began the first public instruction of karate as part of the physical education program in the Okinawan public schools. It is not entirely clear how this came about, but the program was apparently quickly accepted. Public demonstrations of karate also became frequent and well-received in Okinawa after the turn of the century (Kim, 1974).

Funakoshi Gichin introduced Okinawan karate to Japan. Here, the "Father of Modern Karate" poses with his senior student, Nakayama Masatoshi.

The first public demonstration of karate in Japan was given in 1917 by Funakoshi Gichin, at the Butoku-den in Kyoto (Hassell, 1984). This and subsequent demonstrations greatly impressed many Japanese, including then Crown Prince Hirohito, who was very enthusiastic about the Okinawan art. In 1922, Dr. Kano Jigoro, founder of judo, saw Funakoshi demonstrate at the first National Athletic Exhibition in Tokyo. Dr. Kano invited Funakoshi to demonstrate at the famous Kodokan Dojo and asked him to remain in Japan to teach karate. This sponsorship was instrumental in establishing a base for karate in Japan; as an Okinawan "peasant art," karate would have been scorned by the Japanese without the backing of so formidable a martial arts master.

Japanese Karatedo

From the beginning, Funakoshi presented karate to the Japanese people as a *do* form. The traditional Japanese bujutsu included several unarmed disciplines. Two of those, jujutsu and aikijutsu, had been developed around the turn of the century into *do* forms: judo and aikido. Other budo disciplines common in Japan included *kendo* (the Way of fencing), *iaido* (the Way of the sword), and *kyudo* (the Way of the bow).

Funakoshi followed the example of the traditional Japanese budo and presented karatedo as an art of self-defense whose study would lead the practitioner into greater self-awareness and spiritual advancement. He emphasized the development of character and the virtues of honor, sincerity, effort, respect for others, and self-control. In dojo where Funakoshi's style, Shotokan-ryu, is practiced, students recite the *dojo kun* (ethics of the dojo) at every class:

> Seek perfection of character! Be faithful!
> Endeavor! Respect others!
> Refrain from violent behavior!

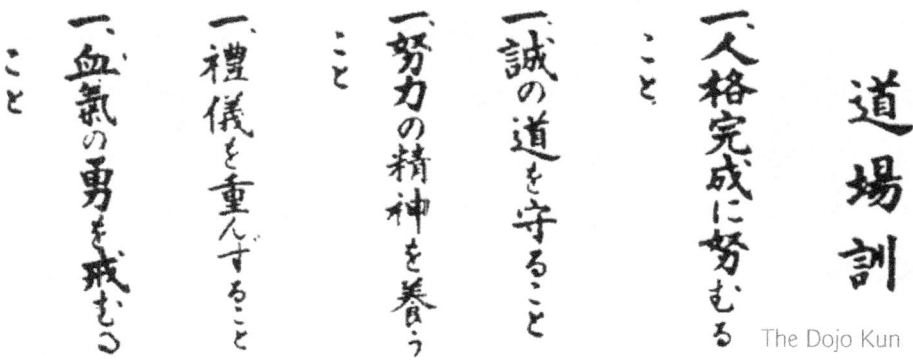

The Dojo Kun

Funakoshi also established the *shoto niju kun* (twenty guiding principles), which are studied by students of Shotokan-ryu. While some of these refer specifically to karate practice, most are philosophical in nature and stress the importance of correct attitude in all things, and the wider implications of karatedo as a way of life:

1) Karate begins with courtesy and ends with courtesy.
2) There is no first attack in karate.
3) Karate is a great benefit to justice.
4) Know yourself first, then others.
5) Spirit first; technique second.
6) Always be ready to release your mind.
7) Misfortune always comes from lack of effort.
8) Do not think that karate training is only in the dojo.
9) You must practice a lifetime to learn karate; there is no limit.
10) Practice karate in everything you do, and you will find *myo* [the mystery].
11) Karate is like hot water. If you don't give it heat constantly, it will be cold water again.
12) Don't think you have to win. Think rather, you don't have to lose.
20) Always think and devise ways to live the precepts every day.

Collegiate karate clubs were essential to the spread of karate in Japan. This photo was taken at the Takushoku University Karate Club early in the 1950s. Nakayama Masatoshi, front row, second from left. Nishiyama Hidetaka, second row, far right. Okazaki Teruyuki, back row, third from right.

Funakoshi and the other Okinawan teachers who brought karate to Japan focused on social groups that they thought would be most receptive to this Okinawan art and most influential in promoting it. University students and the intelligentsia were particular targets. The many clubs established at colleges and universities were essential for the propagation of karate in Japan and have remained the core of the Japanese karate world for several decades. As young karate men graduated and took their places in the world of Japanese business, finance, and government, they took their karate loyalties with them, and before long karate had many friends in high places.

The establishment of karate among young collegians also contributed significantly to the development of sport karate, a development at odds in many ways with karatedo. The effects of this aspect of the evolution of karate have been felt primarily in practice; nevertheless, sport karate has had some influence on the ideology of the art. Most traditional Japanese ryu, however, continue to promulgate karate as a *budo*, or martial Way.

Contemporary Karatedo

Ideologically, the traditional styles and schools of Japanese karate explain karatedo as a way of life, the purpose of which is to develop harmony and awareness within oneself. Over the course of the last few decades, sport karate has become increasingly popular and even in traditional styles has had an enormous influence on the practice of the art. Despite the steadily growing popularity of competition, the ideology of traditional karate continues to be that of karatedo. Sport karate is seen as a limited aspect of the art, not to be pursued for itself alone.

According to Nakayama Masatoshi, Chief Instructor of the Japan Karate Association for thirty years, "karatedo is a martial art for the development of character through training, so that the karateka can surmount any obstacle, tangible or intangible" (Nakayama, 1977: 11). He elaborates:

> If karate is practiced solely as a fighting technique, this is cause for regret. The fundamental techniques have been developed and perfected through long years of study and practice, but to make any effective use of these techniques, the spiritual aspect of this art of self-defense must be recognized and must play the predominant role.
> – Nakayama, 1977: 9

This ideology is reflected in the structure of traditional karate training. Over the last three decades, Japanese karate has been introduced throughout the world. Wherever it is taught, its structure and principles remain the same, reflecting the cultural roots of its Japanese origins. Elements of Zen, of bushido, and of budo can be seen in almost all aspects of traditional karate.

Karate Training

The *dojo*, or training hall, in which karate is taught may take many forms. Some dojos are devoted exclusively to karate training, while others consist of borrowed space in schools, gymnasia, or community centers. Regardless of its form, however, when used for karate training, the dojo is a *dojo*—a training hall for budo. Literally, *dojo* means "a hall for the study of a Way." As such, the dojo is a special place, where different rules and codes of conduct apply.

Upon entering a traditional Japanese dojo, one removes oneself from the ordinary world. The physical space occupied by the dojo may, at other times, be a gymnasium, a meeting room, or a church basement, but when karate is taught there, this space is transformed. Likewise, one's identity in the "outside world" is also left behind. The professional or social status enjoyed (or endured) in daily life becomes irrelevant in the dojo.

Nakayama Masatoshi teaching. "Karatedo is a martial art for the development of character through training."

The traditional Japanese emphasis on respect and form becomes obvious from the moment one enters a dojo. Shoes are removed immediately, and upon entering the actual training space, one bows with respect toward the front of the hall. In a self-contained dojo, the front wall will display a portrait of the founder of the style and possibly flags (Japanese and national) and inspirational inscriptions (preferably Japanese calligraphy).

The bow of respect upon entering and leaving the dojo floor has two meanings. First, it displays respect for the training space itself, as a place where a single purpose will be pursued. Second, the bow demonstrates respect for the traditions and teachings of the art and for those who have gone before.

Karate students in traditional Japanese ryu wear plain white uniforms, or karate-gi. The gi must be clean and in good repair at all times and unadorned except for, possibly, an association patch on the chest. Street clothes, athletic attire, and colored or decorated gi are not allowed. Even when practicing alone in the dojo, a karateka is expected to wear a gi. Inappropriate clothing signifies disrespect—for the style, the dojo, and the individual displaying it.

White uniforms were introduced by Kano Jigoro, the founder of judo, around the turn of the century. In addition to signifying purity, the white gi conceals the "outside" status of the *budoka* (martial artist). Identical clothing reinforces the principle that one's identity in the dojo is independent of his identity outside the dojo. Status in the dojo is determined by seniority and rank.

The social structure of a traditional karate dojo, like that of Japanese social groups, is a rigid hierarchy. Respect and etiquette are of supreme importance, and the relative status of the individuals in any social interaction determines the degree of respect and the forms of etiquette required of each.

The *sensei* (teacher), whether of Japanese ancestry or not, commands absolute respect and authority. His position is patriarchical; he is responsible for overseeing the training and personal development of his students. They, in return, accept his authority and follow his teachings without question. This expectation has led to many misunderstandings between Japanese instructors and their non-Japanese students, but even in dojo with Western sensei, this expectation of unquestioning obedience and deference is maintained.

The dojo is marked by rigid rules of hierarchy and etiquette. The photo shows black belts preparing to bow to judges before an international ranking examination.

The social relationship between *sempai* (seniors) and *kohai* (juniors) is only slightly less rigid. One's sempai is, technically, anyone who has trained longer or is of higher rank than oneself. Sempai are entitled to respect and obedience from their kohai and, in turn, have the responsibility of overseeing their juniors' progress in karatedo. Since direct communication between a sensei and the lower ranks of students is rare, sempai are generally responsible for imparting informal teaching, correction, discipline, and advice.

The lines of communication in a dojo are similarly well-defined. Generally speaking, one approaches only those closest in rank to oneself. For a beginner, for instance, to directly approach an instructor or high-ranking black belt with a question or for casual conversation is considered rude. Likewise, those of high rank will frequently order a student of lower rank to correct or tutor a beginner rather than doing so themselves.

A traditional karate class is highly structured. When the instructor enters the floor, the students cease all activity and quickly line up, according to rank, facing the front wall (*shomen*). The instructor kneels, and at a command from the senior student, the class follows. After a brief period of meditation, the class, upon command, bows to the front, displaying respect for the style, its founders, and its traditions. The instructor turns to face the class, and the command is given to bow to him.

Correct attitude and posture is maintained at all times while training. Students bow to the sensei if they need to turn away from him (to adjust their gi, for instance) and to each other at the beginning and end of any partner exercises. These bows indicate respect for one's fellow student and an intention to do one's best. No conversation is permitted, and questions are only rarely entertained.

Traditional karate is taught in an intuitive manner. Little explanation or correction is offered; it is believed that students will find deeper understanding if they discover correct technique on their own. Training consists of seemingly endless repetitions of *kihon* (basic techniques), *kata* (prearranged forms), and *kumite* (partner sparring drills, also usually prearranged). This repetition is believed to serve two purposes: techniques become ingrained and can then be executed automatically when needed, and by driving the body beyond the point of exhaustion and mental control, spirit is forged.

Students in traditional karate classes are frequently exhorted not to let conscious thought control their bodies. The nature of the training is such that dwelling on a previous or future moment is liable to lead to failure, if not to injury, in the present. The mind is to remain calm, resting in the present moment, and flowing with the activity around it.

While the "official" ideology of traditional karate as expressed in books, handouts, and dojo brochures reflects the philosophical ideals of budo, the ideology expressed on the training floor tends more to *bushido*, the warrior's code. Spirit is stressed above all, sometimes beyond the bounds of safety. Students are exhorted to continue "with spirit" when they become exhausted or injured. Any display of emotion, from friendliness to frustration, is considered a lack of self-control. To leave a training session before its end, even because of sickness or injury, is cause for shame. The karateka should display the ideal spirit of a warrior: one moment calm and intent, ready to meet any attack, and the next, fierce and intense, capable of destroying any opponent. Presence of mind is paramount in either mode.

The elements of karatedo introduced by Funakoshi are emphasized in training as well. Character, sincerity, effort, etiquette, and self-control are the essential components of the martial spirit. Students are encouraged to "just keep training" and not concern themselves with lack of progress or inadequate technique. Sincerity and effort, combined with proper respect and attitude, are sufficient to develop the spirit and techniques of karatedo.

Bushido in Karatedo

Training in traditional karate ryu is deeply rooted in bushido. This heritage is clearly reflected in many of the structures of karate training, as described above. The virtues of etiquette, decorum, obedience, stoicism, duty, loyalty, and self-discipline, central to the ethical code of the Japanese warrior, are strongly emphasized in the traditional dojo as well.

Another aspect of the heritage of bushido is reflected in one of the most popular karate maxims: *ikken hissatsu* (to kill with one blow). Karate *waza* (techniques) must always be executed with the spirit of ikken hissatsu. Students are exhorted that they have but one chance and must make their single technique count. The sparring form considered by many to be the most expressive of karate's essence involves single attacks that are neutralized and countered almost instantaneously, with each partner executing only one technique.

Bushido emphasizes the warrior's need for total commitment to action as well as for courage, discipline, and spirit. In both the armed and unarmed budo, this sense of total commitment is emphasized in training and considered an ideal for which to strive. Training methods, both physical and mental, are designed to encourage and cultivate this attitude of concentration and commitment.

While this karate maxim reflects the fierceness and intensity of the Japanese warrior spirit, it also reflects the practical development of karate. The concept of ikken hissatsu had great significance in the days when

Okinawan te was used to defend against armed opponents. Facing a samurai with *katana* (sword) raised, one could be quite certain that if a single blow failed to kill the opponent, another chance was unlikely.

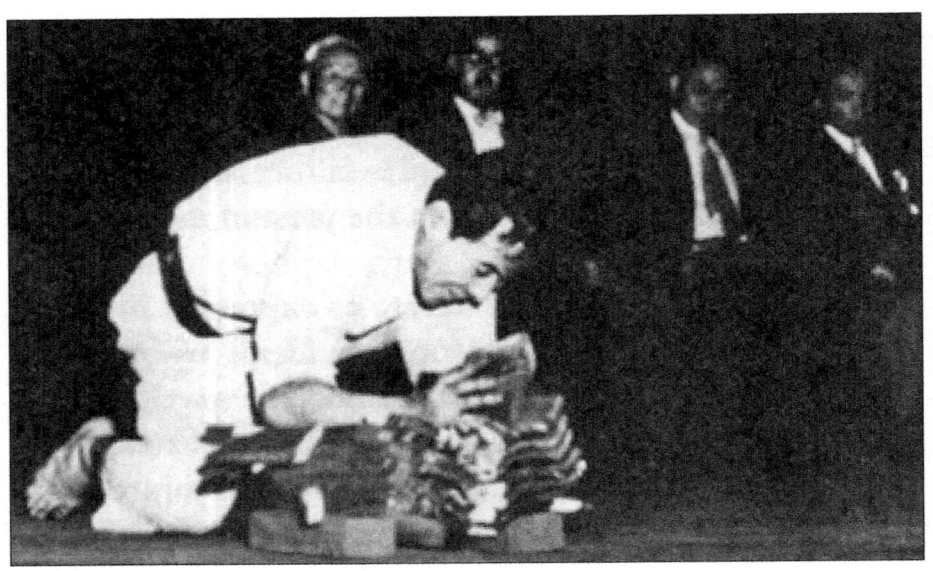

Tameshiwari (breaking) demonstrates the unity of spirit and technique. Funakoshi (sitting far left) looks on as a senior student smashes through a stack of roofing tiles.

Nakayama (1977) comments on this aspect of karate training:

To be capable of inflicting devastating damage on an opponent with one blow of the fist or a single kick has indeed been the objective of this ancient Okinawan martial art. But even the practitioners of old placed stronger emphasis on the spiritual side of the art than on the technique. Training means training of body and spirit. . .
– Nakayama, 1977: 9

Many other aspects of bushido are reflected in the ideology of karatedo; this is inevitable, considering the extent to which Japanese society itself reflects these ideals. Karate-jutsu developed in Okinawa, a country dominated for several centuries by Japan and greatly influenced also by China (whence many aspects of Japanese culture also derived). Karatedo, its offspring, developed in Japan itself and reflects the unique and homogeneous culture of that nation as well as its Okinawan ancestry.

Budo in Karatedo

Because budo evolved from bushido in many respects, a clear separation of the elements of each in karatedo is difficult. The principles emphasized in the structure of day-to-day karate training seem primarily to stress the behavioral mandates of bushido. The philosophical and spiritual elements of budo are sometimes less readily identifiable, but the significance of their influence is nonetheless clear.

If *ikken hissatsu* (to kill with one blow) exemplifies the spirit of bushido in karatedo, then *karate ni sente nashi* (in karate there is no first attack) exemplifies the spirit of budo. One of the key elements differentiating budo from bujutsu is the avoidance of conflict. In bujutsu there is no such thought; conflict is what such training is all about. In budo, however, one practices an art to gain mastery over oneself and, in doing so, finds awareness and enlightenment.

By learning to resolve conflicts within themselves, karateka are better able to avoid conflicts with others. The stories handed down of the exploits of great karate meijin do not describe their greatest fights; rather, they tell of how these men, through wit, wisdom, and benevolence of character, evaded physical confrontations and served the cause of justice (Funakoshi, 1973, 1975, 1988; Kim, 1974).

Karate's emphasis on repetition and intuitive
learning has its roots in budo and Zen.

Karate ni sente nashi emphasizes that karate techniques are for self-defense only and that, ideally, physical encounters are a last resort. "For to win one hundred victories in one hundred battles is not the highest skill. To subdue the enemy without fighting is the highest skill" (Funakoshi, 1973: 248).

Another reflection of budo philosophy in karatedo is the maxim *domukyoku* (no limitation for life).

> Perhaps more than any other saying, this mirrors the essence of karatedo training. Even though human beings have physical limitations which may be reached in middle age, the mind and spirit can continue to make progress. Thus, the practitioner of the *do* forms of martial arts sees his art as an endeavor that may be continued throughout life.
>
> – Rielly, 1985: 91

This saying is repeated by Funakoshi in his *shoto niju kun*: "you must practice a lifetime to learn karate; there is no limit."

Many other sayings express the budo philosophy and Zen heritage of karatedo. Some of these are precepts of the budo in particular, while others come from Zen and apply to all *do* forms.

The budo aspects of karate ideology can be seen in traditional karate training as well as in its precepts. Because Zen was embraced by Japanese culture and the samurai in particular at the same time that budo was developing as a Way, many aspects of budo have a strong Zen flavor.

The intuitive methods of traditional karate instruction come from the traditions of budo and Zen. Unlike bujutsu, whose methods are logical and instructions explicit, the *do* forms tend to depend on intuitive learning and self-discovery. Understanding is infinitely more valuable and enlightening if derived from personal experience; in fact, the nature of *seishin kyoiku* (spiritual education) decrees that true understanding can come only from within.

Special instructor training programs began in the 1950s. Here, Japan Karate Association trainees Nishiyama Hidetaka (far right) and Okazaki Teruyuki (second from left) assist their juniors.

Even today, many traditional karate instructors give little explicit instruction and even less feedback in their teaching. According to true budo philosophy, performance of *waza* (technique) is an outward manifestation of inner enlightenment. The instructor cannot tell a student how to perform or correct waza; the student must find this within himself. Likewise, principles of movement and strategy come from experience and a process of discovery.

In the major schools of Japanese karate, this approach to teaching has been tempered considerably by several factors. In their efforts to export karatedo to the rest of the world, the Japan Karate Association found it necessary to present a more rational and scientific basis for training. To this end, they developed an instructor-training program that provided background in such areas as functional anatomy, biomechanics, physiology, psychology, and other technical subjects (Hassell, 1984).

Despite this intensive and unique training, however, most Japanese karate instructors continued to teach according to the old methods, emphasizing constant drill and repetition. With the development of martial sports, of which karate is one of the most popular, more effective teaching methods became necessary, and it was probably this, in combination with the insistence of Western students on explanation, that led to the gradual adoption of less intuitive methods. These methods are, however, by no means the rule in traditional karate dojo even now, especially those that explicitly emphasize karate training as budo.

Another aspect of karate training that reflects budo philosophy is, of course, the emphasis on spiritual development. While, on the floor of the dojo, little mention is generally made of things spiritual, instructors occasionally provide short (and impromptu) lessons on self-development and personal growth as these relate to training. Such lessons may specifically refer to aspects of budo, emphasizing the tenets of karate maxims such as the *dojo kun* and the *shoto niju kun*, or they may more closely resemble the kind of inspirational talks often delivered by coaches to their teams, emphasizing the importance of good character, personal goals, and enjoyment of the experience. The more esoteric aspects of Zen and spiritual development are rarely discussed but are very evident in writings on karate and the martial arts (Hassell, 1980; Hyams, 1979; Kauz, 1977; Payne, 1981; Stein, 1988; Ueshiba, 1984).

Though little overt acknowledgment is given to the spiritual aspects of budo on the dojo floor, their importance to the ideology of traditional karatedo is manifested in the lip-service paid to these ideals in martial arts writing, lectures, dojo brochures, interviews, and other "official" communications. Furthermore, it is clear that for at least some participants, the spiritual aspects of the art are the main purpose in studying them (Hassell, 1980; Kauz, 1977; Payne, 1981).

The traditions of Zen are seen in
many aspects of karate training.

Zen in Karatedo

It may seem easier to identify Zen influences in traditional karate training than those of budo, and in a sense, this is because, to a great degree, budo is Zen, and the elements of karatedo that clearly represent its Zen roots reflect budo as well.

Perhaps because Zen lacks dogma and doctrine, it is replete with aphorisms and fables that reflect its basic tenets. Many of these have found their way into the literature and ideology of karatedo. Three of the most popular of these sayings are *mushin no kokoro* (mind without thought), *mizu no kokoro* (mind like water), and *tsuki no kokoro* (mind like the moon). (While *kokoro* is often translated simply as "mind," it is more accurately expressed as "mind, spirit, heart, will, intention," and is so defined in most Japanese-English dictionaries.)

Mushin no kokoro (mind without thought) is the ideal state of the *budoka* (martial artist). The mind without thought is wholly aware of the present, unattached to conscious desire or emotion. The Zen master Takuan, in his writings to the sword master during the seventeenth century, discussed the concept of *mushin no kokoro* at length (Takuan, 1986), as did Japan's most famous sword master, Musashi, during the same period (Musashi, 1974). *Mizu no kokoro* (mind like water) is related to *mushin no kokoro*. Such a mind is calm and clear, like the surface of a pool of pure water. It acts like a mirror, reflecting all that comes before it without distortion. Only with a mind like water can the budoka respond quickly and freely in the cause of justice.

When we speak of *tsuki no kokoro* (mind like the moon), we refer to an unclouded mind, shining equally on everything and thus open and aware of all things. In all three of these concepts, conscious thought, desire, and emotion serve only to disturb and distort our perceptions and our ability to act. Total concentration and awareness are necessary for the successful execution of waza, and these are impossible if conscious thought or desire "stop" the mind from perceiving freely. This principle is basic to the practice of Zen as well as to all budo. True enlightenment presupposes the absence of obstacles to perception. Many other Zen adages and countless stories contribute their wisdom to the traditional budo, including karatedo. While these receive little mention on the training floor, their popularity in martial arts writing and lore attests to their significance in the ideology of traditional karate.

Benefits of Karate Training

Individuals engage in the practice of martial arts for many reasons; the most common of these include recreation, exercise, sport, self-defense, and self-development. According to the ideology of karatedo, the art provides all these benefits and more. As a *do* form, karate's raison d'etre is to enhance self-development and spiritual awareness in all who participate. Unlike some budo, karate also claims to provide practical self-defense techniques. The art's value in promoting physical health has been touted for over a century; in the past several decades, karate has become popular as a recreational and competitive sport as well.

In his most widely read book, *Karate-do Kyohan: The Master Text*, Funakoshi Gichin (1973) describes the value of karate under three headings: athletic training, self-defense, and spiritual training. He points out that karate can be practiced alone or in groups, without special equipment, and that the progressive nature of the exercise allows it to be performed by anyone, regardless of initial physical condition. As a method of self-defense, karate also has several advantages: no weapons are needed, and its techniques do not require great strength.

As spiritual training, Funakoshi continues, "karate is no different from the other martial arts in fostering the traits of courage, courtesy, integrity, humility, and self-control in those who have found its essence ... I consider karate to be the most suitable of the many martial arts in leading to fulfillment of the need for training of the spirit" (1973: 13-14). The master does not specify, however, precisely how these traits are fostered nor how such spiritual training unfolds.

Most writers about karatedo agree that the art aspires to improve the character of its participants and to teach a way of life. Few, however, provide details as to how this is accomplished. Two writers who have undertaken this task are Hassell (1980) and Kauz (1977).

Hassell describes the philosophy of Kano Jigaro, founder of judo, as it applies to karate training and self-development:

> For Kano, budo was the basis of everything, but he realized that each individual, even a great technical master, must consciously seek to make budo work for him, or he would gain nothing but physical strength... If we do not consciously seek to apply the principles of karate-do to our daily lives, we will not change at all. – Hassell, 1980: 47

This point is critical in assessing the potential of the martial arts as vehicles for self-development. While certain experiences and examples may lead students to develop in certain ways, without a conscious desire for self-improvement, little real advancement is likely. Hassell is one of a very few writers on the martial arts to acknowledge this necessary condition, akin in many ways to the adage in modern psychotherapy that the patient must really want to get better before improvement will occur.

Like Funakoshi and Hassell, Kauz (1977) also describes the benefits of karate training in terms of self-defense, physical exercise, and spiritual development. He goes on to point out that because the Eastern view of man is holistic rather than dualistic,

> martial arts teachers who share this view see themselves as helping their students develop as a whole. In teaching what Westerners would consider physical skills, they think they are affecting the student's mental and psychological approach to life as well as cultivating his body.
> – Kauz, 1977: 28

Most martial arts writers seem to agree that even without the conscious desire to improve one character, consistent training will provide certain psychological benefits (Funakoshi, 1973, 1988; Hassell, 1980; Kauz, 1977). Hassell remarks that "of course, one who stays with karate training over a period of years will develop courage, self-control, discipline, and awareness" but notes that beyond these traits, perfection of character involves "health, intelligence, judgment, and moral rectitude" (1980: 47-48). Development of these latter traits requires conscious desire.

Though the learning of the physical techniques of a martial art remains largely an intuitive process in traditional training, the instructor's role is of crucial importance. One aspect of this role is the encouragement and cultivation of character development.

> The instructor must constantly exemplify the highest standards of the budo discipline, the whole idea of which is to develop character ... With strict discipline and etiquette, a karate instructor should teach his students to respect everyone, and to be clean and healthy of body and mind. – McCarthy, 1987: 10

Kauz and Hassell likewise emphasize the important role of the instructor in encouraging self-development and correct understanding of the principles of budo. Both point out that though the *sensei* (teacher) must be of the highest character and insight, he is still but a guide:

> While we need a sensei to guide us, we must ultimately learn and understand by ourselves. No teacher can teach us how to feel, or how to have good judgment, or how to be moral, or how to be just. He can only guide us and give us exercises, physical and mental, to help us find our true nature. – Hassell, 1980: 54

In this passage, Hassell refers to the basic tenets of Zen and thus of budo: that real understanding comes from within and that, in becoming enlightened, we are but perceiving our own true nature. While this concept is an essential element of Zen practice and may be easily understood in Eastern cultures, it is considerably more difficult for the Western mind to comprehend. Unfortunately, though many of the traditions and structures of karatedo derive from this principle, it is rarely explained to students of the art, and instructors of both Japanese and Western origin frequently seem to forget that this is the foundation for their methods.

Both Kauz (1977) and Hassell (1980) detail the way in which specific aspects of the training process will benefit karate's practitioners. As each author has devoted an entire book to the topic, their thoughts cannot be conveyed in full here. A summary note that training in karatedo produces benefits in three interrelated ways: (1) through the structure of the training process, one must develop discipline, self-control, concentration, and awareness in order to progress in one's training; (2) through the example and guidance of the instructor and seniors, one is encouraged to strive for self-improvement, and in so striving, one develops in character and virtue; (3) as one continues in the art and develops a deeper understanding of its nature and purpose, one is motivated to adopt attitudes and practices that lead to self-development and spiritual awareness.

McCarthy provides a succinct summary of the method of karatedo:

> The philosophy of karate-do is the most important aspect of training because it is the training of the spirit ... [students of the art] learn the higher virtues, that [sic] of respect, compassion, gratitude, and honor. Karate is a path by which one humbly learns his weaknesses, and it is by these virtues that weaknesses are turned into strengths.
> – McCarthy, 1987: 9

Conclusions

Individuals engage in the martial art of karate for many reasons: as sport, recreation, exercise, and self-defense. Karate, like other traditional martial arts, is widely believed to contribute to the self-improvement and perhaps spiritual development of its practitioners. It is in this regard that we consider karatedo from the ideological perspective.

Since its introduction to Japan in the 1920s, and to the rest of the world in the 1960s, karate has been promulgated as a *do* form, practiced for self-development and spiritual growth. The ideology of karatedo is deeply rooted in the philosophical and spiritual traditions of the East in general and of Japan in particular.

Karate, unlike most Japanese martial arts, developed in Okinawa and was introduced to Japan only in this century. Upon its introduction, however, karate became a *do* form in the tradition of Japanese budo. Like all Japanese martial arts, both classical and contemporary, karatedo derives its spiritual and philosophical traditions from ancient combat arts (*bujutsu*) that evolved during Japan's feudal era into martial Ways (*budo*). Karatedo developed from the cultural traditions of *bushido* (the code of the warrior), *budo* (the martial Ways), and Zen Buddhism (which significantly influenced both bushido and budo).

The ideology of traditional karatedo continues to reflect its identity as a *budo*, or martial Way. The art is practiced for self-improvement, not combat. Its teachings, training, and lore promote perfection of character, the development of virtue, a deeper understanding of self, and an enhanced spiritual awareness.

Regardless of the purpose that brings a given individual to the practice of karatedo, the nature of the art is such that physical and psychological benefits should accrue. The evidence for the latter, however, is weak at best (Wingate, 1990). Several reasons for this lack of evidence are possible: (1)

training in karatedo does not really benefit its participants (in which case we must re-examine both the ideology of the art and its proponents, who make great claims to the contrary); (2) the practice of karatedo in contemporary society (in whatever countries) is greatly at odds with its ideology, and thus the predicted benefits do not accrue (this is entirely possible and even probable, in light of the rise of sport karate and non-traditional styles); (3) benefits do accrue to practitioners of karatedo, as claimed, but researchers have failed to measure them (again, entirely possible, as research has concentrated on personality assessment and self-concept rather than values or morality); (4) benefits accrue only to some practitioners in some styles of karate, and the research has been too muddied to identify these variables (again, very likely); (5) the "truth" lies in some combination of the above.

The accumulated research on the effects of martial arts training is inadequate to address any of these possible explanations. Given the ideological premises of karatedo, our next task is to explore the actuality of practice and the phenomenological understanding of their experience that practitioners express. Once this has been done, well-designed research into the benefits of karate training will be more likely to contribute to our understanding and assessment of the martial arts as vehicles for the enhancement of human potential.

Yaguchi Yutaka teaching in Denver, Colorado.

"the instructor must constantly exemplify the highest standards of the budo discipline."
– Pat McCarthy

References

Barclay, G. (1973). *Mind over matter: Beyond the bounds of nature*. New York: Bobbs-Merrill.

Becker, C. A. (1982). Philosophical perspectives on the martial arts in America. *Journal of the Philosophy of Sport, 9*, 19, 29.

Berger, P. (1963). *Invitation to sociology*. Garden City: Doubleday.

Deshimaru, T. (1982). *The Zen way to the martial arts*. New York: E. P. Dutton.

Draeger, D. F. (1973). *Classical budo*. Tokyo: John Weatherhill.

Fuller, J. (1988). Martial arts and psychological health. *British Journal of Medical Psychology, 61*, 317, 329.

Funakoshi, G. (1973). *Karate-do kyohan* (T. Oshima, Trans.). New York: Kodansha International.

Funakoshi, G. (1975). *Karate-do: My way of life*. New York: Kodansha International.

Funakoshi, G. (1988). *Karate-do nyumon* (J. Teramoto, Trans.). New York: Kodansha International.

Harrison, E. J. (1955). *The fighting spirit of Japan*. Woodstock, NY: The Overlook Press.

Hassell, R. G. (1980). *The karate experience: A way of life*. Rutland, VT: Charles E. Tuttle Company.

Hassell, R. G. (1984). *Shotokan karate: Its history and evolution*. St. Louis, MO: Focus Publications.

Herrigel, E. (1953). *Zen in the art of archery* (R. F. C. Hull, Trans.). New York: McGraw Hill Book Company.

Hyams, J. (1979). *Zen in the martial arts*. New York: Bantam Books.

Japan Karate Association. (1988). Rules concerning qualifications. Unpublished manuscript.

Kauz, H. (1977). *The martial spirit*. Woodstock, NY: The Overlook Press.

Kim, R. (1974). *The weaponless warriors*. Burbank, CA: Ohara Publications.

Konzak, B. (1980). Some comments on the field of sport sociology and its relation to sport psychology: Toward an integration of sport psychology and sport sociology. In P. Klavora and K. A. W. Wipper (Eds.), *Psychological and sociological factors in sport*. Toronto, Ontario: University of Toronto.

Layton, C. (1989). *Mysteries of the martial arts*. Hunstanton, Norfolk, England: Kime Publishing.

Lovret, F. J. (1988). *Budo jiten*. San Diego, CA: Taseki Publishing Co.

McCarthy, P. (1987). *Classical kata of Okinawan karate*. Burbank, CA: Ohara Publications.

Musashi, M. (1974). *Go rin no sho (Book of five rings)* (V. Harris, Trans.). Woodstock, NY: Overlook Press.

Nakayama, M. (1977). *Best karate: Volume 1 Comprehensive.* New York: Kodansha International.

Nakaya, T. (1986). *Karate-do: History and philosophy.* Carrollton, TX: J. S. S. Publishing Co.

Nitobe, I. (1969). *Bushido: The soul of Japan.* Rutland, VT: Charles E. Tuttle Co.

Payne, P. (1981). *Martial arts: The spiritual dimension.* New York: The Crossroad Publishing Co.

Pieter, W. A. (1989). An historical exploration of the martial arts within the context of Japanese strategies of culture. (Doctoral dissertation, University of Oregon). Dissertation Abstracts International, 50/09A, 2830.

Random, M. (1977). *The martial arts.* London: Octopus Books Ltd.

Ratti, O., and Westbrook, A. (1973). *Secrets of the samurai: A survey of the martial arts of feudal Japan.* Rutland, VT: Charles E. Tuttle Company.

Rielly, R. L. (1975). *Karate training: The samurai legacy and modern practice.* Rutland, VT: Charles E. Tuttle Company.

Sato, H. (1985). *The sword and the mind.* Woodstock, NY: Overlook Press.

Scott, D., and Pappas, M. (1985). *The fighting arts: Choosing the way.* London: Rider and Co. Ltd.

Stein, H. J. (1988). *Kyudo: The art of Zen archery* (F. Nevill and T. Nevill, Trans.). Dorset, England: Element Books Ltd.

Takuan, S. (1986). *The unfettered mind: Writings of the Zen master to the sword master* (W. S. Wilson, Trans.). New York: Kodansha International.

Thirer, J., and Grabiner, M. D. (1980). Self actualization through Zen and the martial arts. *Review of Sport and Leisure, 5:* 79-92.

Ueshiba, K. (1984). *The spirit of aikido.* New York: Kodansha International.

Wertz, S. K. (1977). Zen, yoga, and sports: Eastern philosophy for western athletes. *Journal of the Philosophy of Sport, 4:* 68-82.

Wilson, W. S. (1984). *Budoshoshinshu: The warrior's primer of Daidoji Yuzan.* Burbank, CA: Ohara Publications.

Wingate, C. F. (1990). Psychological effects of training in the martial arts: A review of the literature. Unpublished manuscript.

The Makiwara as a Tool for Learning
by John R. Stebbins

Figure 1
A typical karate punch at a makiwara. Upon impact, force (F) is transmitted to the makiwara. The opposite reactionary force (rF) travels into the hand, arm, and body, down the rear leg into the ground. The reactionary force at the metacarpal heads is specifically termed a comprehensions force (FC; see Figure 2). Friction (f) between the feet and ground, created by body weight and gripping with the toes, provides resistance and prevents the rear leg from becoming unstable. Correct angling of the leg is important in maintaining stability. A large angle of the rear leg will decrease stability.

Illustrations by J. Stebbins.

Introduction

This chapter will examine the dynamics of the typical straight karate punch (*tsuki*) against a firm but flexible object, the makiwara. It is a brief review of the physics, physiology and psychology behind a unique and often ignored method of training. Though all of the principles outlined can be applied to any technique, it is not feasible to discuss them all here. Therefore, for the purposes of this chapter, only the tsuki is considered. The interested reader is advised to consult the references cited for information on anatomy, biomechanics, makiwara training and other types of strikes, as well as a more in-depth discussion of the principles discussed below.

The proper formation of the fist and the correct execution of the punch are usually the first technique taught to beginning karate students. It is surprising, however, to see the number of advanced karateka who are not familiar with the kinetics involved in the proper execution of the punch. It is essential that the karateka have a working knowledge of the skeletal system and the biomechanical and basic physiological processes that are employed during training. An injury is usually an unpleasant reminder that some study in these areas must be done. Aside from the personal benefits of this knowledge, teachers have a responsibility to be knowledgeable in these areas and to convey that information to their students. In the case of the tsuki, an excellent way to understand these principles is through makiwara training.

Kinetics of Training

The traditional Okinawan-style makiwara is constructed from an erect, flexible piece of wood approximately shoulder height, secured at the base, with a pad at the tip as the striking surface (Peled, 1993; Higaonna, 1988). Perhaps the most important attribute of the design is its flexible nature, which allows hard focused strikes without the risk of serious injury. When executing a punch at the makiwara, the karateka must maintain good form. The stance must be secure to prevent imbalance, the hips must twist in the direction of the punch, the shoulder must relax and align with the upper arm and the hand must align correctly with the forearm. With the exception of those muscles driving the punch, the body should remain relaxed until contact. When the hand makes contact, the muscles are contracted, thereby insuring force transmission to the target (Nakayama, 1966). The flexibility of the makiwara allows for partial absorption of the force of impact. An opposite reactionary force is then applied back to the hand and is transmitted through the body to the ground via the stance (See p. 44, Figure 1). When contact is made, the karateka should be supported by a firm foundation. Friction between the feet and ground provide resistance to the reactionary forces, preventing loss of balance. Development of a strong stance by angling the rear leg and gripping the ground with the toes serves to increase the friction, adding stability and resistance.

The Skeletal Structure of the Hand

An understanding of the skeletal structure of the hand is imperative for the karateka to execute a technically sound tsuki. By virtue of the arrangement of bone and precise alignment upon impact, the hand is capable of delivering an impact force of over six hundred pounds and withstanding a compression force of over five thousand pounds without fracture (Feld, et al. 1979). With the proper form, the strength of bone enables the karateka to deliver a powerful punch without injury.

A properly executed tsuki impacts at the second and third metacarpal heads (knuckles). The skeletal structure behind these knuckles allows this to occur with relatively little risk of damage or dislocation. Upon impact at the metacarpal heads, a compression force is transmitted from the large bones of the index and middle fingers (the metacarpals) to the radius, ulna and then the humerus, providing maximal support. A fraction of the force is distributed through the ligaments, muscle, and visceral tissue of the arm.

Though the human hand is endowed with a sufficiently strong skeletal structure, it is not enough to insure injury-free impact. It has been reported that there is a high incidence of index metacarpal fractures sustained during karate practice (Kelly, et al. 1980). This undoubtedly occurs due to poor alignment of the hand and arm at the moment of impact. For an injury-free punch, contact must be made so that the compression force can be equally distributed between the second and third metacarpal heads. Since there is a discrepancy in size between these knuckles, there must be a slight abduction of the hand at the wrist and leveling of the carpals and metacarpals with the radius. In addition, impact at the fourth and fifth metacarpals will greatly increase the risk of injury due to the lack of skeletal structure to support the force (Figure 2).

Figure 2
Schematic diagram of the skeletal structure of the hand and arm as viewed from the top. The compression force (Fc) is delivered to the second and third metacarpal heads (A) and is transmitted to the arm via the metacarpals and carpals. Proper alignment of the arm enables the force to proceed through the radius (B) and ulna (shaded bone) to the humerus (C). Note that a force applied to the fourth and fifth metacarpals will travel diagonally through the carpals (D) where there is insufficient bone structure to withstand compression.

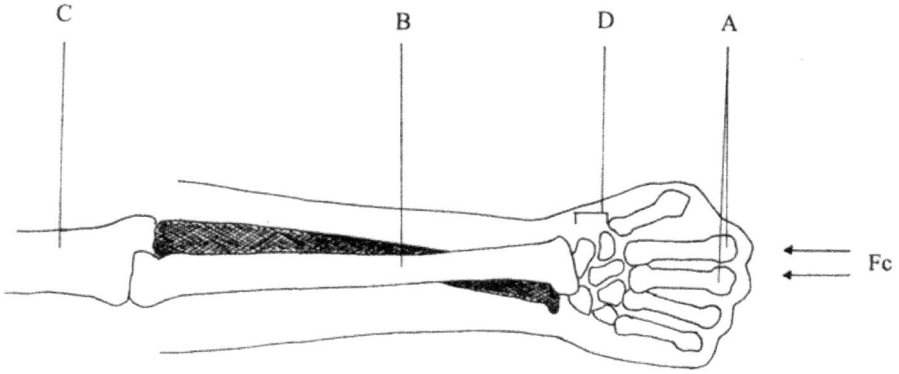

Physiological Adaptation Due to Makiwara Training

Any stress to the body results in a localized physiological adaptation. Probably the most widely recognized adaptation to makiwara training is hypertrophy of the skin at the second and third metacarpal heads (i.e. callusing of the first two knuckles). If the tsuki is performed incorrectly, the skin at the knuckle may lesion. At this point, makiwara training should be suspended to prevent infection and allow sufficient time for the lesion to heal completely. Wound healing at the knuckles is normally slower than at other locations on the body due to the peripheral location of the hand and the low blood supply there. When training is resumed, it is important to prevent further damage to this area while enabling hypertrophy to occur. The resulting calluses develop as a protective mechanism for the knuckles that serves to provide a cushion against the impact, lessening the likelihood of further tissue damage. Contrary to popular belief, this phenomenon will not cause a reduction of hand and finger range of motion. In fact, this adaptation is beneficial to the karateka, but excessive callusing that is greatly elevated from the knuckle is prone to tearing and is not recommended. Moderation in training will help to avoid excessive callusing and it has been reported that certain liniments can also be used to reduce callusing (Higaonna, 1988; Peled, 1993). In any event, it is essential that the makiwara be of flexible design to decrease the chance of serious injury.

A common injury to the hand is fracture and/or dislocation of the metacarpals due to collision with a solid object (Kelly, et al. 1980; Birrer, et al., 1988). These traumas may lead to dysfunctions involving the synovial fluid surrounding the joint, ligament and/or cartilage damage, wearing down of the bone, and chips or spurs lodging in the joint cavity (Kreighbaum, 1985). Cartilage build-up and subsequent new bone deposition in the event of fracture or dislocation can contribute to the enlargement of the knuckles and fusing of the gap between them. In contrast to callusing, damage to the joint can lead to painful movement and a reduction of finger range of motion. Repetitive impact to an inflexible target can also lead to similar injuries at the wrist and elbow, particularly in the elderly and the very young (Canney, 1988).

Strength development occurs via a similar mechanism as a result of makiwara training. A small amount of muscular hypertrophy is often seen at the wrist and forearm. The primary muscles affected are the extensor and flexor retinaculum and the flexors and extensors of the forearm. The extensor and flexor retinaculum are thin, wide sheaths of muscle that wrap around the lower portion of the radius and ulna at the wrist. The primary purpose of these muscles is rotation of the forearm at the wrist just prior to impact, but they are also used to stabilize the radius and ulna. The opposing muscles of the forearm, the families of flexors and extensors, are also extremely important for adding stability to the wrist. The primary purpose of the extensors during a punch is to prevent the downward bending of the wrist upon impact. On the contrary, the flexors are the muscles that pull the fingers into a fist and also prevent the upward turning of the wrist. Both of these muscles work in unison to help abduct the hand and, along with the biceps and triceps, stabilize the wrist and elbow (Wirhed, 1984; Figure 3).

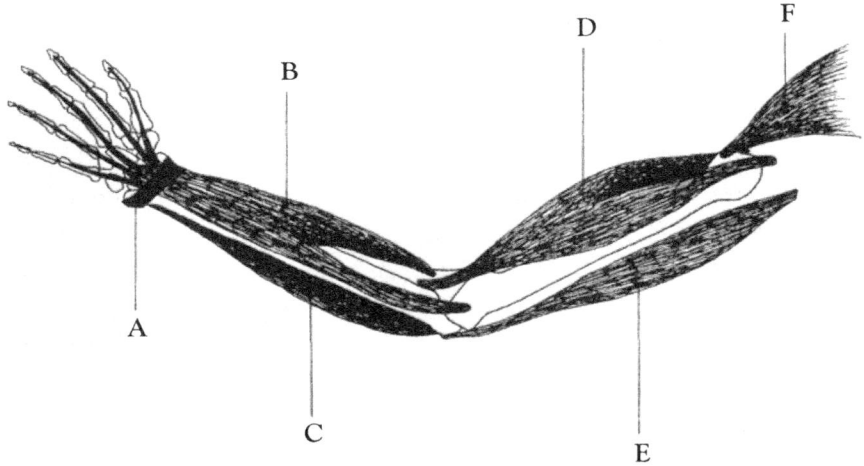

Figure 3
Schematic diagram of the primary muscles used in punching, right hand, palm facing. A) extensor and flexor retinaculum (the flexor is under the extensor), B) the flexors of the forearm, C) the extensors of the forearm [pulled away from the bone for visibility], D) biceps brachii, E) triceps brachii, F) deltoid.

The tsuki is delivered by contraction of the pectoral, deltoid, biceps, and triceps muscles. From the hip, the biceps and the muscles of the upper back hold the arm in the chamber position, the deltoid lifts the humerus and the triceps extend the elbow. Strong contraction of the pectorals will roll the shoulder forward and should be avoided. For the karate punch, contraction is required over a relatively short distance, from the hip to the target. With proper and consistent training, the time of contraction can be reduced, creating a faster punch. It is not necessary to load these muscles for significant speed gains. Power is added to the punch through speed and strength in the contraction. There will be some strengthening of these muscles by makiwara training; however for significant strength increases the muscles must be loaded throughout the tsuki range of motion. All of the muscles used in punching will strengthen in accordance with the stress placed upon them.

The wrist joint is held together by ligaments surrounding the articulation between the carpals and the radial and ulnar heads. Stress in this area is largely a result of the resistance to the reactionary force needed to sustain the joint in its natural position. The reactionary force coming back along the metacarpals into the wrist will cause compression of the carpals and tends to separate the heads of the radius and ulna. The stabilizing effect of the ligaments serves to prevent joint dislocation. If a ligament is subject to a force greater than it can withstand, it will stretch thereby lessening its stabilizing effect. However, a stretched ligament will usually return to its original length after sufficient rest. Extreme forces can tear the ligament from the bone, requiring surgical reattachment. Taping of the wrist joint is inadvisable because it lessens the load on the ligament and without some stress upon it, the ligament will weaken (Wirhed, 1984; Kreighbaum, 1985).

Psychological Benefits

Higaonna (1988) states that makiwara training provides psychological benefits that can help develop character in the karateka. These benefits include the alleviation of tension and the development of persistence. Of course, each practitioner will gain subjective psychological benefits from this type of training, but these two characteristics are probably typical. It has been widely documented that exercise can reduce the effects of tension and this has been attributed to a variety of physiological and psychological factors (Noakes, 1991; Fixx, 1977). It is unlikely that the actual pounding of an object is the means for reducing tension (i.e. pounding out frustrations). It is possible, however, that the rhythm involved in striking places the karateka in a meditative state that is conducive to tension relief. Other Eastern disciplines also employ rhythm as an inducer of this state, such as repeated chants or sounds. Usually, the karateka executes a predetermined number of strikes when training and to continue through high repetition and discomfort requires discipline and persistence. Thus, makiwara training is goal-oriented and the determination required to reach the goal will serve to strengthen these qualities in the practitioner's character. Over the long term, character traits that are developed through training will evolve as less exercise specific and become ingrained in the psyche. Therefore, the manner in which one trains will contribute to the overall development of character.

Another important benefit from makiwara training is that the karateka is able to fully realize the interplay of the entire body when executing a punch. Initially, he or she strives to understand the role of the specific body parts used in punching. During this period, the karateka learns to make the necessary adjustments and corrections to the technique. After continued training, however, the karateka becomes less aware of the details and strives for the overall "feel" of the movement. The highest level of skill is the ability to execute the punch without thoughts about the kinetics of the movement, hereby moving as a "whole." This level is only achieved after proper, long, term training.

As an educational tool, the makiwara is valuable for skill development in punching. Unfortunately, the availability of the heavy punching bag has caused many to view it as a replacement for the makiwara. Most karate dojos are now equipped with a heavy bag and it is difficult to find a traditional makiwara. Though the heavy bag is a valuable tool, the makiwara offers some unique advantages. The design of the makiwara is such that it is firm enough to allow the karateka to feel solid impact yet flexible enough to lessen the likelihood of serious injury in the event of error. It is more economical than the heavy bag, less space consuming and its narrow design is ideal for developing accuracy in punching. Makiwara training can also be done in solitude and the adept karateka is able to immediately distinguish between proper and incorrect execution of the tsuki. This is perhaps the most valuable aspect of makiwara training.

As with any conditioning exercise, moderation and intelligence is the key to success. When injury occurs, training should be suspended until there is complete recovery. Bearing this in mind, the karateka can develop a powerful, technically correct tsuki and resilient spirit through makiwara training.

References

Birrer, R. B., and Halbrook, S. P. (1988). Martial arts injuries: Results of a five year survey. *American Journal of Sports Medicine*, 16 (4): 408-410.

Canney, J. C. (1988). *Health and fitness in the martial arts*. London: The Bath Street Press.

Feld, M. S., McNair, R. E., and Wilk, S. R. (1979). The physics of karate. *Scientific American*, 240 (4): 150-158.

Fixx, J. F. (1977). *The complete book of running*. New York: Random House Publishing.

Higaonna, M. (1988). *Traditional Okinawan Goju-ryu karatedo makiwara training*. San Clemente, CA: Panther Video Productions.

Kelly, D. W., Pitt, M. J., and Mayer, D. M. (1980). Index metacarpal fractures in karate. *The Physician and Sportsmedicine*, 8 (3): 103-106.

Kreighbaum, E., and Barthels, K. M. (1985). *Biomechanics*. New York: MacMillian Publishing Company.

McMinn, R. M. H., and Hutchings, R. T. (1985). *Color atlas of human anatomy*. Chicago: Year Book Medical Publishers, Inc.

Nakayama, M. (1966). *Dynamic karate*. Tokyo: Kodansha International.

Noakes, T. (1991). *The lore of running*. Champaign, IL: Leisure Press.

Peled, M. (1993). Hand conditioning through makiwara training. *Karate Profiles Made in America*, 8 (1): 32.

Wirhed, R. (1984). *Athletic ability: The anatomy of winning*. New York: Crown Publishers.

chapter 4

Three Distinctive Techniques of Pwang Gai Noon-ryu

by Mary Bolz

Characters for *ban* [half *yang* (hard) *ruan* (soft], the Mandarin which with an Okinawan accent is pronounced as Pwang Gai Noon.

Mary Bolz illustrating a blocking maneuver against a kick executed by Nishiuchi Mikio. *Photographs courtesy of Taira Yoshimura.*

Introduction

One of the three most well-known and highly respected karate styles in Okinawa is *Pwang Gai Noon-ryu*, or *Han Ko Nan-ryu* (Japanese pronunciation), which means "half-hard, half-soft style." This name not only reflects the nature of the style, but also reveals what originally was indigenous to all martial arts—the law of *in/yo* (Japanese) or *yin/yang* (Chinese)—that is, hard and soft always go together.

In and *yo* are the complementary, yet seemingly antagonistic forces in nature which together make up the entire universe, including the whole and all its individual parts. Some examples of *in/yo* are light/heavy, day/night, light/dark, women/men, expanded/contracted, negative/positive, hollow/solid, just to mention a few. *In* always appears first when the phrase is used in its general sense, denoting the emphasis placed on *in* (soft). This emphasis is to show the importance of it in the universe. However, in the name Pwang Gai Noon-ryu, *gai* appears first, which is "hard" or *yo*, denoting the emphasis placed on "hard." But both aspects are included.

In the early days of martial arts, traditionally there was no distinction between a "hard style" or a strictly "soft style" as you hear so many martial arts practitioners discussing today. It was only since the "sportinization" (modernization) of karate that these terms were separately applied to different styles. Styles were changed for physical education purposes rather than street self-defense in the later half of the nineteenth century when peace and stability were attained in the Okinawan and Japanese society, thus ending the "samurai era."

Pwang Gai Noon-ryu is one style that has not modernized. Practitioners of this style do not practice for tournament sparring or winning trophies. The purposes of the practice are for self-defense, good health, discipline, and training to develop "guts" and "spirit" in life.

The half-hard, half-soft principle applies to many aspects of the training in Pwang Gai Noon-ryu. Certainly it means that soft defenses are used against hard attacks and hard defenses against softer types of attack. It also refers to the way the body is maintained at all times, hard as a rock on the outside to withstand attacks, yet soft and relaxed on the inside to maintain maximum stamina and flexibility in a fight. Here is where the famous dynamic tension kata, Sanchin, shines. The main purpose of training in this kata is to toughen the body to enable it to withstand any type of bodily attack, yet maintain flexible movements and stamina. The body is kept rigid and tight at all times throughout the kata with emphasis placed on proper breathing. During the time the practitioner performs the kata, he is constantly tested by a trainer who kicks and punches his body, legs and arms in various places, adjusting the power of the punches and kicks according to the level of conditioning of the trainee's body. Eventually, the practitioner can withstand full force and even a two-by-two inch board can be broken across his body, arms or legs, and even across his shins. This style is also famous for the practitioner breaking baseball bats with his shins by kicking the bat with either a *maegeri* (front kick) or *mawashigeri* (roundhouse kick). During the time the practitioner is being "trained" by the instructor, he must also be "soft" on the inside to allow for free movement. Admittedly, this is high technique, to have the body in a "hard" tension yet at the same time in a "soft" relaxed state. That is why it is said that it takes ten years of training to even begin to understand Sanchin kata.

A prime example of "soft against hard" is the *mawashi-uke* or circle block. This is perhaps the only style within the Okinawan and Japanese traditions that uses a circle for a block. Other styles have techniques that appear to be derivations of the circle block, as seen in some Goju-ryu blocks, but they are linear and angular, not circular. In Pwang Gai Noon-ryu *wa-uke* (circle block), drawing an actual circle with the hand is stressed in practice. Many times a beginner is taught to practice the block by using a wall on which to draw an imaginary circle with his hand.

Kamae (ready fighting pose) and details of
the circle block in figures 1 through 4.

The hand *kamae* (ready fighting pose) of Pwang Gai Noon-ryu is always open-handed with the hands held out in front so that the tips of the fingers are about the same height as the shoulders and the elbows are pointed inward, forming a V-shape. This V-shape is very important, for it is what gives the practitioner leverage against an opponent, who is often larger and stronger than the one defending himself in an actual fight.

To perform the circle block from this hand kamae pose, with the arm outstretched straight forward from the body, one must turn the blocking hand outward (thumb side down) and move the hand straight across toward the center of the body and drop it down, covering the groin area and lower part of the body. Then one must cross over and draw a complete circle by raising the hand high enough to cover the head. It is like cleaning a mirror in a circular motion. After the hand drops down and begins to draw a circle directly in front of the body, the circle covers not only the groin area, but the midsection and then the face area as well, while the hand draws the circle upward. In this manner, all three main attack areas (lower, middle and upper body) are covered and the speed of the circle has the effect of blades on a propeller or fan: it can catch the opponent's attack regardless of where on the practitioner's body or face the attacker is aiming.

There's literally another "catch" to the circle block and that is, when the block is completed, the defender catches, grabs, and immobilizes the attacker's arm and the defender then pulls the attacker off balance, into the defender's own counter attack. The defender's elbows must be "inward" as in the original V-shape, thus giving him "leverage." In this manner, a small person can stop and overcome a large aggressor. And this is what self-defense is all about. It is rare that the upper and lower blocks practiced in sport styles of karate are ever used in a fight, and *jodan-uke* (upper block) is rarely used even in tournament sparring by the Pwang Gai Noon-ryu stylists. Even for a skillful practitioner, it is difficult for the blocker to assess where the attacker is going to exactly attack: the face, neck, or body. With the use of the circle block, it is not necessary for the blocker to be able to "see" the target area where the attacker is aiming because the attack will be caught regardless of its target. Most of the time, the common aggressor on the street will use a roundhouse type punch to the face. Because of this, most *bunkai* (analysis of movements with a partner) practiced in Pwang Gai Noon-ryu will be with the attacker punching to the face rather than the midsection. Kicks are not left out in bunkai either, and once again the circle block can do the job. A version of the circle block, *hasami-uke* (scissors block) is equally useful against a roundhouse, front kick or sidekick.

The "soft" block, being circular rather than linear, prevails against the "hard" attack. It is important that technique and deflection be used against the opponent, who is almost always bigger and/or stronger than the defender. A "hard" block, such as the typical *jodan-uke* (upper block) for punches or *gedan barai* (lower block) for blocking kicks are "hard-against-hard" techniques and the weaker defendant will lose as these techniques become a test of the defender's strength against the opponent's strength. The typical tournament-type techniques do not allow for the blocker to stop the attacker by immobilizing him or forcing the opponent into the blocker's counter.

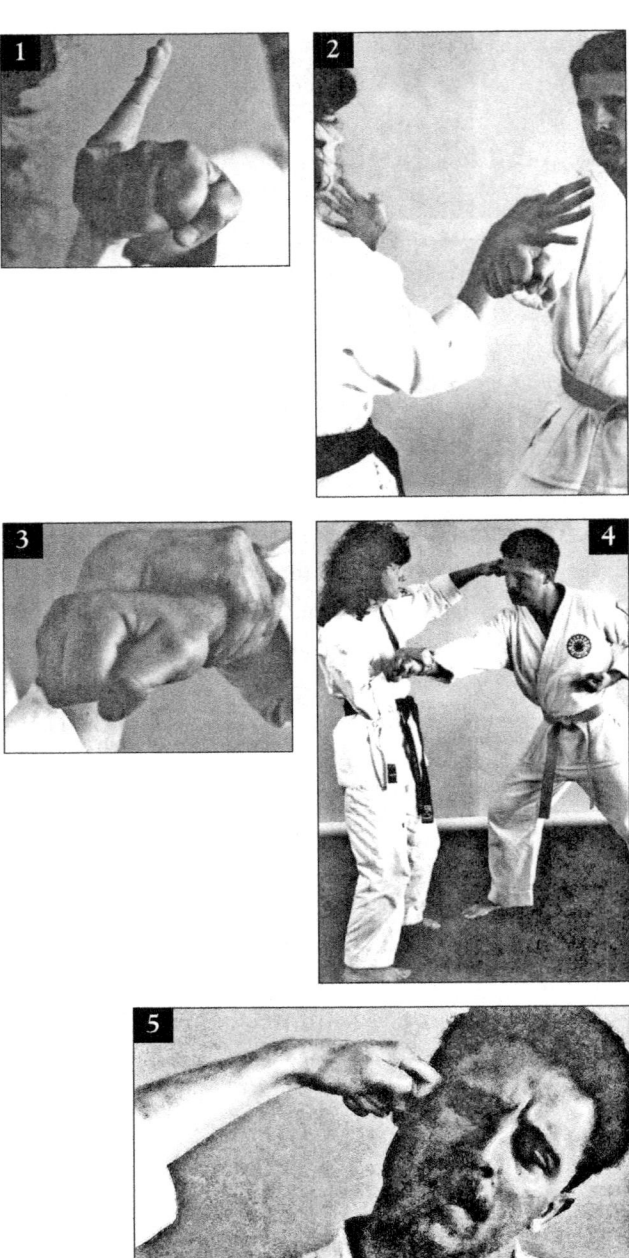

Initial slap-block (fig. 1). Executed with the left hand just prior to catching the opponent's wrist with the right circle block (fig. 2). The right hand then grabs (fig. 3) and pulls the opponent off balance (fig. 4). Bolz ends the sequence with a one-knuckle punch (fig. 5). Special thanks to Mr. Tim Kouris shown here and on the following pages assisting Bolz.

Details on using the circle block to the left side and following through with a right handed one-knuckle punch to the opponent's temple.

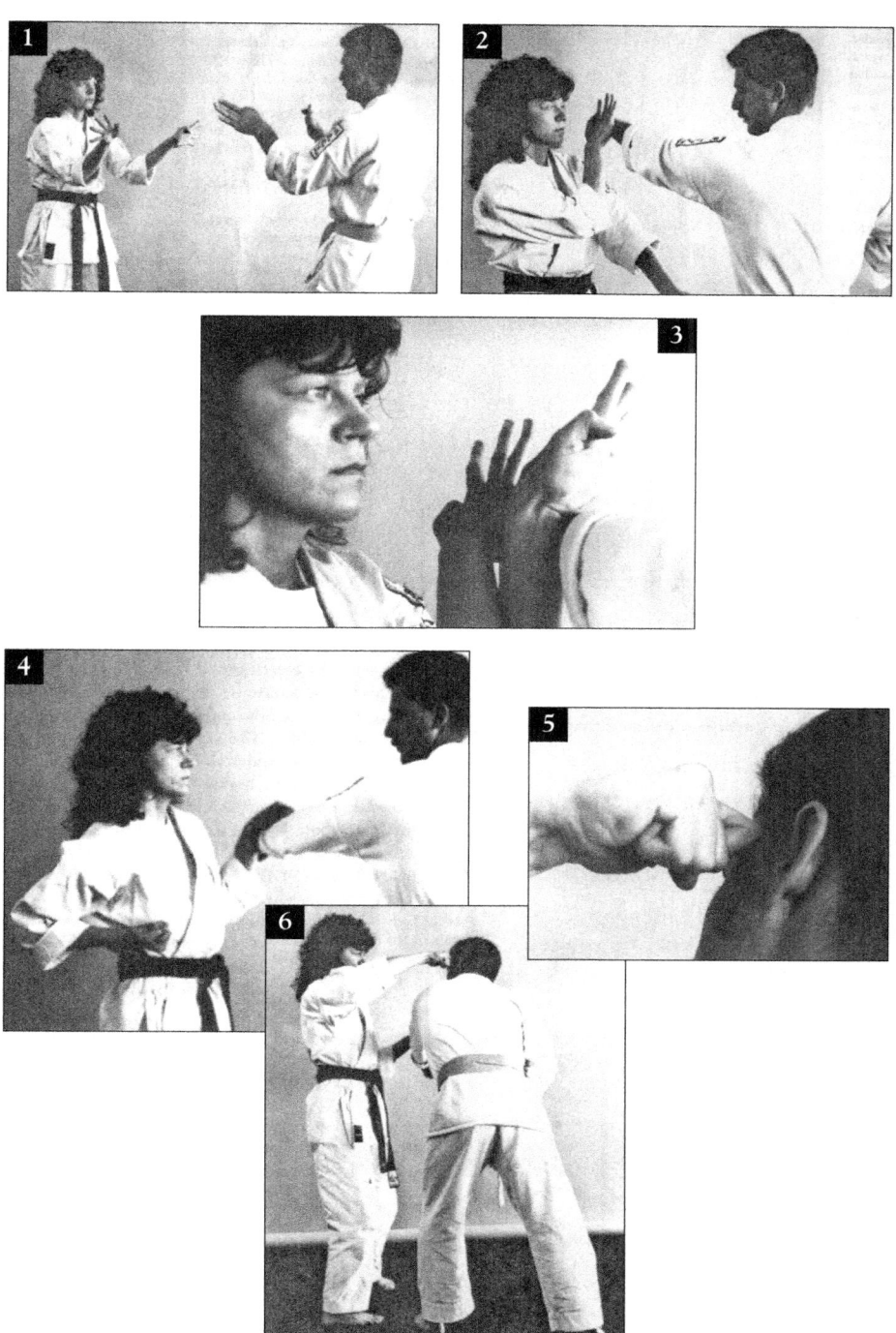

One of Pwang Gai Noon's "hard" hand techniques is *shohken-zuki*, the powerful one-knuckle punch with the forefinger. It is important to first of all be able to make a hard, compact basic karate fist by curling the first knuckle joints near the tip of the fingers very tightly, and without slipping, curl the middle knuckle joints, again, very tightly. The side of the thumb knuckle is placed against the side of the index finger and pressed very tightly towards the center of the fist, while the little finger, acting as a stopper, is squeezed extremely tight. This makes for a very compact, hard fist, while the index finger acts as a small, pointed weapon, having a more painful impact on the receiver than the typical *seiken* (basic karate fist). This "hard" attack is especially useful against larger, soft areas of the body's surface, such as the rib area.

The typical target of shohken-zuki, though, is the *danchu* pressure point of the body, which is in the center of the chest at the nipple line. This pressure point is the relay station, so to speak, of *ki* (Japanese) or *qi* (Chinese). Ki is the electromagnetic energy that is inherent in all things, living and nonliving, in the air and all around us. It is the "life-force." (Of course, the ki power in solid, inanimate objects is less than in expansive, animate beings, including members of the plant kingdom). When the danchu pressure point is attacked, the receiver loses ki, i.e., the receiver loses his fighting spirit and will. If the attacker's will is destroyed, it is difficult for him to continue fighting. The defender will prevail and be safe.

It is recommended that the practitioner make *shohken* (the one-knuckle fist) a habit, rather than *seiken* (the standard or basic fist). It is also important that the fist be usable and not just in "good form." To really be able to use this fist, the practitioner must be able to do deep push-ups on *shohken* (one-knuckle push-ups with a correct shohken fist). The practitioner must also be able to punch the *makiwara* (wooden punching board) and a hard bag at full speed. Then, when it comes time to really be used, shohken-zuki will be as powerful as a small weapon thrust into the opponent.

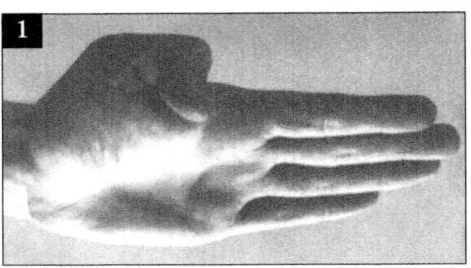

Forming a basic karate fist (figs. 1-1a-b).

The formation of a *shohken-zuki* or one-knuckle punch (figs. 1-2a-2b), allows the index finger to act as a small pointed weapon useful when attacking soft areas on the opponent's body as shown in fig. 3.

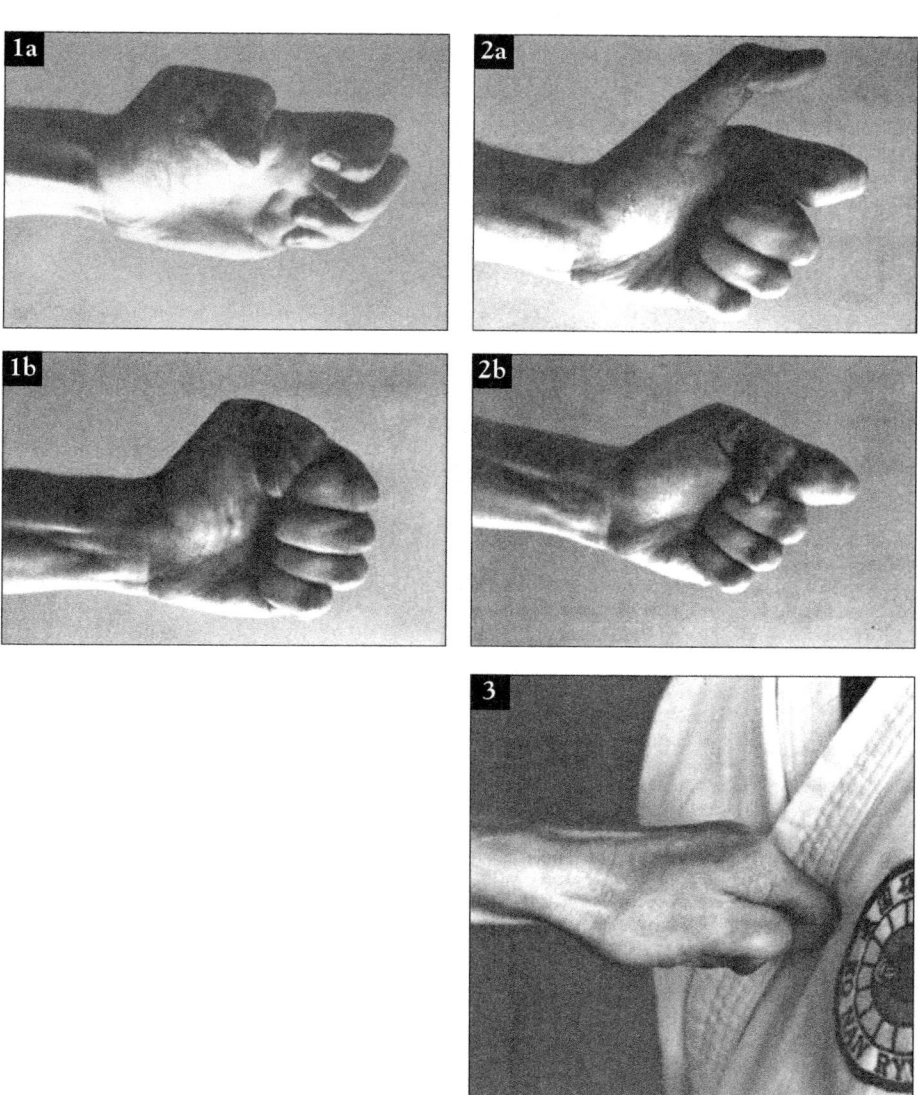

Kicking with the big toe may sound impossible, futile, ineffective and dangerous, but close observation of the techniques may convince one to the contrary.

Once you see in action the dynamic "foot fist" of Pwang Gai Noon-ryu, called *sokusen* (*soku* means "foot and *sen* means "fist"), you will be convinced this is truly an art that turns the body parts into weapons.

Sokusen is to the feet what shohken is to the hands. The big toe turns the foot into a small, sharp weapon in the same way the index finger in shohken turns the hand into a weapon. Although it sounds amazing and even "wrong" to some martial artists who have been taught to pull back their toes and who have even been yelled at by the teachers to do so, it really is quite possible (and very advantageous) with regular and persistent training to attack with your toes. And, once a practitioner gets the hang of it, he'll never want to revert to *sokutei* (pulling back the toes and attacking with the ball of the foot) because he will feel the increase in the power of his own kick, which will give him great confidence.

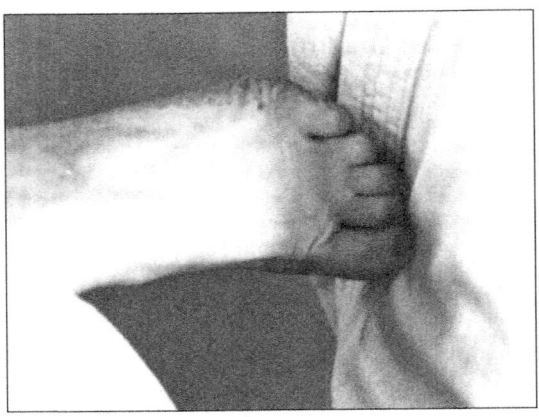

The "foot-fist" (*shokusen*) utilized in
a roundhouse kick to the solar plexus.

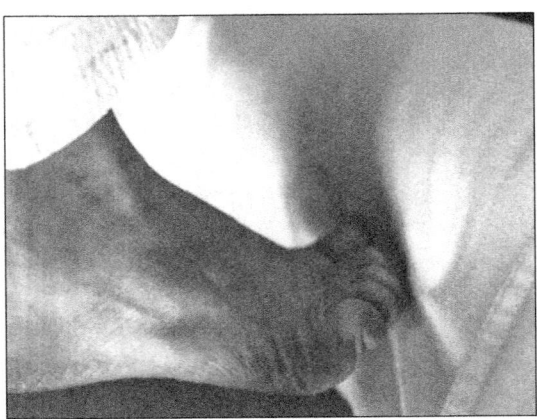

The shokusen strikes a vital point located
on the inner side of an opponent's thigh.

All of the toes are bent at the first knuckle joint from the tips of the toes, not at the second joint as some styles practice when performing sokuto, a kick with the outer edge of the foot's heel. The toes are then pulled inward extremely tight, the same as the fingers are when making a karate fist. The point of attack on the foot is the very tip of the big toe. But all of the other toes must be curled in just as tightly, including the little toe, and the toes must be held very tight laterally against each other. This manner of curling the toes corresponds with the manner of curling the fingers in the fist, and just as the little finger must be squeezed very tight to act as a stopper, so must the little toe. This makes for a tight, compact "foot fist."

Sokusen is always used in *maegeri* (front kick) as the point of contact, except when one is attacking the groin. In the case of a groin kick, the top of the foot is used. The foot is held in sokusen position for all kicks, including *mawashi-geri* (roundhouse) and *sokuto* (side-kick) even if sokusen is not the point of contact. However, sokusen may be used as the actual attack in *mawashi-geri* (roundhouse) depending on the purpose of the technique. Often the top of the instep or shin is used as the point of contact in order to put the entire weight of the body into the kick. It is also easier to deliver a kick using the shin or instep than using sokusen. The practitioner must be very skillful to use sokusen since such a small attack area (the big toes) is being used. Correct assessment of distance, target area on the opponent's body, and power are much more difficult to obtain. For *sokuto-geri* (side-kick), the point of contact on the foot is the outer edge of the heel, but the toes are held in sokusen form to keep the foot as tight as possible, like a solid fist, to make the kick more powerful. To have an effective sokusen, the practitioner must be able to kick the makiwara as well as a very hard punching bag at full speed with sokusen. A kick done properly with sokusen, thrust into the outside or inside of the opponent's thigh, can disable the opponent because he will not be able to continue attacking or even standing, due to the resulting pain. Although most teachers of Pwang Gai Noon-ryu do not stress tournament free-sparring or even care about it, when they do perform *kumite* (free sparring) with another stylist that has not trained in full contact, it is the heavy kicks the Pwang Gai Noon-ryu stylist delivers to the other stylist's legs that will defeat him early on since he can not continue to fight due to the pain in his legs. Another advantage to using sokusen is that the practitioner who always uses it will never have the risk of breaking or spraining his own toes in kumite.

• • •

The training of Pwang Gai Noon-ryu also emphasizes breathing and body training. The body training includes special attacking and blocking exercises in which partners "hit" each other's arms, upper legs, shins, lower legs, and body in an organized and graduated manner. As you have probably realized by now, it is very important for a Pwang Gai Noon-ryu practitioner to be able to "take what one dishes out." There are other training methods that are unique in Pwang Gai Noon-ryu that are not covered in this short chapter, but the three discussed above are the most outstanding and well-known among all martial artists in Okinawa.

Pwang Gai Noon-ryu was founded by Uechi Kanbun* (1877-1948), an Okinawan who had lived and studied martial arts in his earlier years in China. Later the style's name was changed to Uechi-ryu. The influence of Chinese gongfu movements can definitely be seen in the style. Master Uechi's son, Uechi Kanei, carried on the style until he passed away in March, 1991. The organization has since split into four major organizations, one of which is Pwang Gai Noon-ryu. The head of the style is Kinjo Takashi Kaicho, who is well-known as a strong, skillful practitioner in Okinawa. Pwang Gai Noon-ryu's chief instructor in the United States is Shihan Nishiuchi Mikio, who is a student of Kinjo Takashi and a seventh-degree black belt, residing and teaching karate, kobudo, and iaido in Citrus Heights, California.

* Family name listed first in traditional Japanese style.

chapter 5

The World Within
Karate and Kinjo Hiroshi
by Patrick McCarthy

Left: Poem written by Kinjo Hiroshi meaning:
"The performance of technique reveals one's understanding of it."
Right: A perfectionist, Kinjo Hirosi offers detailed corrections to
Patrick McCarthy's punching technique. *Photos courtesy of P. McCarthy.*

Never having won a tournament, made a movie, set a record for knocking people out, breaking bricks, boards or even ice for that matter, Kinjo Hiroshi remains one of Japan's most respected masters of karatedo. At seventy-five years of age, Kinjo Hiroshi has been immersed in the study of karatedo for the last seven decades. And yet, Kinjo remains one of karate's most unpretentious authorities, virtually unknown in the Western world.

With a profound regard for Kinjo, Richard Kim remembers having the privilege of training under this task master during his early years in Japan. Kim describes Kinjo Hiroshi as a "walking encyclopedia of karate history, philosophy and application, a master's master." Although an entire volume might better describe the life of such a remarkable man, this modest presentation examines those convictions most central to his seven decades of experience.

Born on St. Valentines day, 1919, in Okinawa's old castle district of Shuri, Kinjo learned his art directly under the tutelage of the legendary Hanashiro Chomo (1869-1945)[1] and Oshiro Chojo (1888-1935).[2] Taking his first lesson in 1926, Kinjo began to study karate-jutsu while in the second grade of Okinawa's Men's Teachers College "Elementary School."

"That was a wonderful time in my life," recalled Kinjo. "We vigorously embraced a set of standards and kind of austerity no longer valued in this generation. Master Hanashiro and Oshiro both taught that inner-discovery through karate enhanced the value of life and of the world in which one dwelt. They maintained that by transcending ego-related distractions, one could easily get beyond the immediate results of physical training and discover the world within. Pursuing karate under their guidance I ultimately came to find immeasurable happiness and inner peace.

"I have always remained faithful to the precepts upon which karatedo rests and have enjoyed a modest but fruitful life. That is what karatedo, the art of karate, is all about."

Commercialization has revolutionized the practice of karate and brought new interpretations regarding the significance of the art. "The problem with the advent of so many variations is that the moral precepts of karatedo have been overshadowed by the sport and utilitarian aspects of self-defense. I fear that too few truly understand the deeper meaning of karatedo," said master Kinjo.

By pondering the valuable but nearly forgotten teachings of Bushi Matsumura (1809-1901),[3] all can discover a simple message of enormous spiritual value. However, few ever embrace this simple reality because of ego-related distractions and inner conflict. Bushi Matsumura told those whose progress remained hampered by such distractions, to let humility—the spiritual cornerstone upon which the fighting traditions rest—serve to remind them to place virtue ahead of vice, values ahead of vanity and principles ahead of personalities. Matsumura and Itosu were two men who never forgot that they were personal examples of what the fighting traditions truly represented.

The effect Bushi Matsumura had upon Okinawa's civil fighting heritage is immeasurable and yet rarely, if ever, is it described. A subordinate for the Sho Dynasty during the later part of the Ryukyu Kingdom (1507-1897), Bushi Matsumura was, in many ways, regarded as the Miyamoto Musashi of Okinawa. Having studied in both China and Satsuma (present-day Kagoshima prefecture) while enjoying a widespread popularity at home, Matsumura became something of a local folk hero. In addition to a myriad of incredible feats, he was also responsible for introducing the teaching principles of Jigen-ryu kenjutsu to Chinese gongfu as it was practiced in the Shuri district during that time. Matsumura's convictions concerning the precepts of the fighting traditions are clearly outlined in a message he left to Kuwae Ryosei in 1882.

In talking about the advent of modern karate, Kinjo describes how Itosu, like Matsumura, also felt very strongly about perpetuating the cultural self-defense heritage of the old Ryukyu Kingdom. Itosu was the principal force responsible for bringing together several Chinese and Okinawan civil fighting traditions (*kata*) into one modernized format based upon physical recreation.

Students of Okinawa's second middle school pose with their instructor Kiyoda Juhatsu (1887-1968). *Photo courtesy of P. McCarthy.*

"He had his own ideas about how the fighting traditions could benefit the people of Okinawa as well as Japan. He dedicated his entire life to pursuing the very deepest meaning of karate-jutsu and was responsible for bringing together, restoring, and fostering many of the old traditions (*kata*) practiced during his generation. Itosu worked diligently to improve the basic characteristics of karate-jutsu so that it might be approved for the introduction into Okinawa's school system," said Kinjo.

Bushi Matsumura (1809-1902) is regarded as the father of the karate movement which surfaced in and around the castle district of Shuri. *Illustration courtesy of Nagamine Shoshin.*

MATSUMURA'S PRECEPTS ON BU

Through resolve and relentless training one will grasp the true essence of the fighting traditions. No less interesting is the fundamental similarity between the fighting traditions and that of literary study. By examining the literary phenomenon we discover three separate elements: 1) the study of *Shiso*, 2) the study of *Kunko*, 3) the study of *Jukyo*.

The study of *Shiso* refers to commanding words, communicative skills and seeking a position for wages. The study of *Kunko* refers to a comparative study in the philosophy of ancient documents and teaching a sense of duty through example. Yet, in spite of their uniqueness they are incapable of finding the "Way." Capturing only a shallow understanding of the literary phenomenon, *Shiso* and *Kunko* cannot, therefore, be called complete studies.

It is in the study of *Jukyo* (Confucianism) that we can find the "Way." In finding the Way we can gain a deeper understanding of things, build strength from weakness and make our feelings more sincere, become virtuous and even administer our feelings more effectively and, in doing so, make our home a more peaceful place. A precept which can also apply to our country or the entire world. This then is a complete study and it is called *Jukyo*.

Scrutinizing the fighting disciplines we also discover three separate divisions: (i) *Gakushi no Bugei* (ii) *Meimoku no Bugei* (iii) *Budo no Bugei*.

Gakushi no Bugei (practiced by scholars and court officials) is like a psychological game of strategy. It is not actually for fighting but more like a dance or a woman and has no real depth. *Meimoku no Bugei* (nominal styles) are considered purely physical in form and aim only at winning. Without virtue participants are known to be argumentative, often harm others or even themselves and occasionally bring shame to their parents, brothers and family.

Budo no Bugei (the genuine methods) are never practiced without conviction and participants cultivate a serene wisdom which knows not contention or vice. Fostering loyalty among family, friends and country, a natural decorum encourages a dauntless character.

With the fierceness of a tiger and the swiftness of a bird, an indomitable calmness makes subjugating any adversary effortless. Yet, *Budo no Bugei* 1) forbids willful violence, 2) governs the warrior, 3) fortifies people, 4) fosters virtue, 5) appeases the community, 6) brings about a general harmony, and 7) prosperity. These are called the "Seven

Virtues of Bu" and they have been venerated by the *seijin* (sagacious person or persons, most probably Chinese Confucianists) in the document entitled *Godan-sho* (an ancient journal describing the ways of China).

Hence, the way of *bun bu* (literally the study and the fighting traditions often described as the pen and the sword) has mutual features. A scholar needs not *Gakushi* or *Meimoku no Bugei*, only *Budo no Bugei*. This is where you will find the Way. This indomitable fortitude will profoundly affect your judgment in recognizing opportunity and reacting accordingly, as the circumstances always dictate the means.

I may appear somewhat unsympathetic, but my conviction lies strongly in the principles of *Budo no Bugei*. If you embrace my words as I have divulged to you, leaving no secrets and nothing left hiding in my mind, you will find the Way.

>   Signed: Matsumura Bucho May 13th (1882)
>   To: my wise young brother Kuwae (Ryosei)*

*A special way of addressing a youthful friend not related by blood.

Three completely separate kinds of karate came to be known during the turn of the century. There was *toudi*, meaning Chinese-based civil fighting traditions (representing, for the most part, the gongfu disciplines in and around the Naha district), the most prominent headed by Higashionna Kanryo (1853-1915) and brought sporadically to Okinawa over various generations. Then there was *Uchinan-di* (pronounced *Okinawa-te* in Japanese), the indigenous traditions that evolved from *toudi*. And finally, there was the innovative hybrid engineered by Itsosu which surfaced as Ryukyu kempo toudijutsu. His unique system was introduced into Okinawa's school curriculum and represented the very first building block in the foundation of modern karatedo and group instruction. It is interesting to note that group instruction was basically unheard of before that time. This cultural recreation provided the foundation which the competitive format was built.

Itosu's efforts to research, preserve and cultivate the many self-defense traditions practiced during his generation were unprecedented and yet rarely if ever is he given the credit he deserves. While they have revolutionized karate, commercial exploitation and the competitive phenomenon have done little to foster the moral precepts and non-utilitarian values upon which the art form rests (see Itosu's *Ten Lessons*).

"I discovered early in life that one need never leave the dojo to find that which one seeks," said Kinjo. "We already possess what we need to enhance life itself: it resides in our minds, the world within. The point of embarkation is recognizing that the source of human adversity is internal and not external. Hence, the journey must be inward and not outward. Karatedo is 100% holistic and, when embraced deeply, teaches one how to conquer ego, inner conflict and human misery. . . Mastering karate means mastering self. Mastering the self means controlling our world within. Only when we have established this inner harmony and self-control, can we enhance the world in which we dwell, the world without.

"I took part in a karate demonstration for Prince Fushinomiya in 1934. My responsibility was to perform Naijanchin kata and yet all I can remember was the enormous impression my teacher made upon me. The event was held at the Governor's mansion and Oshiro Chojo was the guest speaker. I remember how he captivated the audience with the bojutsu of Shikiyanaka Chinen: the swishing cudgel coming to life and vibrating with every move; his skills were really incredible. However, his true character was revealed when he later described the value of karate. He spoke not of confrontation or strength of fighting, but rather of abstinence, patience and sacrifice, peace and victory without contention: the deepest meaning of karate."

Itosu Ankoh (1832-1915) brought together several martial traditions under the name of Ryukyu Kempo Karatejutsu. Reflecting its Chinese heritage, the new discipline emphasized physical recreation and character development and was introduced to Okinawa's school system as early as 1905. *Illustration courtesy of Nagamine Shoshin.*

At right is a document that was composed in October of 1908 by Itosu Ankoh. Given to Nakasone Genwa by Kinjo's teacher, Hanashiro Chomo, it was first published posthumously in *Karatedo Taikan*, in 1938. Outlining the principles, purpose and potential of karatedo, this document, Itosu's "Ten Lessons," it is believed, was drafted for Okinawa's Prefectural Board of Education to provide a deeper understanding of the tradition for the purpose of having *karatejutsu* (the term then used) accepted into the school system and/or the military. In expressing his convictions he makes it evident that karatejutsu had not yet been officially accepted by the school board regardless of whether it had been informally introduced in 1905 or not.

ITOSU'S TEN LESSONS

Karate (written "Chinese hand") did not descend from Buddhism or Confucianism (as is often thought). In the olden days two schools of karate, namely Shorin and Shorei style, came from China. Both support sound principles and it is vital (in maintaining their true essence) that they be preserved and not altered. Therefore, I will mention here what one must know about karate.

1) Karate does not only endeavor to discipline one's physique. If and when the necessity occurs to fight for a just cause, karate provides the fortitude from which to risk ones own life in support of that campaign. It is not meant to be employed against a single adversary (in trivial circumstances) but rather as a means of avoiding the use of one's hands and feet in the event of a potentially dangerous encounter with a ruffian or a villain.

2) The primary purpose of karate training is to strengthen the human muscles making the physique strong like iron and stone, so that one can use the hands and feet like weapons such as a spear or halberd. In doing so, karate training cultivates bravery and valor in children and it should be encouraged in our elementary schools. Don't forget what the Duke of Wellington said after defeating Emperor Napoleon: "Today's victory was first achieved from the discipline attained on the playgrounds of our elementary schools."

3) Karate cannot be learned (adequately) in a short space of time. Like a torpid bull, regardless of how slowly it moves it will eventually cover a thousand miles. So, too, for one who resolves to study diligently two or three hours every day. After three or four years of unremitting effort, one's body will undergo a great transformation revealing the very essence of karate.

4) One of the most important issues in karate is the training of the hands and the feet. Therefore, one must always make use of the makiwara in order to develop them thoroughly. In order to do this effectively, lower

the shoulders, open the lungs, focus your energy, firmly grip the ground to root your posture and sink your *ki*—commonly referred to as one's life force or intrinsic force—into your *tanden* (just below the navel). Following this procedure perform one to two hundred *tsuki* (thrusts) with each hand every day.

5) In the case of the karate stance, one must maintain an upright posture. The back is aligned, loins are straight up and shoulders down while maintaining power in your legs. Relax and bring together the upper and lower parts of the body with the ki force focused in your tanden.

6) Handed down by word of mouth, karate comprises a myriad of techniques and corresponding meanings. Resolve to independently explore the context of these techniques and observe the principles of *torite* (theory of usage) so the practical applications are more easily understood.

7) In karate training one must determine whether the specific application is suitable for defense or for cultivating the body.

8) Intensity is an important issue for karate training. To visualize that one is actually engaged on the battlefield during training does much to enhance progression. Therefore, the eyes should dispatch fierceness while lowering the shoulders and contracting the body when delivering a blow or blocking such an attack. Training in this spirit prepares one for actual combat.

9) The amount of training must be in proportion to one's physical reservoir of strength and condition. Excessive practice is harmful to one's body and can be recognized when the face and eyes become red.

10) Participants of karate usually enjoy a long and healthy life thanks to the benefits of unremitting training. Practice strengthens muscle and bone, improves the digestive organs and regulates blood circulation. Therefore, if the study of karate were taken into our (athletic) curricula from elementary school and practiced extensively, we could easily produce indomitable men of immeasurable defense capabilities. With these teachings in mind, it is my conviction that if the students at the Shihan Chugakko (old name of the teachers college) practice (karate) they could, after graduation, introduce karate at the local levels, namely elementary schools. In this way karate could be disseminated throughout the entire nation and not only benefit people in general but also serve as an enormous asset to our military forces.

Signed: Itosu Ankoh, October, 1908

This 1936 photo shows standing, left to tight, are Shinpan Gusukuma, Maeshiro Choryo, Chibana Choshin, Nakasone Genwa. Seated, left to right are Kyan Chotoku, Yabu Kentsu, Hanshiro Chomo (Kinjo's teacher) and Miyagi Chojun. *Photo courtesy of Kinjo Hiroshi.*

Hanashiro often described karate as an introspective vehicle through which a journey without distance brought forth a deeper meaning to life itself. However, he also said that austere conditioning, philosophical assimilation and protracted meditation had to be the product of attraction and not promotion. One must discover for one, self that humility builds strength from weakness, cures inner conflict and imparts self-worth. These values cannot be forced upon anyone. Captured by the essence of introspection, this kind of desire often ascends from the blazing furnace of personal adversity.

Chibana Choshin (1885-1969), a man whom Kinjo greatly admired, often said, "It is not that people can't find a solution to their problems; it's that they are unable to perceive that there is even a problem in the first place." Likewise Funakoshi stressed that karatedo teaches one how to recognize character weaknesses and defeat the enemy within.

Mabuni Kenwa (1889-1952), the founder of Shito-ryu and a staunch advocate of the moral precepts upon which karate rests, explained in an abstract poem, "that when the spirit of *bu* (*budo*) is deeply embraced it becomes the vehicle (the world within) to *bu*—island (spiritual emancipation)" [see Mabuni's original poem].

Speaking of the origins of karate, Kinjo said that "the principles of self-defense date back so far into the abyss of history that we will never know where and who actually contrived such skills. However, we can find a provocative explanation about the evolution of the fighting traditions in Miyagi Chojun's publication entitled *An Outline of Karatedo.*"

Miyagi (1888-1953), a prominent authority of the civil fighting traditions and the founder of Goju-ryu karatedo, wrote that "regardless of where and when the self-defense disciplines first unfolded, we can only conclude that they ascended alongside of mankind since ancient times resulting from the animosity inherent in human nature." Miyagi embraced the term *goju* not just because it implied hard and soft but because on a metaphysical plane it also represents the material force of the human body and the humility of one's character as developed through years of uncompromising discipline.

Kinjo mused: "Although there are many paths which lead up a mountain, there is only one moon to be seen by those who achieve its summit. Enlightenment cares not how it is achieved."

The Precepts of Shuhari

Kinjo describes *shuhari* as the three phases of the development from beginner to master. The term *shu* literally means to protect or maintain and represents "learning from tradition." This is the way the chain of tradition is perpetuated and passed on. The initial stage of training is an indispensable step on the infinite ladder of growth and development in karatedo. There are no time limits for each of the three stages, and the transition from one level to the next is neither simple nor immediate. Rather, stages tend to overlap each other in the transition phase, which allows for a gradual emergence from one level to the next. Spiritual development takes one beyond the boundaries of physical training and away from the tyranny of worldly delusion, the preoccupation of materialism and other ego-related distractions.

Ha literally means "to detach" and refers to breaking free from the chains of tradition. It represents a transitional phase from which a person emerges strengthened through the power of introspection. Described as exploring the "world within," the kata and protracted meditation become the focal points through which the supreme power of one's mind is first realized. Having a profound effect upon every aspect of one's life, *ha* takes on a completely new meaning as one continues a relentless pursuit of the next phase of mastery.

Ri is the final stage and literally means "to go beyond or transcend." This is what is commonly referred to as enlightenment or spiritual emancipation. Provoked by relentless austere conditioning, philosophical assimilation and protracted meditation, the intermittent flashes of penetrating wisdom become more frequent as one ascends to the portal. Passing through the portal of the "world within," one is absorbed into its abyss and emerges reborn. Those who fail to enter remain forever unfamiliar with the true essence of karatedo and mastery of the "world without."

This brief description summarizes the doctrine of *shuhari*, which is often referred to in Zen as completing the circle or attaining a primordial state. Although its symbol is an empty circle, it is not void of meaning for those who stand within it. It is filled with life, peace, happiness and fulfillment. The *shuhari* precept knows no time barriers.

When the teacher becomes the student, the master a beginner, and the end a beginning, the beginning will be void of delusion and human misery. In the *Four Quartets*, T. S. Elliot wrote: "We shall not cease from exploration, and the end of all of our exploring will be to arrive where we first started and know that place for the first time."

Bun Bu Ryu Doh of particular significance to the martial arts, this old precept represents balancing martial elements with the literary. *Photo courtesy of P. McCarthy.*

It is said that there can be no limit placed upon kata training. When one is consumed in and by the kata, impermeable layers of silence shield him from both external and internal distractions. Inner confusion gradually dissolves until it no longer exists at all. As one regulates the flow of air from within the body and synchronizes it with the execution of each physical contraction, the kata becomes a powerful vehicle of introspection through which external performance and internal thought correspond harmoniously. Into a muffled roar both external and internal disturbances fade away until they are no longer any more disturbing than the distant sound of rolling thunder. As one gradually building up an immunity to life's trivial distractions, detachment from illusion becomes easier and quicker in time. In this light, kata is often described as moving Zen. Beyond exhaustion, despite aching muscles, we have all experienced a peacefulness flowing quietly within the brutality of karatedo. And it is through this tranquility that our pursuit of fulfillment is realized. The ancient proverb *"bun bu ryu doh"* represents the principles of spiritual emancipation as realized through balancing austere conditioning with philosophical assimilation and protracted meditation.

Kinjo Hiroshi (right) was an instrumental force during Richard Kim's early years in Japan. This photo was taken to commemorate Mr. Kim's kyoshi eighth dan indicated then by the red and white belt. *Photo courtesy of K. Hiroshi.*

When asked to describe what he thought was lacking in karate today Kinjo simply responded by saying "teachers of karatedo!" We need more teachers to pass on the essence of this cultural heritage. Anyone can learn to kick and punch! The meaning of kata is practically unknown these days, even by those anxious to be called sensei. That's why karate is so misunderstood. Karate was never meant to be used against expert fighters as such, but rather was contrived to subdue an attacker who was completely ignorant of the methods being used against him.

With the passing of time, in the history of the civil fighting traditions, moral precepts were deeply embraced in an effort to govern the behavior of those who learned its secrets. Affected by ancient customs, inflexible ideologies and profound religious conviction, the study of the civil fighting traditions took on introspective elements. In modern karate, however, this history has been overshadowed. With the absence of philosophy and introspection, karatedo becomes unbalanced and is reduced to little more than a competitive sport or even a sophisticated means of brutality.

Learned in an orthodox custom karatedo is enlightening. Physical training promotes a healthy body which helps to prevent sickness and is the basis for all happiness. Philosophical assimilation nourishes moral fortitude and "right thinking." Introspection (protracted meditation) completes the regimen by which immeasurable self-conquests are made possible. Together, the non-utilitarian values of karatedo help us to discover our "world within," cultivate its enormous power, and promote modesty, pacifism and harmony while fostering a deeper understanding of life and of the world in which we dwell.

Heeding the wisdom of Kinjo, we are able to perceive karatedo in ways never before imagined. Rather than encouraging us to accumulate excess baggage in life, karatedo advocates simplicity in application. Instead of only taking from karatedo, we must also consider, like Kinjo, establishing a symbiosis with karatedo so that our lives are just as much a product of the art as the art is a product of our lives. All power, happiness and success has to do with putting knowledge into action through mastering the world within. As enthusiasts of this ancient fraternity, we are all responsible to some degree for cultivating the growth and direction of karatedo, a responsibility which extends beyond the dojo and into society as a whole.

Being absorbed in the study of karatedo for the last seventy years, Kinjo Hiroshi assures us all that the fighting traditions are a deeply personal experience which affects each of us in different ways. But the only way of discovering the magnitude of its value is through resolve, sacrifice and perseverance. Only those who have made the journey can testify to the immeasurable personal conquests that are made possible through karatedo.

In discovering the world within, the journey reveals the essence of karatedo. However, a provocative question remains unanswered, inviting each of us to seriously consider not only what we can get by continually taking from this humble tradition, but as responsible enthusiasts concerned with its future direction, what we can put back into karatedo, the art and way of karate.

Notes

[1] A prominent disciple of Itoshu Ankoh (1832-1915), Hanashiro Choma (along with his contemporary Yabu Kentsu (1866-1937) first brought attention to karate-jutsu after being commended for his superb physical conditioning during his army enlistment medical examination in 1891.

[2] Oshro Chojo was a student of Itosu Ankoh's but is perhaps better remembered for his eminent skills in *bojutsu* which he learned directly under Yamane no Chinen Sanda (c. 1846-1928).

[3] The two classes of pechin officials included the *satunushi* (from the upper class) and the *chikudoun* (from the common class).

Editor's Note: Matsumura's *Precepts on Bu* and Itosu's *Ten Lessons* were translated by the International Ryukyu Karate Research Society.

chapter 6

The Karate of Miyagi Chojun
by John Porta and Jack McCabe

Senior students are shown in this 1946 photograph taken at
Miyagi's residence. From left to right are Yagi Meitoku,
Master Miyagi, Miyazato Eiichi, Toguchi Seikichi and Eiko Miyazato.
All photos courtesy of John Porta and Richard Strait.

In the early part of this century, a style of karate was developed on Okinawa that made it possible for many people to learn the benefits of a traditional self-defense system. Eventually becoming known as Goju-ryu (the hard/soft style), the art combined traditional Okinawan techniques with both internal and external Chinese principles. The soft, internal Chinese styles concentrate on circular movements and the development of *qi* (vital energy), while external, hard principles rely upon physical strength. The combination of these principles makes Goju-ryu a close-range, infighting system that concentrates on efficiency of movement as well as personal development.

Master Miyagi Chojun, the founder of Okinawan Goju-ryu karatedo, saw the martial arts as being more than just effective methods of self-defense, and the system that he developed reflected this belief. Through the influence of Master Miyagi, Goju-ryu karate became an educational subject that could be taught in schools, and the creation of new *katas* (forms) made the art more understandable to the public. Miyagi thus became one of the pioneers that brought karate out of its exclusively Okinawan enclave of relatively few practitioners to worldwide acceptance.

Devoting his life to the promotion of the martial arts, Miyagi reportedly made more than ten trips to China, made more than seven to the Japanese mainland, and also visited Hawaii and Korea. It has been said that he spent millions of dollars travelling to promote karate and helping friends with their debts. Since Miyagi was prone to seasickness, he seldom travelled alone and often was not fully recovered from his ailment when giving a demonstration or lecture.

Very pleasant in nature, Miyagi was called *Bushi Miyagusuku* ("Gentleman Warrior Miyagi") on Okinawa. Possessed of tremendous physical strength, he was known far and wide for his extraordinary gripping power and performance of kata that displayed his great devotion to martial arts training. However, Miyagi's gentle manner was his strongest asset. Despite stories that may contain more fable than fact, Miyagi never fought, keeping a promise to his teacher that he would not use the martial arts to hurt another human being.

The Early Years

Born Miyagi Matsu on April 25, 1888, at Higashi Machi, Hana, the son of Miyagi Chosho came to inherit the fortune of one of the wealthiest families on Okinawa ("Miyagi" is the Japanese derivative of the Okinawan name "Miyagusuku"). Involved with the importing of pharmaceuticals, the family owned two trading ships, which were used to supply the government and private merchants. Miyagi was adopted at the age of five by an uncle after the death of the main successor to the family, and his first name was changed to Chojun, as he became heir to the family fortune. Being born into great wealth allowed Miyagi in later years to devote all his time to study and travelling to promote the martial arts.

Left: Higashionna Kanryo, the founder of Naha-te and teacher of Miyagi Chojun. Right: Miyagi Chojun, successor to the Naha-te system and founder of Okinawan Goju-ryu Karate-do.

At the age of eleven, the strongly built youth began training under karate master Aragaki Ryuko. This early instruction consisted mainly of exercises designed to develop the body, using Okinawan implements such as the *chishi* (stone lever weight), *nigirigame* (clay gripping jars), and *makiwara* (punching post). From this strong foundation, Miyagi later carried over the principles of strength development to his own teachings, and he always encouraged his students to engage in supplementary weight training. As a physical culture enthusiast, Miyagi developed scientific methods of exercising that reflect his early training, which stressed the importance of a sound body.

In 1901, Miyagi was introduced to Higashionna Kanryo (1853-1916), a master of Naha-te, who had studied in China before returning to Okinawa, where he became very well-known as a teacher of the martial arts. Miyagi studied under Higashionna for fifteen years and became the successor to the art form that eventually evolved into form Goju-ryu karate.

Master Higashionna became interested in Chinese boxing while working for an import/export company, a job which enabled him to travel back and forth from Okinawa to China. An 1868 trip to Fuzhou in Fujian Province in southern China resulted in his studying under martial artist Ryu Ryu Ko, a master of Shaolin Kempo of the Southern School. When he eventually returned to Okinawa, Higashionna established a style of self-defense known as Naha-te, which was a combination of Chinese Kempo and Okinawan techniques. With his home in Nishi Machi serving as a dojo, Higashionna's fame as a teacher spread, and he became the martial arts instructor for the royal family. In 1905, Higashionna taught the physical and philosophical values of his art at a public high school in Naha.

A modest, quiet man, Master Higashionna stood only five foot one inch tall, but was very strongly built. He was called *Kansei* (sacred fists) on Okinawa and was known for his extremely fast footwork and low kicking techniques. However, Higashionna believed that the integral purpose of the martial arts was to help society, not to hurt people. This philosophy was passed on to his students, especially to Miyagi, on whom the lesson was never lost.

Miyagi Chojun left Dai Ichi Junior High School in Naha in the ninth grade to study Naha-te exclusively and became the only student of Higashionna to learn all the katas of the system. Under Higashionna's instruction, a student would usually concentrate on only one kata over the years and become highly proficient in the particular movements; however, Miyagi was able to learn all aspects of Naha-te. The training was extremely harsh, with a concentration on the *Sanchin* (three battles) kata, which is a breathing form that involves dynamic tension. Miyagi was one of the few who remained a student of Higashionna, despite the rigors of a demanding schedule.

After getting married at the age of nineteen, Miyagi entered the army in 1908 and served the Fifth Division of Kumamoto for three years. In 1915, he made his first trip to China, going to Fuzhou to study Chugoku Kempo, accompanied by his friend Gokenki (1886-1940), who adopted the Japanese name "Yoshikawa" and taught a southern Shaolin form of White Crane in his tea shop in Naha. It is possible that Gokenki's influence on the young Miyagi may be seen in the katas that were developed for Goju-ryu, since they contain movements similar to those of White Crane. This Chinese system is also known as *Paihaoquan* or, in the Japanese translation, as *Hakutsuru Ken* and was developed by Fang Chiliang, a woman who lived in Tan Yong Chun in Fujian Province.

Miagi's relationship with his teacher was a close one, as his wealth allowed him to house Higashionna and pay for instruction. Since he remained in the constant company of Higashionna, Miyagi was able to learn all the Naha-te kata under the master's close scrutiny. Saddened by the death of Higashionna in October of 1916, Miyagi took care of all funeral arrangements, then went back to China in search of the dojo of Ryu Ryu Ko but was unsuccessful in the attempt. When Miyagi returned to Okinawa in 1917, he became instructor at the Okinawa-ken Police Training Center, Naha City Commercial School, Okinawa Normal School, and the Prefectural Health Center.

Miyagi Chojun with a group of his high school students. Note the different types of equipment that were used for supplementary strength training, which was always a major part of Miyagi's instruction.

Early Goju-ryu Development

The influences of Chinese styles combined with Naha-te principles eventually formed the Goju-ryu system of karate. Having studied hard, external styles along with the soft, internal systems of yiquan, baguachang, and taijiquan, Miyagi Chojun used his extensive knowledge of the martial arts to develop Goju-ryu. Adding closed fists to the Sanchin forms, Miyagi also created the *Tensho* (turning palm) kata to emphasize softness in movement. Like his teacher, Higashionna, Miyagi strictly believed in the benefits of the Sanchin kata but included the softer White Crane-influenced techniques in his instruction. However, Sanchin always made up the heart of Miyagi's art. Designed to train and build the body through breathing techniques, the physical strength developed through the practice of Sanchin remains a characteristic that distinguishes traditional Okinawan Goju-ryu from other, less physical styles.

To describe his system, Miyagi compared it to a willow tree standing against the wind, remaining stable because of its strong roots, while the branches flow and give with the force. The twelve katas originally taught by Miyagi, which have their foundations in China, still form the basis for Goju-ryu today, though the names may differ in translation from Chinese to Japanese to English. Along with the aforementioned Sanchin and Tensho, the other katas include *Gekisai-Ichi* and *Gekisai-Ni* (attack and smash I and II), *Saifa* (smash and break), *Seienchin* (to grab and pull in battle), *Sanseiru* (thirty-six hands), *Seipai* (eighteen hands), *Shisochin* (four directions battle), *Seisan* (thirteen hands), *Kururunfa* (to destroy with ancient mantis techniques), and *Supairenpei* (108 hands) forms.

The movements contained within Goju-ryu katas are intended for self-defense and not for sport. Short, circular blocks, powerful holds and locks, efficient punching maneuvers, and kicking techniques targeted to the lower body characterize the art that Miyagi so carefully developed. These techniques are not flashy or acrobatic, which makes Goju-ryu an excellent style for defending oneself in a street situation.

As a teacher, Miyagi was very strict and placed a great emphasis on basics. His dojo was actually a courtyard surrounded by a stone wall and illuminated by oil lamps, where kata were taught step-by-step and a student did not progress to the next movement until thoroughly learning the previous one. Miyagi would not accept payment for his instruction and did not promote his students, since there was no ranking system.

Among those who studied under Miyagi and later carried on his original teachings were Higa Seiko, Yagi Meitoku, Toguchi Seikichi, and Eiichi Miyazato. Another student, Yogi Jitsuei, was the teacher of Yamaguchi Gogen, who went on to gain fame in his own right with the development of Japanese Goju-ryu karate. On occasion, Yamaguchi also sought advice and training instruction from Yagi Meitoku throughout the years. Higa, who had trained under Higashionna since the age of thirteen, assisted Miyagi when Miyagi became successor to the Naha-te system and was the only person ever authorized by Miyagi to teach Goju-ryu karate.

Like Higashionna, Miyagi believed in teaching the Sanchin kata for an extended period of time, then instructing a student in another form according to that student's physical build and personal preferences. For example, Yagi learned Supairenpei, Toguchi was taught Seipei, and Miyazato studied Kururufa as a second kata. Unlike the Goju-ryu testing system of today, Miyagi picked the second kata to be taught to a student and did not follow any predetermined regimen. The organizational ranking system of Miyagi's art was developed after his death in 1953.

While Miyagi was sought out for his instruction by many potential students, not many stayed due to the extremely demanding procedures that made up the original Goju-ryu training regimen. Demanding as much from his students as he did from himself, Miyagi taught in an intense manner that belied his gentle nature. Stories abound concerning the necessity of hanging ropes above toilet facilities, because students would be so tired from the hard training that they could not arise from a squatting position if they did not have something to hang onto. Also, it was said that Miyagi's students were always recognizable in public bath houses due to the red marks that were left as a result of Sanchin kata testing.

Promoting Karate and Naming the Art

Exemplified by his public demonstrations and performances in front of royalty, it seems that Miyagi's primary goal was to make more people aware of the benefits of studying a martial art. In 1921, Miyagi impressed Crown Prince Hirohito with a demonstration of Naha-te that was part of a ceremony marking the prince's stopover in Okinawa's Nakagusuku Bay while on tour. Four years later, Miyagi was equally impressive in performing for Prince Yasuhito Chichibu. As he became more famous, Miyagi was able to meet people who could help him realize his desire to open up the Okinawan arts to the public.

In 1922, judo founder Kano Jigoro gave a lecture on Okinawa that greatly influenced Miyagi. Several years later, Kano returned to the largest island in the Ryukyu archipelago and saw Miyagi demonstrate his unique skills in the name of Okinawan martial arts. That demonstration became legendary in Okinawan martial art circles. It is said that Miyagi remained uninjured while being struck with a *bo* (long staff) and displayed his tremendous gripping strength by tearing the bark off a tree with his fingers and ripping pieces off a large slab of meat with his bare hands. The performance was not forgotten by Kano, who would use his influence to allow Miyagi to take part in Japanese martial arts demonstrations.

Miyagi's first trip to Japan took place in 1928, when he lectured and demonstrated at Kansai, Kyoto, and Ritsumeikan universities. Returning to Okinawa in 1929, he became instructor at the Prefectural Police Dojo and later at Naha Courthouse, Prefectural Physical Culture Association, and the Prefectural Teachers' Training College. It was around this time that it became necessary to name the system that was growing in popularity throughout Okinawa and Japan.

As to the naming of Miyagi's system, it has been recorded that his senior student, Shinzato Jinan (1900-1945), was demonstrating in Japan when he was asked the name of his style of self-defense. Unable to accurately reply, he returned to Okinawa and consulted Miyagi, who came up with the title "Goju-ryu," taken from a line in the *Bubishi* (called *Wubeizhi* in Chinese), a record of the eight precepts of Chinese Kempo. In this way, Miyagi became the first Okinawan karate master not to name a system after the area in which it was practiced (such as Naha-te, Shuri-te, and Tomari-te).

Miyagi performed for the *Dai Nippon Butokukai* (Greater Japan Martial Arts Association, the official governing body for Japanese martial arts) in 1930, and at the Sainei Budo Temple in 1932. His influence then led to the official recognition of karate as a martial art of Japan with the formation of the Dai Nippon Butokukai Okinawa Branch, to which he was appointed representative. Miyagi received a commendation from the Japan Ministry of Education for outstanding service in the physical culture field in 1934, the same year he published a paper on karate and made a trip to Hawaii to promote the art.

Miyagi called for martial arts unity and expressed the opinion that karate instruction should be made available to the rest of the world during a lecture in Japan's Sakaisuji Meiji Syoten Hall in January of 1936. The Goju-ryu founder also stated his belief that karate could not grow with solely classical kata and that new kata should be developed to help the public learn the martial art. The Gekisai-Ichi and Gekisai-Ni kata were created with this intention around 1940. Miyagi originally planned to develop a series of Gekisai forms, but World War II interrupted training and instruction on Okinawa and the other kata were never developed.

Miyagi received a medal for excellence in the martial arts from the Japanese Ministry of Education in 1936 and also became the first person in karate to be granted the *kyoshi* (assistant professor) degree from the Dai Nippon Butokukai. In October of the same year, he attended a conference that adopted "karate" as official name of the martial art of Okinawa. A trip to Shanghai for further study of the Chinese arts took place, with Miyagi staying for over two months.

Further promotion of karate took place in 1937, as Prince Nashimoto Moriwasa, commissioner of the Dai Nippon Butokukai, authorized Miyagi and several judo headmasters to create the *Dai Nippon Butokukai Karate Jukkyoshi* (Greater Japan Martial Arts Karate Teachers' Association). This organization would regulate karate throughout Japan. At the time, karate fell under the same classification as judo; therefore, in order to gain independence, Miyagi and a group of Okinawan karate masters established the Okinawan Karate-Do Preservation Society. Those founding the association included Choshin Chibana, Hanashiro Chomo, Motobu Choki, Shinpan Shiroma, and Yabu Kentsu.

War and Its After-Effects

Master Miyagi taught in Japan for the last time in 1943, when he lectured in Kyoto at Ritsumeikan University. Shortly thereafter, karate instruction was interrupted by the war that was raging in the Pacific. Shinzato Jinan, Miyagi's senior student, was killed during the early fighting of the Battle of Okinawa in 1945, and Miyagi's third son, Jun, also died in this most bloody conflict.

Karate spread throughout Japan and Okinawa in the wake of the devastation created by World War II, and Miyagi resumed teaching in 1946, using the backyard of his home in Tsuboya-cho as his dojo. Though plagued by ill health in the form of high blood pressure and a heart condition, Miyagi continued to promote his art and was appointed as an official of the *Okinawan Minsei Taiiku Ken* (Okinawan Democratic Athletic Association) and as director of the Okinawan Civil Association of Physical Education. He also taught at the Okinawan police academy at the time.

According to Toguchi Seikichi, who studied under both Miyagi and Higa Seiko, it was in 1952 or 1953 that Miyagi was made president of the Goju-ryu Shinkokai, an organization that was established for the purpose of promoting the art. At this time, Miyagi's students approached him and asked if he would grant promotions, feeling that karate lagged behind the Japanese martial arts of judo and kendo because there was no formalized ranking system. However, Miyagi still refused to grant promotions to any of his students. As a person of great humility, Miyagi believed himself unworthy of granting black-belts and that a true black-belt degree should only be awarded by a member of the emperor's family or a sanctioning body such as the Butokukai.

Master Miyagi died of a heart attack on October 8, 1953, at the age of sixty-five. Since his death was so sudden, there was no official successor to Goju-ryu named. Higa Seiko, who was always considered as more of an assistant to Miyagi than a student, was accepted as the master's successor by all the senior students and continued to teach Goju-ryu until his death in 1966.

Carrying on the Tradition

After the death of Miyagi, his senior students formed an association known as the All-Okinawan Goju-kai, which was a reorganization of the Goju-ryu Shinkokai, and a promotional ranking system for the art was established. Yagi, Toguchi, and Miyazato assumed the *hachidun* (eighth degree) black-belt ranking, and various schools of Goju-ryu were opened, with Yagi teaching at his Meibukan school, Toguchi at Shorikan, and Miyazato at Jundokan. Yagi, as Miyagi's senior student after the death of Shinzato Jinan, came to inherit the master's gi and black belt from the Miyagi family in 1963. Eventually, all three senior students of Miyagi, as heads of their respective Goju-ryu organizations, were elevated to the rank of tenth degree black-belt.

As the only person Miyagi ever authorized to teach Goju-ryu, Higa Seiko had opened up a dojo in Shioizumi Village, Naha, in 1931, and moved the school to Matsushita Village also in Naha two years later. Higa was awarded the *renshi* (teaching) grade from the Dai Nippon Butokukai upon his return from the South Pacific island of Saipan, where he taught Goju-ryu from 1937 to 1939. In 1956, Higa became the first vice-president of the All-Okinawan Karatedo Renmei, an organization that represented the major Okinawan karate styles. Choshin Chibana was the founding president of this group, which was renamed the All Okinawan Karatedo Federation in 1967 and remains the largest karate organization on Okinawa today.

Higa received the hanshi grade by mutual consent of all members of the All-Okinawan Karatedo Renmei in 1958 and built the Shodokan dojo. Formerly an elementary school teacher, Higa was serving as a policeman in Itoman City when he formed the International Karate and Kobudo Federation, also in 1958. This organization was established for the purpose of researching Goju-ryu and unifying the katas. After World War II, Higa opened a dojo in Itoman and taught at Itoman High School.

On Okinawa, a Goju-ryu master named Shinjo Masanobu emerged and, like Miyagi before him, became known for his gentle nature and extraordinary strength. Those who knew Miyagi described Shinjo as being closer to the master in the way he performed kata and techniques than any other

Goju-ryu practitioner. This similarity may have resulted from Shinjo's seeking out anyone on Okinawa who had trained under Miyagi for the purpose of studying their individual kata, since Miyagi usually had his students specialize in only one kata, along with Sanchin. In this way, Shinjo was able to learn all aspects of Goju-ryu as Miyagi had previously done with the study of Naha-te under Higashionna.

While in his childhood, Shinjo studied under Miyagi Chojun and later with Toguchi Seikichi and Yagi Meitoku. In 1990, Shinjo succeeded Yagi as president of the All-Okinawan Goju-kai, while still serving as chief instructor of the Okinawan Goju-ryu Shobukan Association, which he had founded. Through this direct lineage, the teaching and integrity of Miyagi's art were maintained.

Left: Shinjo Masanobu performing the Supairenapai kata during the 1990 Uchinan-chu Fetival on Okinawa. Right: Master Shinjo exercising with *nigirigame* (clay gripping jars).

The karate world suffered a serious setback in October of 1993 with the untimely passing of Master Shinjo after a year-long illness. Like Master Miyagi, Shinjo had spent his life promoting Goju-ryu, making trips to China and the Shaolin Temple, and visiting his United States Shobukan headquarters and branch schools in 1987.

As one of the more popular systems of karate today, Goju-ryu has now become accepted around the world. But with this increased popularity comes the problem of authenticity, since there are numerous organizations and individuals, especially in the United States, that operate under the Goju-ryu name that actually have little or no connection to the lineage of Miyagi Chojun. Though claiming otherwise, such systems may teach in a manner that is a far cry from the original instruction of Miyagi, sacrificing through a lack of traditional knowledge the basics and integral components of the art that were so carefully developed by the founder and followed by his successors.

It is the task of today's schools of Goju-ryu to maintain the principles set forth by Masters Higashionna and Miyagi so many years ago and by their successors such as Master Shinjo. The art that was born on the island of Okinawa has now spread worldwide, seemingly in keeping with the wishes of the founder, who always believed that karate should be made available to the public. As such, Goju-ryu is first and foremost a means of personal development that builds the confidence to enable someone to become an outstanding citizen. In developing the concepts of Goju-ryu to a high degree, Master Miyagi served society by making life better for anyone who has the opportunity to train in his system.

Photo of Shinjo Masanobu and John Porta
taken in Shinjo's Shobukan dojo in Yaeshima.

Bibliography

Alexander, G. W. (1991). *Okinawa: Island of karate*. Lake Worth, FL: Yamazato Publications.

Babiadelis, P. (1993, January). The sensei who received Chojun Miyagi's belt. *Martial Arts Masters*, pp. 60-74.

Bishop, M. (1989). *Okinawan karate: Teachers, system, and secret techniques*. London: A&C Black.

Corcoran, J., and Farkas, E. (1983). *Martial arts traditions, history, people*. New York: W. H. Smith.

Funakoshi, G. (1987). *Karate-do nyumon*. Tokyo: Kodansha International.

Funakoshi, G. (1973). *Karate-do kyohan*. Tokyo: Kodansha International.

Higaonna, M. (1985). *Traditional karatedo–Fundamental techniques*. Tokyo: Minato Research and Publishing.

Iwai, T. (1992). *Koden Ryukyu karate jutsu*. Japan: Airyudo.

Kim, R. (1974). *The weaponless warriors*. Los Angeles: Ohara Publications.

Nagamine, S. (1976). *The essence of Okinawan karate-do*. Rutland, VT: Charles E. Tuttle Co.

Nakaya, T. (1986). *Karate-do history and philosophy*. Carrollton, TX: JSS Publishing Co.

Nakayama, M. (1960). *Dynamic karate*. Tokyo: Kodansha International.

Oyama, M. (1965). *This is karate*. Rutland, VT: Japan Publications.

McCarthy, P. (1990). *The bubishi*. Kanagawa: International Ryukyu Karate Research Society.

Random, M. (1984). *The martial arts*. London: Peerage Books.

Reid, H., and Croucher, M. (1983). *The fighting arts*. New York: Simon and Schuster.

Toguchi, S. (1976). *Okinawan Goju-ryu*. Burbank, CA: Ohara Publications.

Toguchi, S. (1986). *Interview with Seikichi Toguchi*. [Video tapes]. (Vols. 1, 2, and 3). Toguchi Productions.

Urban, P. (1967). *The karate dojo*. Rutland, VT: Charles E. Tuttle Co.

chapter 7

The Sources of Power in Karate
by Kazumasa Yokoyama

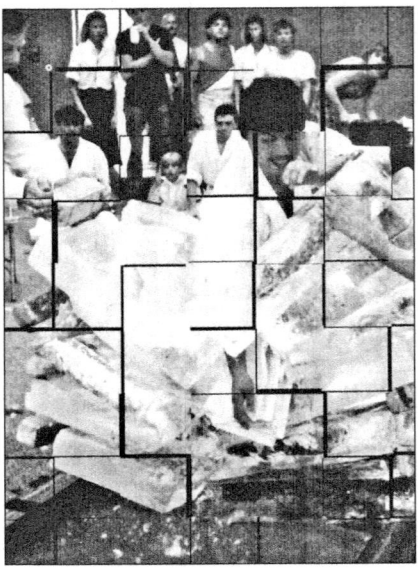

All photos courtesy K. Yokoyama

Power: Where Does It Come From?

Karate is an organized system of acquired martial skills in which, by using the entire body, one can successfully dominate an adversary. During karate practice, you learn how to utilize the body naturally and rationally, which enables you to defend yourself. It is important to keep in mind that there is already an innate capacity for self-preservation in everyone, and when physically confronted, a person will instinctively resist by employing punches, kicks and other defensive movements. However, the level of innate abilities differs greatly from person to person. And those who only have these attributes to rely on will discover that in a confrontation their natural abilities may be considerably inferior to those of their adversary. Why? . . . Because each person is structured differently: tall or short, light or heavy, etc.

A large person naturally possesses a greater body mass than a smaller person. It is, therefore, logical to assume that the larger person will be able to exert greater power with less effort, but reliance on muscle strength alone neglects other sources of power. Karate compensates for inherited disadvantages, such as body size, through training and mastery of martial skills.

For example, two people may engage in batting competition. One is a small individual who has ten years experience playing baseball. The other is a large person who has never played before. Even if the larger person is "stronger," he will not be able to hit the ball farther than the smaller, more experienced person. The reason for this is the smaller person has acquired the skill of using his body in the most effective manner, which enables him to hit the ball farther. Most believe that "power" is in direct proportion to a large, muscular physique. This in not necessarily true. Additionally, the average person uses a maximum of only thirty percent of his body's muscular capabilities. There are a few reasons why this is so.

There certainly are many different types of power. Among these are the kinds of power employed when lifting, pushing, pulling, flexing, etc. Every type of muscular power requires effort from start to finish in order to attain a given goal. Therefore, the power found within a karate technique is derived from motion and the concentration necessary to execute the techniques. Motion includes the balance, speed, degree of movement and timing which are required for the correct execution of the technique. These factors form the source upon which the power in karate techniques is derived. It is possible to attain incredible power by combining and properly utilizing these elements. Furthermore, these factors do not depend on innate abilities or physique, but can be learned and adapted by anyone. One reason why karate is so beneficial is that it teaches all of these aspects which deal with psychosomatics.

By transferring these principles to self-defense, one learns how to create more power through practicing and perfecting basic karate movements. Karate's basic movements fully utilize the natural attributes of the human body, which students learn to integrate to achieve a higher level of martial skill. However, the practice of karate without true understanding of basic body principles and correct movement is merely a ritual in which the movements have no meaning and the true essence of karate will always remain out of reach.

In order to experience the essence or spirit of karate, you must not only understand the doctrines of power but also always practice the principles and movements together as a whole. This concept of power is based on the "theory of opposites."

The "theory of opposites" was inspired by the Chinese theory of yin and yang, called *in* and *yo* in Japanese. *In* represents dark, cold, sadness, internal, low, left, crooked, defensive, etc. *Yo* represents light, heat, motion, happiness, external, high, right, straight, aggressive, etc. For instance, everything in nature possesses a beginning and an ending and evolves and progresses according to a natural order. Nature is a product of such balances and cannot survive without them. For example, if a sudden drop in temperature occurs in the north, the temperature in the south will rise. The difference between the two temperatures creates winds, and if the difference is great, powerful winds will occur.

A simple example to illustrate the *in/yo* concept can be found in the positive (+) and negative (−) ends found on batteries. The battery will not function with only a positive charge or only a negative one. Only if both charges coexist together can any electrical flow be brought about. After objectively seeing the *in/yo* duality work in nature, we can then apply the same principles to body mechanics. If *in/yo* are applied in martial art practice, a one-hundred percent use of power becomes possible rather than the mere thirty percent used by the beginning student.

The *in/yo* principles are also applied to the physiology of the human body. Walking, for example, is generally taken for granted, but analyze the process and you will find some important principles. When you step forward with your right foot (+), your left arm (−) naturally swings forward, and vice versa. This balanced motion provides a fluidity to movement. Even when you use a more rapid arm motion, the speed of your legs will automatically increase to the same pace. Slow down your leg speed and your arms will respond in the same manner. The same theory of opposites applies to martial arts. For example, if a boxer receives a blow to the left side of his head, the right side of his body may go numb. Or if he is struck in the jaw, his feet may be affected. This is indicative of the human body's relationship to the principles of *in* and *yo* and is called the "cross-power theory." According to this theory, the power in karate techniques comes from the ground up through the feet and legs, the shoulders being positioned to keep the body balanced. To obtain a clearer understanding of this, imagine a diagonal line drawn from the left foot up to the right shoulder and another line drawn from the right foot up to the left shoulder. The area where these two lines intersect is in the abdominal region and is the seat of power.

It is generally believed that punching requires proper use of the hips because the hips are located where the imagined lines intersect. When one executes a right reverse punch from a forward stance, power ideally travels from the right back leg through the intersection point and down the left forward leg. When this principle is put into practice, greater speed and power can be achieved by pulling the left hand back quickly and strongly as the right hand is punching. Power is amplified by using stored energy in the intersection point and twisting the upper body until the fist is within a fraction of an inch from the target. At the moment of impact, arm and fist power is added. To execute the roundhouse kick, face your opponent with the upper body and bring your kicking foot up in a crescent motion. As the foot makes contact, twist the upper body towards the kicking leg. In this way, even a beginning karate student can have relatively good kicking power. The key is in using the twisting motion of the entire body. This is the basis of the cross-power theory, which is founded on *in* and *yo*. Virtually infinite power can be created by applying the *in/yo* theory to the practice of karate techniques in which power can be exhibited using a much shorter attacking range than is normally required. The "one-inch punch" technique is only one of the many applications of this principle.

The principles regarding the source of power in classic karate involve the fluctuating relationship between *in* and *yo*. The reverse punch is a basic karate technique which illustrates this principle of movement.

Up to this point, the examples have been concerned with body movements. Now combine the physical mechanics with the respiratory system, and the result is the ability to use one hundred percent of the body's abilities instead of only thirty percent. Respiration is a system designed to maintain life by continued inhalation and exhalation from the moment we are born to the time we die. Inhaling creates tension and exhaling releases tension. Therefore, if respiration is erratic then the bodily functions are also erratic, and vice versa. We can discern the body's condition by observing the rate of respiration.

There are two major kinds of breathing: thorax and abdominal, each with different characteristics of its own. Thorax breathing is very light and shallow and involves the upper body. Abdominal breathing is heavy and deep and is concentrated lower in the body,

Some believe that roundhouse kicks spontaneously evolved from irregular front-kicks during tournaments in the 1950s.

Thorax and abdominal breathing each has its own advantages and applications, but the reason abdominal breathing is so important in martial arts and meditation is that the oxygen, which is the fuel that maintains life, is assimilated through the nose and absorbed internally. It is then mentally gathered in the pelvic region where the entire process smoothly unifies the mind, body and power and circulates throughout the body's cardiovascular system. At this point, all worldly thoughts and cares are banished from the mind. The body and spirit are in their most natural state, enabling the latent abilities to be awakened and enhanced. Thorax breathing is not suitable for projecting the power outward because this type of breathing primarily utilizes the upper body. It keeps the body's balance high and thus makes it unstable. The legs are also affected in that they are not able to be firmly rooted to the ground.

In Japanese martial arts and Zen, the oxygen and bodily energy which are assimilated internally and brought together at the point at which the two diagonal lines intersect is called the *tanden* (Chinese, *dantian*). The tanden is located within the pelvic region and is the source of internal power. Imagine the pelvic region as a circle, and the tanden as the general area where the lines intersect. In other words, the tanden is the pivotal point around which the pelvis rotates, and is the intersection point (cross-power point) of the two diagonal lines.

Before one can understand how to obtain power utilizing the tanden and respiration, one must first grasp the relationship between the body's reflexes and respiration. Respiration is comprised of three basic parts to which the body unconsciously responds: inhalation, exhalation, and a momentary pause before reinhalation. During inhalation the body will expand, lengthen, and arch slightly. These are visible reactions to the power moving inward. During the momentary pause between breaths, the body's natural reflexes also pause. When you work on small or complex tasks, your breathing is very quiet and subtle. This is the body's unconscious method of controlling respiration and thereby avoiding excessive movement. Many people believe inhaling is preferable to create outward power, but during inhalation the body expands, arches, and is, therefore, more vulnerable. In this position it is impossible to make power. Exhaling is also nonconducive to making power because the power, or air, which has been collected internally is expelled.

These weaknesses are the reasons for the "air compression theory," which takes advantage of abdominal breathing. In this theory, before you make real power you must first make air power. To accomplish this, inhale the normal amount of air sharply just before executing a technique, and push the air down to the tanden. Here, air is compressed top to bottom, and side to side by the cross-power theory. Then, as the compressed air expands the technique is executed at the same time. If you were to hit a fully inflated ball against a wall, it would bounce well because at the moment of impact the shape is changed, and the air within the ball compresses since it cannot find an outlet. However, the ball's shape returns to normal, which is its most stable state. The result is that the compressed air radiates energy to the outside of the ball. But if the ball has a hole in it, there is an outlet so that when the ball hits the wall the air does not compress because it can now escape. Therefore, the ball does not bounce as well as a fully inflated one.

This is one of the principles of the power (air compression theory) of abdominal breathing. In addition, the body and respiration must be accompanied by conditioned reflexes of which there are numerous martial applications. All body movements must be done rationally, based on correct breathing and knowledge.

The "tespiration theory" involves taking air that we inhale and converting it into energy. On the other side of the same coin is the "kiai theory," which states that something latent within the body is converted into energy. *Kiai* is a word used among martial artists that has considerable meaning. *Ki* means mind, spirit, and air; *ai* means to harmonize or combine. Therefore, *kiai* refers to the unification of the mind and body.

There are several methods of kiai, all of which utilize a shout or some other application of the voice. The aim of the kiai theory is to push the body past normal boundaries by using the voice and thus give both mind and body the encouragement and confidence necessary to achieve any goal. During the kiai, your body is in the same state as during exhalation, which by itself is not conductive to the making of power. However, when used properly, kiai can eliminate all other thoughts, fears, and uncertainties, thereby giving the body purpose and direction which acts as a form of energy.

According to this theory as well as the previously mentioned abdominal theory, it is preferable for the oxygen to be expelled forcefully using the voice and the tanden. Also, by timing a kiai just before the execution of a technique, at the precise moment of execution and just after execution, several results are brought about. The most important of these is that when the kiai concentrates internal energy and expels it, it leaves the body prepared to receive new energy to be assimilated. By practicing basic movements with kiai, you circulate oxygen, which is the source of energy, thus increasing power, endurance, spirit and mental focus. Both the respiration and kiai theories emphasize the circulation of oxygen at the source of life—the tanden. The application of both theories exhibit a tremendously positive effect on health and discipline. This utilization of the body to make superior use of power in basic movements is absolutely vital to karate.

If one learns and practices constantly, the techniques will become instinctive. In order for someone to train properly in karate, the curriculum should be taught sequentially, one level at a time, with basics as the first level, then kata, techniques, and finally kumite; each level utilizing its own applications and examples.

It is not difficult to imitate karate movements, disregarding the applications and meanings, but no matter how closely such movements resemble to be true karate, they are devoid of substance just like an empty water glass. This is completely different from a glass full of water, which, though upon first glance it appears to be the same, is not able to meet the same needs.

Karate, which has been passed down from generation to generation, must be an art of the mind, body, and skills based on fighting techniques. The martial arts have progressed tremendously since their journey from China to Japan and elsewhere and have survived the good and bad of many decades. However, if it is to continue to survive, we, the practitioners, have a responsibility to study diligently and keep our minds selfless and our bodies strong and never forsake the basics. For it is the basics which are the foundation of all martial arts, without which they become just another form of exercise.

What martial arts will be in the future depends on us, right here and now, and it is up to us to keep the spirit alive and preserve the "art" in the martial arts.

TECHNICAL SECTION

The following techniques illustrate the "cross power" and "air compression" theories. Mr. Yokoyama demonstrates sequences from two Okinawan Shorin-ryu katas. Techniques "A" and "B" are illustrated by the advanced Gojushiho form. Technique "C" is illustrated by Naihanchi Shodan, usually used for close-fighting in a small area.

"A" — Gojushiho: Elbow Strike

A-1 Yokoyama gathers energy towards his body while inhaling naturally. Air is compressed at the tanden, the pivotal point around which the pelvis rotates. This is the intersection point, or "cross-power point," of the imaginary diagonal lines described on page 91.

A-2 The outward motion of the arms and legs explosively releases the compressed air, which in turn releases energy from inside the body.

A-3 The opponent prepares to attack Yokoyama.

A-4 The opponent quickly grabs Yokoyama's left arm in preparation for a sweeping technique.

A-5 As the opponent attempts to sweep the leg, Yokoyama defends by raising and moving his left-leg in the direction of the sweep, while positioning his right hand to control his opponent.

A-6 Yokoyama demonstrates *in* and *yo* by simultaneously grabbing his opponent's arm with his right hand while moving closer to the opponent with his right leg.

A-7 Yokoyama executes a crossing movement by stepping behind his opponent and stomping the ground with his left leg as he pulls his opponent with his right arm. His right leg shifts to his right to provide the angle for his left elbow to strike his opponent's rib cage. The simultaneous execution of both moves forces energy from the ground diagonally up through the legs to the opposite shoulders and creates the crossing movement at the tanden. As the crossing movement is being executed, Yokoyama forces compressed air down into his tanden to maximize the power.

"B" — Gojushio Palm-hand Strike

B-1   Mr. Yokoyama prepares to demonstrate a cross movement technique. The power comes from the ground up through the feet and legs, with the shoulders positioned to keep the body balanced.

B-2   The application of the cross-power theory is demonstrated by the combination of the twisting motion of the body to the left while crossing the right arm and left leg with the left arm and right leg.

B-3   The palm hand strike to the lower body illustrates combining crossing power with the principle of *in/yo*. Turning into the opponent transfers energy from the ground, through the legs, diagonally to the opposite shoulders. Greater speed and power are achieved by using the twisting motion of the right leg (*in*) to support the left hand (*in*), which is pulled back quickly and strongly, as the right hand (*yo*) and left leg (*yo*) advance to attack.

B-4　The opponent attacks Yokoyama's left shoulder.

B-5　Yokoyama turns to his left and his left hand deflects the opponent's right arm.

B-6　Yokoyama completes the circular motion with his left arm and traps his opponent's right arm.

B-7　Mr. Yokoyama uses a palm hand strike to the opponent's groin. The left hand (*in*) controls the opponent (defensive/negative). The left leg steps into the opponent and the right hand (*yo*) strikes the opponent's groin (aggressive/positive).

Special thanks to Mr. Kirk Weaver for assisting Mr. Yokoyama in the photo illustrations.

"C" — Naihanchi Shodan: Elbow Strike

C-1　This is an important technique in Okinawan Shorin-ryu and Shuri-te. It uses the Naihanchi stance, a very important one for karate because it shows the crossing technique of *in* and *yo*. Yokoyama demonstrates energy being compressed by inhaling naturally while crossing over to step sideways.

C-2　Compressed air is forced into the tanden as weight is shifted into the Naihanchi stance. Energy is transmitted from the ground diagonally to the shoulders, crossing the tanden. A hook strike is executed with the right hand (*yo*) as the left hand is pulled back (*in*).

C-3　The elbow strike is executed by bringing power from the ground up through the legs as the right hand reaches out to grab and then crosses to the striking left elbow.

C-4　The opponent prepares for an attack.

C-5　The opponent attempts a middle punch, but Mr. Yokoyama steps to the side and with a circular motion lifts and controls the opponent's right arm.

C-6   Yokoyama's left hand (*yo*) strikes the opponent's neck while his right hand (*in*) controls the opponent's arm.

C-7   The left hand becomes the *in* hand and controls the opponent's neck. The right hand becomes the *yo* hand and provides the strike.

C-8   As Mr. Yokoyama's left hand continues to control the opponent's neck, his left leg twists toward the opponent, pulling him in. At the same time, Yokoyama's right elbow strikes the opponent's lower rib.

chapter 8

The Okinawan Sai:
A Kobudo Weapon for Self-defense
by Mary Bolz, B.S.

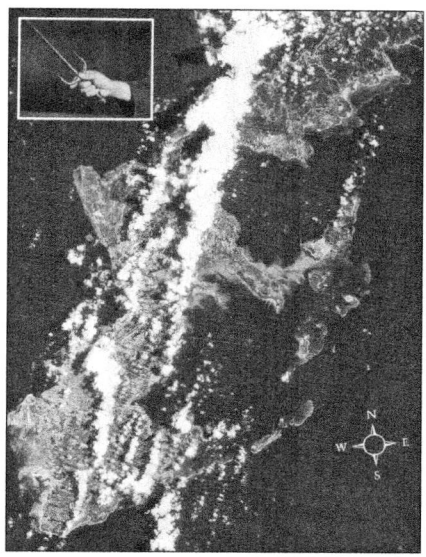

Landsat view of the southern half of Okinawa. Photograph available from the U.S. Department of the Interior, U.S. Geological Survey EROS Data Center. ID#: LM8290300574500.

Kobudo (古武道) is a Japanese word which translated means "ancient stop-fight way." The character 古 means "old" or "ancient." The character 武, pronounced *bu*, consists of two sub-characters: one is 止, *to(maru)* or *shi*, which means "to stop," and the other is 戈, *hoko*, which means "an arrow," a symbol of war or fighting. The last character 道, *do*, means "road," (path, or way).

Originally, the word kobudo was a general term for all old martial arts. Today, however, in Japan and in Okinawa the word kobudo is used to refer to the martial arts in which weapons are used as opposed to the "empty hand" or karate. One reason for this may be that the use of weapons for combat is such older than weaponless combat. Karate was later incorporated into kobudo training and eventually was separated from kobudo and practiced as a combat art on its own. Karate became extremely popular after the Meiji era (1868-1912), since the feudal age of warriors had ended and a new age of peace had arrived until World War II. During this new era (1912-1930s), kobudo almost completely died out in Okinawa. In the "MacArthur Era," which followed World War II, kobudo, along with all other martial arts, was officially banned in Japan and Okinawa. According to the book *Iaido*, published by the Zen Nihon Kendo Renmei, this ban was lifted in 1952, and the practice of kendo and other martial arts was again permitted.

In spite of the MacArthur Era edict, a few Okinawan kobudo practitioners continued to practice, thereby keeping the art alive. One such practitioner was Matayoshi Shinko (1888-1947) from Naha City, who passed on the art to his top-ranking disciple and son, Matayoshi Shinpo, who is teaching kobudo to this day. The sai techniques in this article are those originally taught by Matayoshi Shinpo to Nishiuchi Mikio, President of the International Okinawa Kobudo Association, U.S.A. The weapons recognized and taught by this association are *roku-shaku bo* (approximately a six-foot staff), *sai*, *tuifa* (also pronounced *tonfa*, *tungua*, or *tunkua*), *nunchaku*, *iyeku* (oar), *kama* (sickles), *timbei* (Asian shield), *suruchin* (two rocks on a rope, somewhat like a bola), *tekko* (Okinawan version of brass knuckles), *tetchu* (looks like a miniature *tuifa* which fits in one's palm), *nunti* (*manji sai* attached to the end of a long staff), *kuwa* (hoe), and *san-setsu-kon* (three-sectional staff).

Almost all of the Okinawan kobudo weapons originated from farming and fishing tools. The sai is one that more than likely did not and, according to the Okinawan kobudo masters, seems to have been designed as a defensive weapon. It has been stated in some English-language publications that the sai was originally a pitchfork-like tool used to pick up hay. This seems to have been a theory surmised by Western martial artists. None of the numerous Okinawan kobudo masters interviewed by Nishiuchi Mikio nor any historical information written in Okinawan or Japanese language researched by him mentions such a theory. If one is familiar with Okinawan land and culture, one would think that the idea of the sai coming from a pitchfork is very unlikely. The Okinawans did not harvest hay, they did not use pitchforks, and their farming methods are much different from those in the West. Rice straw was picked up and hung on bamboo stands in the fields by hand just as it is today. The size of a farm in Okinawa is very small compared to a standard American farm. Okinawan farming fields are similar in size to a large garden in the United States; therefore, farming in Okinawa involves much more actual hand labor with less tools. Since the development of the sai was not recorded in writing (it was practiced in secret to prevent enemies from learning the techniques), its exact place of origin is unknown. Some Okinawan kobudo masters say that it was designed as a weapon to be used against professional warriors, such as those wielding a sword, but this has not yet been proven. What is certain is that the sai was carried by the Okinawan police officers (*chikusaji*) and became their symbol, much like a badge is the symbol of police officers in the West.

According to Sotoma Tetsuhiro and Kinjo Masakazu, authors of *Kobudo-gu Okinawa no Tanren Dogu* (only available in Japanese), and many other kobudo masters interviewed by Nishiuchi, four main theories as to the origin of the sai are prevalent among the native Okinawan masters. One theory is that the weapon comes from the Okinawan ladies' hairpin, called *kanzashi*, which had a similar shape to that of the sai. The kanzashi were used to keep the woman's hairdo in place and also were worn as a prized piece of decorative jewelry. Even today in Japan the old-style kanzashi can be seen in almost any good antique store and in some museums. They were made of wood and lacquered in beautiful colors or were made of metal. Authentic wooden lacquerware is highly prized in Japan today. Most modern kanzashi are made of plastic.

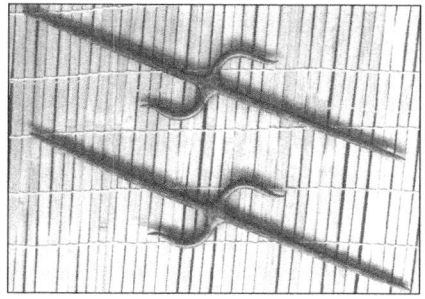

The mangi sai.
Photographs courtesy of T. Yoshimura and M. Nishiuchi, except where noted.

Some Okinawan kobudo authorities believe the shape of the sai came from the *manji sai*. The tale has been told that the manji sai came about when a very imaginative person, observing the Buddhist symbol called *manji*, was inspired to use such a shape for a weapon. This Buddhist symbol looks somewhat like a backward swastika. It represents of the philosophy of *in-yo* (*yin-yang* in Chinese) with each pair of tails that make up the symbol running in opposite directions. The direction of these tails represents the cycles of nature. If all of the corners of the tails were extended, a complete circle would be formed, representing the universe. Whether the Chinese or Okinawans first invented the sai cannot be ascertained, but it is certainly one of the popular weapons used in Okinawan kobudo.

Buddhist manji symbols.

Another theory states that the shape of the sai was devised by someone who was inspired by the *kanji* (Japanese writing based on Chinese characters) for "right" and "left." These contain the sai-shaped radical for "hand."

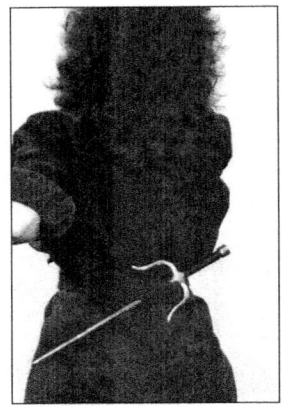

The third sai is stored in the belt behind the back.

Still another theory is based on the traditional Okinawan belief that the human form itself represents authority. While looking at a sai, one can visualize a stick figure human being. Okinawan police officers would hold up the sai to show their authority upon their arrival on a scene to make their identity known, in a similar manner as a badge is worn or shown in the West.

Two common *kata* (forms or routines) practiced in Okinawa are called *Ni-cho-sai kata* (double-sai form) and *San-cho-sai kata* (three-sai form). Although the San-cho-sai kata is the least common in the United States, it is considered the main kata of the International Okinawan Kobudo Association, U.S.A., because a "set" of sai is usually considered to be three sai, not a pair. Besides, one sai is held in each hand when in use, and both sai are held in one hand when at attention. A spare sai is kept in the belt behind the back. Of course, in older times this would be the belt of the Okinawan-styled kimono, which was designed differently than the kimono worn by the people of the main archipelago of Japan. Some of the major techniques from both of these kata, as well as the *bunkai* (analysis with a partner), are shown and explained in the following section.

Choosing the Right Sai

Just as it is important for a carpenter to choose the best tool available to fit a particular job, it is important for the kobudo practitioner to choose the most suitable weapon for the techniques being applied. There are many kinds of sai available on the commercial market. Some are designed for practical use as a weapon, but many are designed only for looks. Please refer to the listing which shows the vocabulary used for the anatomy of the sai.

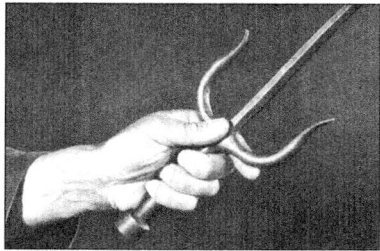 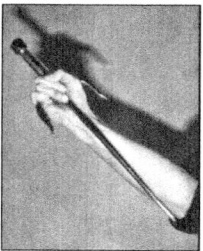

Left: Correct grip of sai for sticking. Right: correct reverse grip.

In the photograph of three sai, you will notice that the area between the two prongs (*yoku*) is quite flat. This provides a good gripping surface on which to press the thumb firmly and also on which to place the side of the index finger. Many sai available on the market are humped or rounded in this area, which makes a firm grip difficult and unstable. The shape of the prongs is also important. Some sai have very wide prongs and are not curved in the correct place to provide for good catching and immobilizing techniques. The length of the handle (*nigiri*) should vary according to the length of the sai from the prongs to the end point (*saki*). The longer the sai, the longer the handle should be because a person with longer arms usually has larger hands as well. Some sai sold commercially do not vary the handle portion at all, even though different lengths of the sai from the prongs to the end point are made. Choose a sai so that the end point reaches slightly past the elbow when you are holding the sai in the reverse position. This is important for blocking as you would soon find out when attacked with a sharp sword or a staff at full speed!

The end point should be sharp and sturdy because throwing of the sai is one of the useful and important techniques of this weapon. It should, therefore, be made of solid steel. Some sai are not solid, but consist of hollow chrome plating covering a thin steel skeleton. These kind of sai will not hold up for *bunkai* (practice with an attacker) and usually cannot be thrown. The sai commonly made in Okinawa are of one solid steel piece that is not chromed. This same solid version is available with chrome plating, however, for a fancier look and are used sometimes for demonstrations.

PARTS OF THE SAI

- *sai-gashira* (sai head)
- *nigiri* (handle)
- *yoku* (prongs)
- *mono uchi* (part for striking)
- *saki* (endpoint)

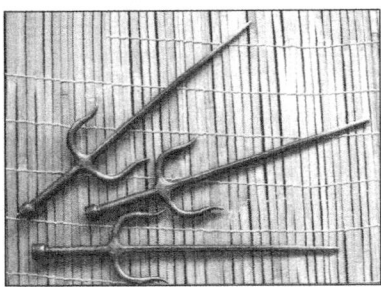

These sai, usually used three in a set, exemplify the ideal shape.

Basic Techniques and Applications

When gripping for an attack, one should hold the sai firmly between the thumb and index finger, and the fingers should never cross over the prongs, for these are used for blocking, catching, and immobilizing the opponent's weapon. This gripping position will allow for various techniques such as jabbing with the long end and the pronged ends, blocking and catching the opponent's weapons, and throwing the sai.

The reverse gripping position is used for blocking and hooking, and then pushing the opponent's weapon away from the defender, allowing an opening for an immediate counterattack. Holding the long end of the sai very firmly against the forearm is of utmost importance for two main reasons: 1) to effectively block so the defender's arm is not broken or cut; 2) to prevent the attacker from hooking on the defender's sai and disarming the defender.

BASIC POINTS FOR ATTACK

- **Danchu (fig. 1):** The *danchu* is a pressure point in the center of the sternum which is an important "relay station," so to speak, of *ki* (*qi* in Chinese), one's life-force. Danchu is also referred to as *chu-tanden*, or middle center of ki. In Oriental medicine, the danchu pressure point is believed to be a great source of will power and fighting spirit. Therefore, any fighter who is successful at delivering a powerful strike to the danchu of his opponent has won three-fourths of the battle and will most likely be successful with the follow-up attacks.
- **Throat (fig. 2):** Shows an attack to the throat with the point of the sai prong. The point of the long end of the sai is also often used.
- **Groin (fig. 3):** The sai is used in a sweeping, slapping motion to the groin. In this case, the sai is not used as a jab.

- **Foot (fig. 4):** Shows a throwing technique called "thief's foot" (*nusuru-guhu*). The name of this technique is derived from the Okinawan language, not Japanese. The name implies that is the sai is thrown at a thief's foot, the thief would not be able to run away and would be caught.
- **Back of the hand (fig. 5):** After sliding the sai down the staff from an upper block position (*jodan uke*) and hooking, the prong of the sai is jabbed into the back of the hand.

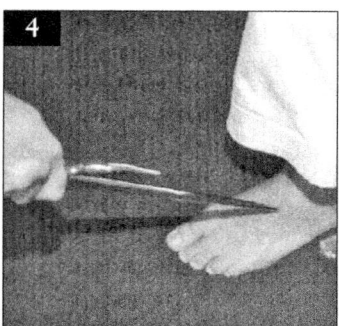
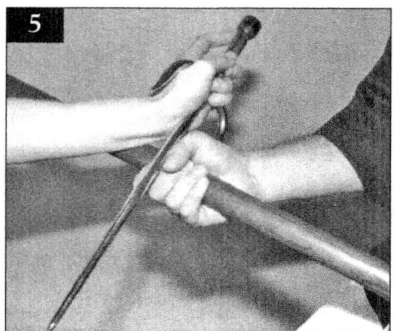

Movements Explained

A-1 The opponent begins to attack, but the defender counterattacks immediately with a feint before the attacker actually executes his move. The attacker avoids the defender's counter.

A-2 The attacker comes in with a side-strike to the knee. The defender deflects with the long end of the sai.

A-3 The defender follows immediately with an attack to the throat.

B-1 The opponent initiates an attack with the staff.

B-2 The defender steps in to attack the solar plexus area before the attacker can complete the movement. The attacker therefore steps back in retreat to avoid the defender's thrust.

B-3   The opponent attacks again with a side strike, which the defender blocks by deflecting with the long end of the sai.

B-4   The opponent then begins to attack with the opposite end of his staff, but is interrupted by the defender attacking to the throat with the end point of the sai. However, the attacker successfully avoids the counter by leaning backward.

B-5   The opponent moves again with an attack to the midsection, while the defender counters with a lower block.

B-6   The defender strikes with the sai to the side of the opponent's neck.

B-7   Upon executing the side-strike, the defender finishes off the attacker by immediately sliding one prong into the attacker's throat.

C-1 The attacker strikes to the midsection. The defender deflects quickly with the long end of the sai.

C-2 The defender counterattacks with a strike to the throat, which the opponent avoids by leaning backward.

C-3 The defender again moves in immediately with a simultaneous double-strike, one to the groin and one to the danchu with the head of the sai.

D-1 Starting position for throwing the sai.

D-2 For close-range throwing, the sai is held with the prongs lying in a flat plane, and the sai also lands in this position after thrown.

E-1　The opponent attacks with a downward sword strike aimed at the top of the defender's head. The defender blocks with a scissors block (*hasami-uke*).

E-2　The defender traps the opponent's sword by pushing the sai together from the scissor's block position, then, while holding the sword in the trap with one hand, reaches behind his belt for his third sai.

E-2a　Close-up of the hasami-uke trap before switching to a one-hand hold.

E-3　The defender uses the third sai to move in quickly and counterattacks at the opponent's throat with the prong end of the sai.

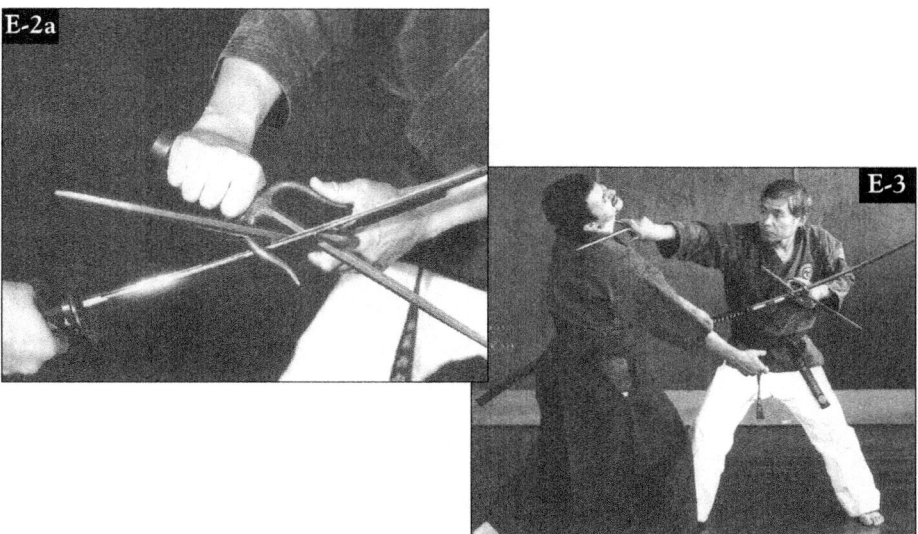

F-1 After already having thrown two sai at the feet of other opponents, a third opponent initiates an attack from behind. The defender turns with the one sai remaining in her hand.

F-2 The attacker executes a strike aimed at the top of the defender's head, but she protects herself with an upper block with the sai.

F-2a Close-up of the upper block (*jodan-uke*).
F-2b Close-up of the hook.

F-3 The defender catches the staff between the prong and stem of the sai and pulls it downward and safely to the side.

F-4 The defender immediately steps in and attacks with an empty-handed punch to the opponent's solar plexus.

 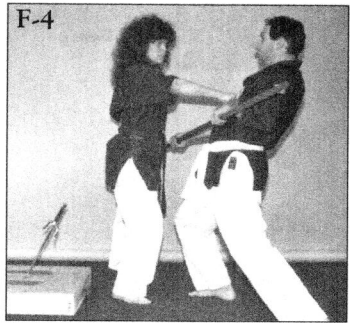

F-5 This photo shows what can happen to the defender if she did not catch the staff with the prong of the sai and immediately pull the staff downward and away from her body. The attacker could easily use his staff to hook into the prong and by pushing downward, actually pull the defender down. The defender is then in the most vulnerable position and the attacker can easily follow-up by another side strike with the reverse end of the staff.

G-1   The opponent side-strikes, but his attack is deflected.

G-2   The defender counters with a strike to the side of the attacker's neck.

G-3   The defender follows up with an attack to the throat with a prong of the sai.

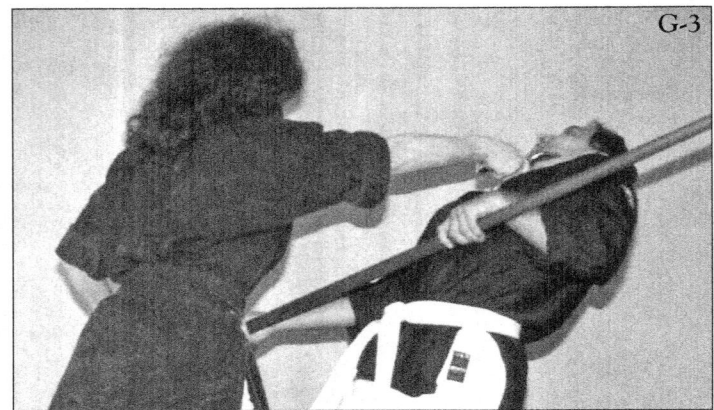

Conclusion

The above techniques show some of the most commonly used techniques of the sai, although not all of them. Within the San-cho-sai kata, the sai is thrown twice, so the defender has only one sai remaining, and the kata ends with a punch, as shown in figure F-4. In this kata, the defender throws the sai at the feet of an opponent after executing a 450-degree turn by pivoting on one foot. The second sai is thrown at another opponent's foot after a 180-degree turn. These turns in the kata are meant to provide practice in balance and coordination. It is not likely that the defender would ever turn around to such an extent in a real self-defense situation. And, of course, throwing the sai into the opponent's foot will not kill him, but slows him down so that the defender may then move in with a deadly attack if necessary.

Tactics such as throwing and deflecting are very valuable when defending with the sai because the attacker's weapon is likely to be longer than the sai. Longer weapons, such as the six-foot staff, long swords, or even the shorter staff, provide more reach for the opponent. Therefore, the person defending with the sai must be highly skilled and extremely fast to successfully defend himself. The cat stance (*neko-ashi*) is often used to enable the defender to spring back-and-fourth and side-to-side rapidly.

You can imagine trying to defend yourself with the sai against an attacker with a sharpened *katana* (long samurai sword). In a life-or-death situation, this is no easy task! Realizing this, we can appreciate the blood, sweat, and tears that was shed by the Okinawans in developing these techniques at which we "play" today.

The author wishes to express special thanks to Nishiuchi Mikio for his guidance in the way of kobudo, for his advice for this chapter and his demonstration of techniques. A special thanks likewise goes to Evan Cosden and Dale Sussdorf for their help in demonstrating the techniques.

chapter 9

Control of Center: The Technical, Strategic, and Spiritual Foundations of Ko-ryu Karatedo
by Robert E. Wolfe, II, B.A.

Photography by John S. Zeedick.

Of the myriad factors affecting the potential efficiency and effectiveness of karate techniques, few are as significant as control of center. The ability to identify and exploit the center can substantially offset disadvantages in size or strength and enhance all the relative advantages of a particular *karateka* (practitioner). Of even greater consequence, an intensive study of center is an exceptionally powerful tool for personal development, the spiritual implications of which extend well beyond the realm of martial technique. The process of coming to understand and employ center is not a difficult undertaking—the tool is well within the reach of the average student of karate—and can form the basis for many challenging and enjoyable hours of practice. In recognition of the importance and accessibility of the concept, Ko-ryu karate focuses its training syllabus and methodology on the acquisition of techniques mechanically executed and strategically applied in accordance with the principles of control of center.

The Japanese concept of *chushin* (center) has two aspects: the personal center of an individual and the center of an interaction between two or more individuals. Control of the center can be effected on a scale ranging from the individual, through small groups of interacting individuals, to armies in combat or nations in contention. There are both physical and psychological components to center at all points along the range of applicability of the concept (Lovret, 1987: 159).

In the individual, control of center is most readily appreciated in terms of balance. Even outside the dojo, it is not uncommon to hear someone described as being centered, and the description usually implies physical poise, emotional equilibrium, and focused intent, as evidenced in day-to-day interactions. The same qualities are prized within the dojo as well as in groups of individuals—such as military forces—expected to function as a unit.

As it relates to an individual person, chushin is associated with the "one-point" spot (*itten*) in the lower abdomen (*hara*) defined by the center of mass of the human body (Lovret, 1987: 96). This point is also referred to as the tanden point, considered in Japanese tradition to be the seat of the soul. Although the exact center of mass can vary from individual to individual in consequence of differences in body structure, in a general sense the *itten* is located about three to five centimeters below the level of the navel (Stein, 1988: 33, 171).

Along the same lines, an organized group of individuals has a center to its corporate body (Pater, 1988: 171). The center may be an individual or a relationship or even a philosophy that guides the actions of the group. There is nothing new or unusual in this notion as evidenced by the fact that various sports have long used the term "center" to designate a specific position on the team that plays a pivotal role in the action.

For both individuals or groups acting in concert, control of center is related to mobility and especially to maintenance of freedom of movement. The greatest range of potential physical actions remains accessible only through avoidance of imbalance or generation of inappropriate momentum.

In physical altercations between individuals or groups, whether sparring in the controlled conditions of the dojo or actual, unrestricted warfare, the center is a position in space that dominates the exchange by virtue of delimiting the point or area through which force must be projected for optimal efficiency and effect. The location of the center in many instances can be difficult to determine. Rather than necessarily being a point simply midway between the opposing sides, the center in combat will be placed in three-dimensional space by a number of factors, including the relative strength, size, reach, mobility, technical skill, and spirit of the combatants and the attributes of local topography.

While there is always a center, the location and duration of the center is specific to each distinct engagement. The duration of the center in a particular location is determined primarily by the number of participants in the exchange: the larger the number, the more durable the center because larger groups of people are more ponderous and embody greater inertia, thus lengthening the time required to effect repositioning.

At the scale encountered most frequently in karate training—sparring between two individuals—the center is constantly relocated and endures statically for only moments at a time. To have any chance of employing strategies and techniques based on chushin, karate practitioners must be trained to remain cognizant and in control of their own, personal centers, while simultaneously assessing and exploiting the center of the exchange.

Successful control of personal center results in greater balance, the ability to move freely in any direction, and an enhancement of the power and precision of striking techniques. Achievement of a balanced physical state has important psychological benefits as well. It is much easier for a karate practitioners to feel confident and focused when he is not fighting himself, as well as the opponent, because of improper body mechanics (Millman, 1979: 13).

The best way to insure control of personal center is by paying careful attention to *kamae* (stance). When Western martial artists discuss stance, they are usually talking only about the physical positioning of the body (Schlesinger, 1982: 6). The Japanese concept of *kamae*, however, includes both physical and psychological elements (Lovret, 1993: 53). Japanese martial artists use the term *tachi* (standing) to refer to physical position alone, from the hips down (Nakayama, 1977: 28). Believing that the body influences the mind just as the mind influences the body, Japanese martial artists have long paid equal attention to the ways one element can be used to effect conscious control of the other (Deshimaru, 1982: 69). If a person exuding confidence stands a little taller than would ordinarily be the case, strategists of old Japan believed it should be possible to induce a feeling of confidence by standing a little taller. Consequently, different kamae may be associated with specific mental states designed to optimize the use of techniques appropriate to the stance (Sato, 1985: 63; and Shimabukuro and Pellman, 1995: 102).

The primary stance of Ko-ryu karate is *chudan-gamae* (middle-stance). Derived from the middle-stance of Tenshin-ryu kenjutsu (fig. 1, the Ko-ryu middle-stance is a forward-facing, stable posture that is optimal for engaging the opponent (fig. 2). By pointing the hara and the feet toward the opponent, the middle-stance reinforces the resolve of the karate practitioner by placing himself physically and spiritually "in the fight," retards the tendency to turn away from an attack, allows all primary weapons to be brought to bear in decisive strikes, and facilitates projection of spirit through the center of the engagement. Psychologically, the middle-stance is neither offensive nor defensive in spirit. The shoulders and hips are angled forty-five degrees to the center line, and body weight is divided evenly between the feet. The karate practitioner assuming the middle-stance aims for the state of *mushin* (no mind), advocated by the Zen priest Takuan to sword master Munenori Yagyu as the mind that "... has neither discrimination nor thought but wanders about the entire body and extends throughout the entire self" (Takuan, 1987: 33). Mushin is the mental equivalent of a balanced stance, enabling the karate practitioner to act spontaneously and appropriately in seizing the opportunity to attack.

In contrast to the characteristics of the middle-stance, the typical "fighting stance" used in modern, tournament karate (fig. 3) is optimal for defense in competition. Usually strongly angled (more than forty-five degrees) to the side, with feet pointing away from the opponent, the tournament stance is adapted from the stance used in kickboxing, and is predicated on "protecting" the main targets used in point competition (Theriault, 1983: 68). Although target zones are covered, the angle of the stance limits the weapons that can be brought to bear at any moment, which has induced many point fighters to emphasize the use of lead-side techniques, in particular the round kick (*mawashi-geri*) and backfist strike (*uraken-uchi*). These two techniques almost always must travel around the center of the engagement, compromising power and decisiveness. The round kick and backfist strike certainly score many points in tournaments, but the strikes usually don't connect solidly enough to have realistic potential to fell an opponent in a fight.

The tournament stance, because of its strong angle relative to the center, makes it more likely that the tournament fighter will be turned completely around in the course of an engagement and be caught with his back to the opponent. Even worse, pointing the *hara* away from the opponent weakens the resolve of the karate practitioner. Turning away in the establishment of a stance reflects a desire to avoid being hit rather than a desire to engage the opponent, and the action reinforces a defensive and reactive state of mind. Ko-ryu karate makes no use of the tournament stance because it offers nothing to support the primary objective of control of center.

The benefits of control of center, both personal center and the center of action, are readily illustrated through two examples. In the first example, a karate practitioner employing a middle-stance to manage his own center engages an opponent using the tournament stance (fig. 4). Since his stance is optimal for defense, the tournament fighter must first turn in toward his opponent in order to throw a strong punch or kick (fig. 5). The necessity to prepare to attack means that the tournament fighter can not launch his techniques across the center of the action as quickly or readily as can the centered karate practitioner, who is already poised to counter with the "bread and butter" technique of traditional karate, the reverse punch (*gyaku-zuki*), as demonstrated in figure 6. By managing his own center, the karate practitioner cognizant of chushin dominates the center of the engagement.

Control of Personal Center — Middle-Stance

In the second example, a karate practitioner uses control of his personal center to redefine the center of action to his advantage. To fully appreciate the principle detailed in this scenario, it's necessary to examine the technique chosen for the attack. Most, if not all, styles of karate in the United States employ what is commonly called the "side kick," but styles vary in the degree of consideration devoted to how the technique might best be applied. Serious oversights can occur in schools relying entirely on English terminology for techniques. The Japanese term for what we call side kick is *yokogeri*, which actually carries a meaning more like "to the side kick" (Nelson, 1974: 511). The difference in meaning is subtle but important because it yields a significant clue to increase the effectiveness of the kick. "To the side" refers to the side of the individual kicking, who is assumed to be facing forward. The side kick was originally intended for use against an enemy attacking from the side (fig. 7), in which application the kick tracked directly through the center of the engagement. In modern tournament play, however, the side kick delivered from a "fighting stance" usually tracks slightly outside the center, which makes it much easier to block. The kick is off line, because drawing the rear foot straight forward to increase the range of the technique angles the fighter even more away from the center of action (fig. 8). Sacrificing control of center in this fashion allows the opponent to block the kick and turn the kicker, with very little effort (fig. 9). The remedy is to apply "yoko-geri" in accordance with its original purpose. In kumite, this is achieved by redefining the center of action.

Control of Center Action—Side Kick

Figure 10 illustrates two karate practitioners in kumite, with neither fighter at the moment clearly in control of center. The attacker (*uchite*, "striking hand") leads with a thrust toward her opponent's eyes intended as a distraction to cover an advance and to reposition (fig. 11). As the defender (*shite*, "responding hand") reacts to the feint, the attacker slides forward and pivots to place herself in position to execute a side kick at an angle consistent with the alignment for which the technique was originally designed (fig. 12). Because the defender is still positioned to contest the former center of the action and has not recognized and reacted to the fact that the attacker has redefined the center, the defender is unable to prevent the attacker from kicking with *yoko-geri* (fig. 13). With control of center established, the attacker presses her attack to a decisive conclusion (fig. 14).

Control of Center Action — Redefining the Center

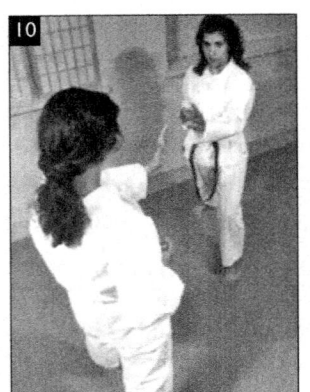
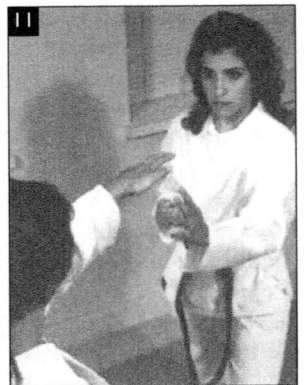

There are several drills useful for recognition and development of control of personal center. A good way to start is to provide students with examples of what it feels like when the control of one's personal center is lost.

The Japanese word describing the loss of center is *kuzushi* (off-balance). Kuzushi is a concept most often related to arts like jujutsu, aikijutsu, or aikido because causing kuzushi in an opponent is prerequisite to a successful throw. From a physical perspective, *kuzushi* can be analyzed in terms of the lines of the shoulders and hips: a person will be out of balance if the line of the shoulders is not parallel to the line of the hips in a vertical plane. If the shoulders are tilted or twisted relative to the hips, or if the shoulders are to the front or back of the line of the hips, a centered stance is impossible.

In the aikijutsu of the Yamate-ryu, a simple exercise is used to convey the principle of kuzushi. In the most basic form of the drill, one student (*shite*) stands in a natural manner. A second student, acting as an attacker (*uchite*), lightly grasps the first student's uniform at the shoulders (fig. 15). Applying very slight pressure, the attacker tilts and/or twists the defender in anyone of the eight cardinal directions, and attempts to poise the defender on the very edge of falling or having to step to regain balance (fig. 16). Both students work to develop a sense of the precise moment at which the defender is off-balance.

Balance Drill

The drill can be repeated with the defender assuming a variety of stances. Students may also find it very interesting to experiment with simulating different emotional states and assessing the effect, if any, on one's ability to achieve or resist kuzushi.

Once students have begun to develop awareness of the physical limits of their centers, they can undertake exercises designed to enhance recognition and utilization of personal center. The Tenshin-ryu utilizes the following drill to teach fledgling swordsmen the basic physical and psychological components of chushin.

In this exercise, the role of the defender is to provide resistance. He assumes a deep and anchored stance and extends an arm to the side to obstruct the attacker's path (fig. 17). The attacker approaches in a natural posture and attempts to walk through the arm and destroy the defender's stance without having to break step, lean into the defender, unduly exert himself, or in any manner even recognize that the defender is present (fig. 18). This effect is achieved by specific measures. The attacker must expand his hara by pushing strongly outward with the muscles of the abdomen (fig. 19) and maintain the configuration of his abdomen even when exhaling. Psychologically, the attacker imagines himself becoming heavier and settling in the abdomen's itten. The attacker must also look past the arm of the defender. Fixing the gaze through a distant object is helpful. If the attacker approaches the defender with his center high, "in his shoulders," or allows himself to focus on the extended arm, he will be completely unable to advance without a gross distortion of posture (fig. 20). Through repetition of this exercise over time, students learn to establish their centers and maintain the necessary physical and psychological components in the face of a challenge.

Balance Drill

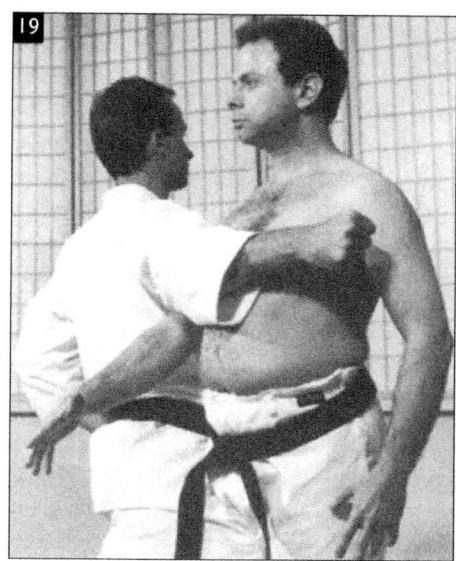 

The expanded *hara*, sometimes referred to as the "iron kettle" by instructors of the Tenshin-ryu, is the key to control of personal center and, by extension, control of the center of action. Ko-ryu incorporates the "iron kettle" in its middle-stance. From a middle-stance, the practitioner controls the center of action by means of a strategic emphasis on counter-fighting, not in a defensive or reactive sense, but in the sense of attacking decisively the opening(s) presented by the opponent as a natural consequence of his aggressive action or intent.

When an attack is manifested in a physical technique, the technique must be dealt with in some fashion. *Uke-waza* (receiving techniques) are the class of techniques employed to manage an attack. While *uke* is often translated as "block," Ko-ryu finds it much more useful to emphasize the more neutral "receiving" aspect of the term. The word "block" conjures an image of force applied in opposition to an attack; blocking is something one does to counter an incoming technique. "Receiving," on the other hand, does not necessarily imply an application of force or even physical contact with an incoming technique. Receiving techniques are actions that are taken with, rather than against, an attack. Thinking in terms of blocks can tend to limit the focus of a karate practitioner's attention because of the need to apply a block against something specific, such as a moving arm or leg. Any such limiting of attention is contrary to the desired state of mushin. By thinking in terms of receiving, however, a karate practitioner is empowered to deal with attacks with a focus that is broader than focusing solely on the closest limb of the opponent.

The source of receiving techniques is the *hara*, and the techniques are applied from the center outward. Most importantly, Ko-ryu receiving techniques are applied ideally to a point or along a line in space and not directly against the opponent. The intent is to de-emphasize the sense of the opponent, to make it less likely that the karate practitioner's attention will be focused on and limited by each individual attack, and to preclude the tendency of smaller karate practitioners to feel they must "load up" against larger opponents.

Applying more than optimal power against a perceived attack by a stronger opponent can reduce the effectiveness of a karate practitioner because failure to receive and counter an attack with a centered, resolute spirit can reinforce the perception of physical inferiority that leads the karate practitioner to believe he must strain to manage the attack in the first place.

The form of a particular receiving technique does not vary whether the technique is executed in solo practice or in kumite, which facilitates execution of the receiving technique in accordance with the standard pattern under the duress of sparring. Ko-ryu receiving techniques are usually executed as cuts, again reflecting the influence of kenjutsu and aikijutsu on the style. The motion of cutting allows the receiving technique to move with the inbound strike. This "soft method" (*juho*) flows with the advance of the opponent on or nearly along the original line of his attack. An old maxim of jujutsu states that "five and five are ten, or two and eight are ten," alluding to the fact that the more energy an opponent carries into an engagement, the less energy the recipient of the attack needs to exert to accomplish a decisive counter (Lovret, 1993: 25). Ko-ryu receiving techniques are designed to allow the opponent to "run into" the counter-technique and facilitate the application of the counter-technique on the same "beat" as, or within one-half beat of, the attack itself.

In contrast, the *goho*, or "hard method" of receiving an attack, tends to rely on power applied in opposition to an incoming strike. *Goho uke-waza* are what most people think of as blocks. The techniques tend to stop or redirect the force of an attack, which might permit the opponent to continue his attack by working off the energy imparted by the block, and often dictate that the block and counter must be applied on a one-two beat. Hard-method blocks are intended to inflict injury on the attacking limb, but that goal can be difficult to realize against a larger or stronger opponent. The force required to apply *goho uke-waza* can often only be generated in a static, anchored stance, which makes the karate practitioner vulnerable to follow-up attacks. These perceived deficiencies have inclined Ko-ryu toward the use of soft methods of blocking whenever possible.

Conventional Rising Block

A comparison of the conventional and Ko-ryu versions of *age-uke* (usually translated as "rising block") illustrates the relative strengths and weaknesses of hard and soft blocking. The rising block is used to receive an attack directed against the upper level of the body. A conventional rising block is chambered in the center of the chest (fig. 21), snapped to extension (fig. 22), and recoiled to a position with the arm angled forty-five degrees up and out from the chest (fig. 23). A conventional rising block is quite powerful and can be used to good effect against an empty-hand strike descending toward the top of the head, but the technique is less useful when the striking hand is holding a flexible weapon that might wrap around the block, or in instances in which the attack is a thrust toward the face.

While a conventional rising block will deflect a thrust, the vector along which force is applied tends to shift the weight of the attacker to his rear foot, stopping his advance but keeping him in balance and allowing his follow-up strike (figs. 24-26).

The hip mechanics used to generate power in a conventional rising block nearly preclude a simultaneous counter-strike. In the moment subsequent to the impact of the block, both karate practitioners are able to strike (fig. 27). Rather than facilitating a decisive counter, the conventional rising block in this application has returned both fighters to an even footing.

The Ko-ryu rising block utilizes a different configuration and execution to set up the opponent for a counter strike. Instead of chambering and snapping the arm, the Ko-ryu rising block requires no change in the arm's formation used in a middle-stance (fig. 28). In response to an incoming strike, the arm is rotated at the shoulder (fig. 29) into a position covering the upper level of the body (fig. 30) in a manner derived from the aikijujutsu *uke-waza aiki-dome*. While the final positions of both the conventional and Ko-ryu rising block appear to be similar, the path taken to those positions is very different and is the basis for the effectiveness of the softer version of the technique.

Application of Conventional Right Block — Ko-ryu Rising Block

Applied against the same attack described above, the Ko-ryu rising block gently removes the incoming strike from its trajectory through the center without altering the momentum of the attacker (fig. 31) and enables the defender to counter simultaneously. The attacker absorbs a strike combining the energy of the counter-technique and her own advance. The key is to apply the blocking technique as though one were performing a solo kata with no physical opponent and not against the arm of the attacker. Any significant force applied to the incoming arm will change the dynamic of the engagement in a way that may not be to the advantage of the defender.

The strategy of seizing the center (*chushin-dori*), represented in the Ko-ryu rising block, can also be applied in a manner by which the same movement becomes both defense and counter-offense. When the attacker commences a punching attack with either the lead or rear hand (fig. 32), the defender simply counter-punches on the same side as the attacker, relative to the center (fig. 33). This technique is known as *nagashi-zuki* (flowing thrust) and is closely related to the Itto-ryu kenjutsu strategy *hitotsu-no-tachi* (sword of one).

Flowing Thrust

The flowing thrust is mechanically simple and requires only that the defender punch straight and turn the thumb side of his striking hand completely downward (fig. 34).

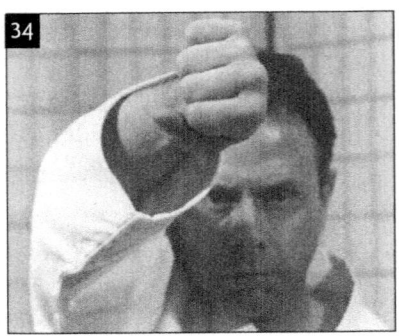

The alignment of the arm resulting from turning the hand thumb-down makes it virtually impossible for the attacker to connect with his punch. Even so, beginners may find it hard to muster the resolve to stand fast in the face of an inbound technique. Experience with the devastating effectiveness of flowing thrust, however, will reinforce the ability to stay in a middle-stance and wait for the moment to strike. As with the rising block, it is absolutely critical that the flowing thrust not be thought of as a block; any motion other than a straight punch toward the attacker's face will fail to control the center and will allow the attacker to press his attack.

It should also be kept firmly in mind that the flowing thrust is potentially very dangerous to practice. If an attacker strikes with determination, it is unlikely that the defender can "pull" his counter in time to prevent injury. The technique is definitely not well suited to friendly sparring.

Many other receiving techniques based on seizing the center can be applied safely in sparring. Methods of responding to kicking attacks, in particular, provide good opportunities to explore uses of the strategy. Kicks carry a considerable amount of energy, so receiving techniques that do not depend on matching the power of the attack offer great utility.

One of the most difficult kicks to counter is the basic kick to the front (*maegeri*). Executed correctly, the front kick itself is an excellent technique for use in dominating the center. Receiving techniques must "steal back" the early advantage of the kick and facilitate the delivery of a decisive counter before the attacker launches a follow-up attack. Ko-ryu depends on several variations of *gedan-barai-uke* (lower-level sweeping receptions) to counter kicking attacks targeting the middle and lower regions of the body. Two of the variations are especially effective against a front kick.

In figure 35, the attacker prepares to kick to the front. The defender responds with *nagashi-gedan-barai-uke* (flowing, lower-level sweeping reception) by advancing slightly with a sliding step (*tsugi-ashi*) while cutting down and just a bit to the outside rear corner with a hand-sword (*tegatana*), as demonstrated in figure 36. The defender's slight advance allows her hand-sword to cut almost directly along the line of the incoming kick, engaging and neutralizing the power of the attack at the center and turning the attacker away from the defender. The motion of her hand-sword enables the defender to scoop the kick and counter-strike with the palm of her lead hand while the attacker still carries most of the momentum of her charge (fig. 37). The defender can conclude the engagement with a takedown and/or a pin. For the maximum effect of this receiving technique, the defender must direct her hand-sword along the line of the front kick in space and not against the leg of the attacker. Any energy exerted by the defender against the leg of the attacker may enable the attacker to pivot away from the impact and continue her attack with a spinning backfist or elbow strike.

Flowing Low-Level Sweep

For situations in which a defender must deal with a front kick without the luxury of receiving the technique in a middle-stance, *gyaku-gedan-barai, uke* (reverse, lower-level, sweeping reception) is the receiving technique of choice. Standing naturally when the attacker executes a front kick (fig. 38), the defender pivots outside the line of the incoming kick while turning her lead arm hard to the inside (fig. 39). The configuration of the defender's arm is essentially a hand-sword, with the hand closed to a fist and the thumb-side turned toward her navel. Interposing by turning her arm as she pivots towards her opponent, the defender redefines the center and opens the opportunity to counter with a foot sweep, takedown, and finishing punch (figs. 40-42). Even though it appears that the defender is starting in a relaxed posture for this application, she must still maintain the iron-kettle of the hara and apply her receiving technique to a point in space rather than to the oncoming kick.

Reverse Low-Level Sweep

Chushin-based receiving techniques applied along the center line or to a point in space also work well against the head-high kicks seen in tournament competition. As mentioned earlier, lead-leg round kicks are a staple of competitive karate, but because the techniques tend to circle around the center, they are typically less dangerous than front kicks and are readily countered.

Hiki-age-uke (pulling-upward reception) is a technique used to seize the center line. Although this receiving technique is contained in a variety of kata, including Sanchin and the Isshin-ryu form Sunsu, it is seldom shown in application. Hiki-age-uke should be taught more openly because it works marvelously well, even against a larger and much stronger opponent. As the attacker leads with a round kick, the defender resolutely advances with a sliding step while making a motion with his rear hand as though to grab the knot of the attacker's belt and pull it up and back to his own ear (figs. 43-45).

Pulling Upward Reception

As he pulls up and back with his rear hand, the defender strikes with an uppercut to the attacker's solar plexus (fig. 46) and finishes with a strike to the head (fig. 47). Through the course of the receiving technique, the defenders's arm must move absolutely along the center line, and the defender must suppress any desire to step or lean away from the attacker's kick. Leaning the least bit away and thereby surrendering the center or executing the receiving technique as a block to a leg (in the manner of a boxer covering up to avoid a hook) will cause the technique to fail.

There is no question that *hiki-age-uke* demands an aggressive and unflinching spirit, but diligent practice of proper stance and execution of the technique against initially slow and gentle, but progressively vigorous, attacks will convince the karate student that he can master the center.

Soto-uke (outside reception) can also be used to counter a round kick in a manner that is less complex technically than *hiki-age-uke* but still requires the karate practitioner to advance in the face of an attack. As the attacker kicks, the defender steps forward and snaps an outside reception to the center point (fig. 48). Without waiting for the round kick to bury itself in her block, the defender pivots around her arm (fig. 49) to strike with turning backfist (fig. 50). This counter is very useful in defeating an opponent inclined to "head hunt" with high kicks because even taller opponents often lean back as they throw a lead-leg round kick, thus delaying the moment at which they could follow up with a punch. The centered and spirited karate practitioner can fill that gap in the attacker's approach with a technique of her own.

Outside Reception

While kumite and competition afford numerous occasions to experiment with the means to control center, traditional kata embody elegant and sophisticated applications of *chushin-dori* that are sometimes too risky to practice in other than carefully controlled circumstances. The Okinawan kata Kusanku contains a hidden technique that presents us with a spectacularly effective application of *chushin-dori*.

One portion of the kata contains the sequence depicted in figures 51 through 54. The standard version of these movements is explained (see also page 137) as receiving two strikes from the first of two attackers (figs. 55-56) and countering with a kick (fig. 57), then pivoting and dropping to receive a kicking attack (fig. 58), and finishing with a punch to the groin of the second attacker (fig. 59). The clue that this sequence is other than what it appears is provided by the fact that, in figure 57, the defender is really too close to the first attacker for the effective use of a kick at the level dictated by the kata.

Kusanku Kata

Kusanku Kata — Standard Version

A close analysis of the sequence of techniques veiled in the section of the Kusanku kata reveals that this receiving technique does not really contain a kick at all or at least not a kick directed against the opponent. In a natural stance, the defender meets the strike by the attacker (fig. 60) by pivoting to *kake-dachi* and using hand-swords to simultaneously deflect the inbound punch while striking the attacker's carotid sinus (fig. 61), a potential knockout point. The defender raises his leg as though to kick (figure 62) but then pivots and drops to the ground (fig. 63) with his leg extending past the attacker. The attacker is felled with a really nasty throw (fig. 64) that is intended to break his spine, and the defender concludes with a strike to the head (fig. 65). As in the other examples of receiving techniques deployed along the center line, it is absolutely necessary that the defender execute this counter in the same spirit as his kata, without any focus on the physical presence of the attacker.

Kusanku Kata — Hidden Technique

Throughout all applications of center, the spiritual component can not be overemphasized. A strong spirit effectively projects the presence of the centered karate practitioner far beyond his physical reach and allows him to dominate the center of the action without making a move. An especially intense spirit can smother the spirit of the opponent, even at a distance, robbing him of initiative and ending the combat before it is manifested in an exchange of techniques. The acquisition of such an intensely strong spirit and development of the ability to control the center in the dojo and in the arena of life in the outside world is of great value to anyone seeking enhanced balance and the ability to act decisively in the face of unexpected opportunities or dangers.

Creation of a strong, centered spirit and an understanding of its power is the primary objective of training in Ko-ryu karatedo.

Acknowledgment

Special thanks from the author and publisher to those who helped by posing for the photo sequences: Jonathan M. Barton, Edward T. Dix, Donald R. Dodson, Rhonda Farley, Joshua G. Fealtman, Randy M. Manning, Rodney C. Snyder, Alan R. Starner, Debra L. Starner, Rosanne S. Wolfe, and photographer John S. Zeedick.

Glossary

age-uke	rising block	kuzushi	off-balance
ashi-barai	foot sweep	mae-geri	front kick
chudan-gamae	middle-stance	mushin	no mind
chusin	center	mawashi-geri	round kick
chushin-dori	seizing the center	mawashi-uraken-uchi	spinning backfist
embusen	center line	nagashi-zuki	flowing thrust
gedan-barai	low sweep	shite	"responding hand"; defender
goho	"hard method"	soto	outside
gyaku-zuki	reverse punch	tegatana	hand-sword
hiji-ate	elbow strike	tsugi-ashi	sliding step
hiki-age	pulling upward	uchite	"striking hand"; attacker
itten	"one point"	uke-waza	receiving technique
juho	"soft method"	uraken-uchi	backfist strike
kamae	stance	yoko-geri	side kick
karateka	karate practitioner		

Bibliography

Deshimaru, T. (1982). *The Zen way to the martial arts*. New York: E. P. Dutton, Inc.

Lovret, F. (1987). *The way and the power: Secrets of Japanese strategy*. Boulder: Paladin Press.

Lovret, F. (1993). *Budo jiten* (2nd ed.). San Diego: Taseki Publishing Co.

Millman, D. (1979). *The warrior athlete: Body, mind and spirit*. Walpole: Stillpoint Publishing.

Nakayama, M. (1977). *Best karate comprehensive*. Tokyo: Kodansha International, Ltd.

Nelson, A. (1974). *The modem reader's Japanese-English character dictionary*. Rutland: Charles E. Tuttle, Co.

Pater, R. (1988). *The black belt manager*. Rochester: Park Street Press.

Sato, H. (1985). *The sword and the mind*. Woodstock: The Overlook Press.

Schlesinger, T. (1982). *Fighting strategy: Winning combinations*. Hollywood: Unique Publications, Inc.

Shimabukuro, M., and Pellman, L. (1995). *Flashing steel: Mastering Eishin-ryu swordsmanship*. Berkeley: Frog, Ltd.

Stein, H. (1988). *Kyudo: The art of Zen archery*. Longmead: Element Books, Ltd.

Takuan, S. (1987). *The unfettered mind*. Tokyo: Kodansha International, Ltd.

Theriault, J. (1983). *Full contact karate*. Chicago: Contemporary Books, Inc.

An Interview with Brian Frost on Testing Through Tameshiwari
by John C. Taylor, B.A.

As an example of speed breaking, Brian Frost removes the top of a bottle while leaving the remainder of the bottle standing.
Photos courtesy of B. Frost.

Personal Background

Mr. Brian Frost is a sixth degree black-belt and holds a *kokusai shihan menkyo* (international instructor's license) in karate. He is a direct pupil of Onishi Eizo, founder of the Japanese Koei-Kan Karate system and chairman of the All-Japan Karatedo Association. Mr. Frost served his apprenticeship under Onishi and studied in Japan as a live-in disciple (*uchideshi*). As one of Master Onishi's senior pupils, Mr. Frost currently serves as the Chief Technical Instructor of the United States Division for the International Koei-Kan Karatedo Federation. A veteran martial artist with more than thirty years experience, he has taught, competed and demonstrated throughout the United States, Canada, Latin America, and Japan. In 1972, he captured the All-Japan Koei-Kan Karate-Do Championship held at the Kamata Sports Stadium in Tokyo. Presently based in Detroit, Mr. Frost is in the process of completing a soon-to-be-published book entitled *Koei-Kan Karate-Do: Practice and Precept*.

INTERVIEW

- **Mr. Frost, will you please explain the meaning of the word *tameshiwari*?**

It is, of course, Japanese and it is actually comprised of two words. *Tameshi* means "to test or experiment; a kind of trial." *Wari* means simply "to break or separate."

- **Can you give an historical synopsis of its development?**

Near the end of the sixteenth century, Japanese practitioners of swordsmanship (*kenjutsu*) tested both the quality of their blade and the skill of their technique by making various cuts on cadavers. This practice was defined as *tameshigiri* (test cutting).

It was in this way of testing a technique that the practice of tameshiwari spread and developed among karate practitioners into the nineteenth century. It also became a tool in exhibiting the power of karate to the public. In China, many exhibitions were arranged highlighting martial prowess, including breaking, to attract potential customers to buy various herbs and medicines. In the twentieth century, the primary use of tameshiwari is to improve technique and strengthen spirit and devotion.

Left: As an example of active breaking, Brian Frost cracks a ten-pound stone into two pieces with a hammer-fist strike. Right: Sensei Brian Frost poses with his teacher, Onishi Eizo, founder of the Japanese Koei-Kan Karate system.

- How many kinds of tameshiwari are there?

There are many types of breaking techniques, and they can be demonstrated with a vast assortment of random objects—baseball bats, bricks, rocks, cement, wood, and so on. The two main categories are speed breaking and power breaking.

- What is the difference between them?

The dichotomy is not simplistic because speed is crucial to both types of tameshiwari. But within this division, speed breaking refers to a technique such as removing a bottle top while leaving the remainder of the bottle standing. In speed breaking, a very rapid striking and retracting motion is needed to cut or penetrate. This technique is almost always done with the hand because it can generate the most speed.

Power breaking includes speed, but requires an increased amassment of force. In order to break ten cinder slabs or ten pieces of wood, a total body thrusting and follow-through is mandatory. This technique can be done with either the hand or foot, since both can generate enough power with the body follow-through.

- Are there other categories in tameshiwari?

Breaking techniques can be both active and passive. "Active" refers to the aforementioned power and speed, or breaking with an offensive motion. "Passive" breaking means having an object or objects broken over or across the body. Usually the chest or abdomen is used, but it can also include the shin, fist, leg, or even the head. In Koei-Kan, this type of passive breaking is best exemplified during the performance of the *Sanchin kata*, wherein dynamic tension, or storing of energy, creates a deeply tensed form of *kokyu-ho* (methods of breathing).

- Does *kokyu-ho* aid in tameshiwari?

Kokyu-ho is integral to tameshiwari. Inhalation aids in muscle relaxation, and exhalation provides muscle contraction. Dynamic tension in active breaking is a matter of timing, focus, and force, since you are concentrating on one target. In passive breaking, it is important to inhale the same way, but exhalation must be longer, slower, and much deeper because in this technique you must prepare a certain part of the body to neutralize the concussion and shock of an opposing force or object.

It should be noted here that proper breathing in tameshiwari is centered in the *saika tanden* (area between the navel and groin). The upper and lower muscles in this part of the body are very powerful and must always be utilized in both active and passive breaking. In passive techniques, focused breathing becomes crucial.

- **Why is a scream or yell often heard in breaking techniques?**

  This is known as *kiai*, but "yell" is not the correct translation. Kiai is a combination of two Japanese words. *Ki* means "life-force or intrinsic energy"; *ai* is a contraction of the verb *awaseru*, which mean "to unite."

  Kiai is released at the exact point of impact and is often defined as "spirit-letting." In tameshiwari, it enhances and bolsters confidence by expelling fear and doubt. It also releases adrenaline into the bloodstream and aids immensely in contracting the muscles necessary for breaking.

- **Can you explain some of the different strikes used in tameshiwari?**

  This is a difficult question because almost every part of the body can be used as a breaking vehicle—from the forehead to the tips of the toes. Our bodies contain an arsenal of weapons that can be used in self-defense. Consistent with technique, however, there are more common strikes: first, the *seiken* (two knuckle); second, the *kensui* (hammer-fist); and third, the *tegatana* or *shuto* (swordhand). These are the three techniques most often employed in active breaking.

- **Are there methods used to strengthen the body for tameshiwari?**

  The most common and well-known method used to temper the various striking parts of the body is *makiwara* training. The proper Japanese translation is "straw/sheath" and describes a variety of striking posts, pads, and other devices. Usually a makiwara is a wooden post with the upper striking area also made of wood and wrapped with rope. Makiwara training originated in the sword arts where it was used in lieu of cadavers.

  Makiwara training and repetition can harden, callus, and form scar tissue on any striking surface of the body that is useful for tameshiwari. The *seiken*, using the first two knuckles of a strike, can be calcified and callused for more effective penetration. The *shuto* and *kensui* utilize the padded cushion of the palm which lies underneath the little finger. Since some muscle exists here, it can become very strong and callused. Also, the cushion helps to absorb the shock of impact and minimize injury when properly developed.

- **What about passive breaking?**

  In addition to using the makiwara, another method used is termed *kotekitai* (arm-forging). In this technique, partners strike each others' arms during the execution of certain blocks. The most common are *uchi uke* (inside block) and the *soto uke* (outside block). This form of body forging is very useful in preparing both types of breaking, since it strengthens the hands and the arms.

Passive Breaking

Brian Frost demonstrating: 1-2) a two-by-two inch board broken across the forearm and the shin; 3) three one-inch boards broken over the forehead.

Active Breaking

Brian Frost breaking: 1) a two-inch board with the fingertips, 2) a baseball bat with the shin, 3) a house brick with a swordhand.

- **Is there a certain approach used prior to the execution of tameshiwari?**

Yes, there are two interrelated segments. First is the initiation stage and, second, is the focusing and impact stage. In the initiation stage, an advanced karateka gathers energy, momentum, and the speed necessary to perform the particular break. This is done by compressing the proper muscles. The variety of objects tameshiwari includes requires differing sets of muscles for proper delivery. To use a simple metaphor, the body must become like a compressed spring. The feet must be firmly rooted to the floor, and all muscles tensed and locked at impact. In this way, the body becomes a conduit or repeated source of energy. The shock wave of the strike is dispersed and diverted throughout all muscles of the body. Also, at this point, breathing must become deeper, slower, and focused toward the *saika tanden* which aids in achieving body balance and power. In the second stage, focus and impact, this gathered energy is released to the target. Compressed muscles are now set in motion to release the power necessary for the break. In power breaking, total body follow-through is required, but in speed breaking, the focus shifts to only the muscles needed to penetrate or cut.

- **How important is *kime* (focus)?**

In every area of technique or demonstration, *kime* is the one postulate for karate—it is the essential imperative. In tameshiwari, *kime* is the instant concentration of force at the exact point of impact. It is this principle which ensures utilizing one hundred percent of the body's potential power in any breaking technique.

- **Are there principles in physics which apply to tameshiwari?**

Yes, sometimes too many. We often hear words like "mass, momentum, energy," and so on. These words are often used in everyday conversation and usually inaccurately. In tameshiwari, there are three words used in physics that do apply—speed, velocity, and force. These terms form a kind of continuum, one phase being built upon the other.

Speed consists of generating enough magnitude to accomplish the break, but alone it is without direction. Velocity, however, involves both speed and direction. It is aimed toward a specific point of impact, and at this time *kime* becomes crucial. Velocity and focus are now interdependent because together they pinpoint the exact placement of the break.

Force, for the purpose of tameshiwari, can be interpreted as impact. Force is the potential striking power one object exerts on another. The faster your hand or foot moves toward a target, the greater the force generated. As you can see, we have now come full circle and returned to speed.

- **Are there breaks which are considered more difficult or dangerous?**

In power breaking, the amount or type of materials to be broken must be carefully considered. The critical factor is expertise. One possible scenario in demonstrations might have an advanced practitioner break ten one-inch thick cinder slabs with a *shuto* or *kensui*. Some demonstrators find this number adequate, while others might wish to increase it to twelve or even fifteen. Again, this determination of quantity is based on the rigorous examination of skill and experience. The most difficult objects to break are common house bricks simply because they are extremely dense.

Within the speed breaking category, removing a bottle top is probably the most difficult break and, therefore, rarely seen. Hundreds of advanced karateka perform tameshiwari demonstrations in the United States every year, but only a handful of these attempt this particular technique. Even these few sometimes fail. The primary obstacle to success is the development of enough speed. When I perform this technique, my mind concentrates on the impact point for only an instant. Once this is achieved, focus is fixated on creating speed. This is done by rotating the hips, knees, and arm rapidly and visualizing not only the strike but also the very rapid snapping-back action.

This cut is always done with the *shuto* because it can create the most speed. Injury may occur because the broken bottle top can cut the hand or break the fifth metacarpal bone.

- **Are there methods used to avoid pain?**

Yes, as stated earlier, *kotekitai* and *makiwara* training aid immensely in developing calluses and forging the arms and hands. One other important aspect is visualizing, or imaging, which is done prior to the actual break to be performed.

Whether active or passive, a mental or psychological dry run of the specific technique is a prerequisite to success. First, the mind pictures the object to be broken and, second, a very strong position or posture is taken in relation to the object. These two strategies enhance completion of the break. Visualizing and imaging instill confidence in ability and aid in precluding any hesitation or self-doubt, which would be disastrous to success.

To help explain pain negation, I should mention an example from passive breaking. In regard to breaking a two-by-two inch thick board across the shin, success is not always guaranteed on the first attempt. Through imaging, a karateka has already anticipated this possibility, and so the second attempt is no more painful than the first.

- **Is it true that the object to be broken is considered nonexistent?**

In a sense this is true. Actually, the target is considered as merely an obstacle to a further objective; the bricks, boards, or stones are simply "in the way." The true object is not a brick or board—it lies beyond.

When this mental state is applied, every strike becomes a penetration. You focus beyond the object. In this way, tameshiwari becomes a concomitant quality. The mind dominates the suspicions of the body, eradicating any doubt as to what must be accomplished. A karateka must be resolute in doing what seems improbable and possibly painful.

- **Are strength and body size important in tameshiwari?**

In relation to strength, the human body contains two types of muscles: voluntary and involuntary. The latter group refers to those muscles which are found in various internal organs. Voluntary muscles are exterior and are attached to the skeleton. We have no control over our involuntary muscles; they respond automatically. The voluntary muscles, however, can become very fast and can be controlled, intensified, and trained for tameshiwari. Weightlifting and body building, while physically beneficial, have no bearing on the ability to break an object.

As for size, a large person can break many objects simply because of weight and applied strength. But assuming you have had no training in karate, you risk doing damage to yourself. While immense size and mass can generate great power, the necessary skill must also exist.

In addition, a large, untrained person will often attempt to break objects through the use of strength and size alone. Such a person has no concept of using all body muscles—he delivers the blow with the use of the arm and hand alone.

As part of his regular practice routine,
Sensei Frost trains on the makiwara.

A smaller person well-trained in tameshiwari realizes it is imperative to lock and utilize every muscle in the body at the impact point, thereby greatly augmenting strength and power. The large person's arm may weigh twenty pounds, but this is all that is brought to the target. The smaller karateka whose total body weight may be only 150 pounds brings all of this weight to the target. It now becomes obvious who can do the most damage and with little or no risk of injury.

The advanced karateka bringing years of tameshiwari training to the target is vastly superior. In self-defense, a large person will defeat a small one—all things being equal. These last four words are the critical ones: knowledge is truly power.

- **Is tameshiwari ever used as a testing or measure device for analyzing a student's progress?**

Absolutely not. Karate is not a science; it is an art. Therefore, each karateka must seek his or her own appreciation of technique. Perhaps a student does not wish to perform tameshiwari but prefers, instead, to perfect a certain kata or excel in kumite. These are desirable goals and should be pursued. Every student brings a unique set of abilities to be developed through karate. It becomes the teacher's duty to help in developing this uniqueness of gifts.

- **Mr. Frost, do you have any final thoughts on this topic?**

Although it often appears violent and destructive, tameshiwari is but one facet of karate—merely a training device or tool, of which there are many. The larger and more important perspective is goal oriented. A karateka, while developing in self-defense, grows, emotionally toward self-illumination. Karate, therefore, becomes an ideal. It is an art to cultivate for physical *and* emotional prowess.

chapter 11

Supplementary Weight Training for Miyagi Chojun's Goju-ryu Karate
By John Porta and Jack McCabe, B.A.

Master Miyagi Chojun (center) with a group of his students. The many types of supplementary exercise implements are displayed, all of which Miyagi placed great value upon in his instruction. *Photos courtesy of John Porta and Richard Strait.*

Traditional Okinawan Goju-ryu karate is a system designed primarily for self-defense. Founded by Miyagi Chojun (1888-1953) in the early part of the twentieth century, Goju-ryu uses both hard and soft fighting principles to incorporate circular blocking movements with linear and circular strikes, forming a flexible style of karate that is geared toward close-range combat, but can also adapt to deal with long-range attacks. Since there are numerous grappling and grabbing maneuvers contained within the twelve *katas* (forms) that make up the system, it is important for students to strengthen their bodies and maintain overall body flexibility, to properly perform the Goju-ryu techniques that require quick responses to put an end to an altercation in the least amount of time. For this reason, supplementary conditioning with traditional Okinawan weights is a major part of the system, which Master Miyagi taught to all his students.

Building a Strong Foundation

Master Miyagi's early training consisted mainly of strength and development work with various resistance devices. Beginning at the age of eleven under the tutelage of Aragaki Ryuko, the young Miyagi was instructed in the use of the *chishi* (single-ended stone lever weight), *nigirigame* (clay gripping jars), and the *makiwara* (straw-padded striking post). In 1901, Aragaki introduced Miyagi to Higashionna Kanryo (1851-1916), who was well-known throughout Okinawa for his expertise in the style of self-defense that he called Naha-te. The training under Master Higashionna was very harsh, with an emphasis on the Sanchin conditioning kata, and few students were able to withstand the physical demands placed upon them by the practice of techniques and supplementary developmental work, which for the most part consisted of running and lifting progressively heavier stones. However, Miyagi thrived on the difficult training, and he eventually came to learn all of the Naha-te katas.

When Master Higashionna died in 1916, Master Miyagi took over the leadership of the Naha-te system and traveled extensively to promote the art. A person of great wealth, Master Miyagi made frequent trips to China before and after the death of Master Higashionna, and combined the principles he learned from the great martial arts masters of the time with Naha-te techniques to establish the art he later called Goju-ryu (the hard and soft system). His travels also took him to mainland Japan, Hawaii, and Korea, where Goju-ryu was promoted to the extent that it became famous not only in Okinawa, but in other areas as well.

A man of great strength and power, Master Miyagi was also known for his gentle nature and desire to serve humanity by making available to the public a martial art system that concerned itself with producing outstanding citizens. Despite very few rumors to the contrary, Master Miyagi never fought, keeping a promise to his teacher, Master Higashionna, never to use the martial arts to harm another human being. However, his demonstrations were anything but gentle, as his tremendous physical and mental strength allowed him to overcome obstacles that would have felled most other people. One of Master Miyagi's performances on Okinawa in the 1920s has become legendary, and eventually paved a way for promoting his art in budo demonstrations in Japan. In this particular instance, after an extraordinary display of techniques by visiting judo founder Kano Jigoro, Miyagi was asked to perform on behalf of the Okinawan martial arts. It has been reported that he responded by carrying out such tasks as ripping bark from a tree with his fingers and tearing chunks off a large slab of raw meat with his bare hands. Master Miyagi also kicked a hole in a kerosene can with his big toe, thrust his hands into a bundle of bamboo and pulled out stalks from the center of the stack, and remained uninjured while being struck with a *bo* (six-foot wooden staff). Kano was so impressed with this performance that he later used his considerable influence to enable Miyagi to take part in demonstrations on the Japanese mainland.

As a physical fitness enthusiast, Master Miyagi maintained a strict training regimen, pushing himself physically and mentally to reach a state where he was always alert and always aware of what was happening around him. Taking every opportunity to practice, the Goju-ryu founder would start off a typical day by practicing kata, running, weight training, and then more kata. Using his vast knowledge of the internal and external workings of the human body, Master Miyagi developed scientific methods of supplementary exercise and calisthenics that directly corresponded with the demands placed upon Goju-ryu practitioners, and his students were instructed to properly perform the intricate exercises that strengthened the body to enhance the performance of kata. As a teacher, Master Miyagi was very strict and pushed his students as hard as he pushed himself, concentrating on the basics and on supplementary exercise. The usual training session that took place in the courtyard that served as a dojo would begin with a warm-up, then weight resistance training, and then the practice of Sanchin. After the death of Master Miyagi, his students carried on the tradition and preserved his teachings, never forgetting the benefits of supplementary exercise that began with the basic instruction of Aragaki Ryuko so many years before.

Another Goju-ryu master, whose life paralleled that of Master Miyagi in many ways, was Shinjo Masanobu (1938-1993), the founder of the prestigious Okinawan Goju-ryu Shobukan Association. Dedicating his life to Goju-ryu, Master Shinjo became famous for his outstanding martial arts skills as well as his community service, and he was sought out on a worldwide basis by people who wanted to train under such a knowledgeable teacher. Like the founder of Goju-ryu, Master Shinjo traveled extensively to promote the art, and his very untimely death marked the passing of one of Okinawa's most respected karate masters, whose deeds have now become legendary on the largest island in the Ryukyu chain.

Along with being known for performing kata in a manner most closely resembling that of Master Miyagi's, other parallels between the two great teachers can be drawn through Master Shinjo's incredible feats of strength, as he was able to exercise with weights that people much larger physically could not even lift off the floor. Another similarity concerns their great dedication to supplementary exercise as a major part of karate training. Like Master Miyagi before him, Master Shinjo passed on to his students the valuable instruction of the correct utilization of the various resistance devices. In this way, the scientific knowledge Master Miyagi so carefully cultivated years ago has been preserved for the benefit of today's Goju-ryu students.

Shinjo Masanobu, a world-renowned Okinawan karate master, firmly believed in supplementary weight training.

The Basics of Supplementary Training

Long before scientific studies of exercise and its effects on the human body became as popular as they are today, Master Miyagi knew the importance of a strong, well-balanced physique and had the knowledge to apply resistance training to the art of karate to enhance the overall performance of technique. For this reason, Master Miyagi designed a system of exercises that would correspond directly to the movements within his art. Through the use of traditional Okinawan weights, the muscles, tendons, and ligaments of the body are strengthened, and the speed at which a technique is delivered is increased, which are the major purposes for this supplementary training. To carry out this task, Master Miyagi was well aware of the importance of a balanced approach to resistance training.

The old saying "a chain is only as strong as its weakest link" applies to Master Miyagi's supplementary system, as he saw the body as a whole unit and designed his training regimen to work all of the major muscle groups equally. Muscles do not work alone, and whenever a movement is performed, the whole body is involved to a certain degree. For every movement, there are prime mover, synergist, and stabilizer muscle groups that act together to complete a given task. Prime movers are the muscles called upon to do most of the work to perform a movement, synergists assist the prime movers, and stabilizers hold the body in place. To use a very common weight training exercise as an example, the bench press, where a person is lying in a supine position on a bench with a barbell across the chest and then presses the weight up to arm's length, involves many muscle groups for completion. In this case, the pectorals (chest muscles) are the prime movers; the anterior (frontal) deltoids and the triceps (the large three-headed muscle on the upper arm) are the synergists; and the lateral and posterior deltoids (side and rear shoulder muscles), along with the upper and lower back, help to stabilize the body.

Muscle fibers provide force for movement by contracting (shortening) to approximately two-thirds their original length when called on to perform a task. By training with progressively heavier weights and forcing the body to work harder, the overload increases the size of the muscle fibers and increases the number of fibers that can be employed to complete a movement. A larger recruitment of working muscle fibers adds strength and power to a technique without decreasing overall speed. However, an imbalance where one antagonistic muscle group is overly developed or under-developed can negatively affect the quickness of delivery. For optimum speed potential, antagonistic muscle groups must function in a cooperative manner without dominance of one particular group over another. When delivering a punch, the triceps contract to straighten the arm as the biceps relax to allow the extension to take place. Upon recovery, the biceps contract to pull the arm back while the triceps relax and let the arm return to a position where another technique can immediately take place. In this context, the term "muscle bound" can apply to an imbalance between the biceps and the triceps if one group is more developed than the other, which could result in a loss of flexibility and decrease the speed potential of delivery and/or recovery of the technique. For this reason, the exercises developed by Master Miyagi concentrate on balanced development, working the body as a whole unit and exercising the various major muscle groups at the same time within a routine.

While muscular imbalance can occur with the improper usage of free weights (barbells and dumbbells) where one muscle is favored exclusively over another, this condition is more likely to be realized when exercising solely with the various resistance machines that can be found in most well-equipped gyms and health spas. Though these machines may serve as an invaluable means of rehabilitating a specific injury, there is no need to balance or control the load being moved, which limits the role of the stabilizing and synergistic muscle groups. The range of motion is also limited to the design of the machine in working an isolated muscle group, and if the user concentrates on exercising one muscle while neglecting others, the specific muscle may be developed out of proportion. With most free-weight exercises, and especially with traditional Okinawan weights, the whole body becomes involved in the movement to a certain extent, which strengthens not only the prime movers but the synergists and stabilizers as well.

Exercising in a manner that strengthens the entire body and enhances the communication between major muscle groups is the primary purpose of supplementary resistance training for karate, as the muscles learn to work together to adapt to the stress that is imposed by the resistance device. According to Philip M. Potacco, D.C., C.C.S.P., "more muscles and more joints are stressed with free weights than with machines. Muscles across the multi-joint areas begin to communicate with each other in a neuro-muscular education to coordinate the amount of stress and respond with the appropriate effort. In other words, the muscles learn to respond to the amount of load on them with the recruitment of additional fibers, and the percentage of each muscular contraction to the total amount of force required to perform the movement is increased. The muscles grow in response to this stress (load); it is a positive adaptation. The bones, tendons, and ligaments are also made stronger in response by the addition of calcium into the bones and at the site of attachment of the tendons and ligaments to bone. The result is larger and stronger muscles and stronger attachments" (personal interview). Though traditional Okinawan weights differ from barbells and dumbbells in many ways, the principle of improved overall body strength and neuromuscular education is very applicable to karate training.

Training with traditional Okinawan resistance devices is not like body building or weight lifting in the purest sense, as the working muscles are not "pumped up" to a degree where they become instantly larger; nor is the concentration on lifting the maximum amount of weight for a single repetition. Instead, Master Miyagi's methodology takes advantage of working at a slow, deliberate pace for each repetition; and the weight being used is kept under control at all times without any sudden movements, "jerking," or extra, forced contractions designed to increase muscle size. Stated simply, "strength" refers to the amount of tension a muscle can apply when contracting; and keeping movements at a slow, controlled, even rate optimizes the potential for a muscle group to exert the strongest contraction when called upon to do so. In Master Miyagi's style of exercise, the use of progressively heavier weights will increase the size and number of muscle fibers that can be recruited when performing a certain movement, which is similar to other methods of resistance training; however, the main emphasis for the Okinawan method is to supplement the techniques within the martial arts system by making them more powerful and explosive.

Traditional Okinawan Goju-ryu karate students must learn to balance their training sessions to include stretching, supplementary resistance work, and the performance of kata in a manner where the body remains strong, flexible, and in a position of readiness to react quickly and explosively when necessary. Reaction time concerns the interval between the recognition of a stimulus and the consequent start of the movement that takes place with regard to the stimulus. The dedicated practicing of kata and *bunkai* (practical applications of kata) teaches the student to react in a corresponding manner to a threat or lack thereof, and supplementary resistance training enhances the techniques by making the movements faster and more powerful.

The Chishi

One of the most versatile and effective traditional Okinawan resistance devices consists of a concrete weight attached to one end of a wooden handle that is approximately eighteen inches long. The *chishi*, or stone lever weight, provides resistance by forcing the user to overcome the effects of leverage and load, which aids in strengthening muscles, joints, tendons, ligaments, and bones. The range of motion with the chishi is greater than with a conventional dumbbell, and since it is unbalanced on one end, more effort is required to control the weight, and various muscle groups can be exercised at one time within a sequence of movements. One sequence with a single chishi illustrates these points; when starting with the arm straight down and the weighted end of the chishi pointing down and then rotating the weight upward to a position behind the head (see photos A-1-5). The rotation of the weight around the shoulder joint and behind the head puts great stress on the tendons and ligaments because of the greater range of movement as compared to a conventional dumbbell, and also produces an increased amount of pull at various angles, The momentum of the chishi must also be controlled, which places additional stress on the joints.

A-1 The *chishi* is a versatile piece of exercise equipment, as it can be used in a variety of ways to work the muscles from different angles. John Porta assumes the starting position for this particular sequence with a single chishi, and demonstrates the proper posture that should be maintained throughout the movement.

A-2 With the weight completely under control, the chishi is moved slowly upward.
A-3 The wrist is turned over as the weight descends to the right side, closely relating to the middle-block position. Note that Porta keeps his shoulders square and in line, despite the pull being asserted to the right side of the body.

A-4 Moving the elbow forward and up, the weight now goes to a position behind the shoulder.
A-5 In the final movement of the sequence before returning to the starting position, the weight is brought forward out in front of the body.

The versatility of the chishi can be realized in training with various amounts of weight, eventually working up to heavier loads when the body becomes accustomed to this type of stress being placed upon it. However, form and technique are the essential factors when working with free weights, and should never be sacrificed for an increased workload that cannot be controlled with good form. When using the chishi, it is extremely important to pay close attention to one's posture, keeping the shoulders straight despite the pull being asserted to one side. Maintaining a strong stance and keeping the body low helps to restore balance, and aids the supporting muscles. Performing the exercises in front of a large mirror can help a student observe postural guidelines to carry out the movements in a most effective and safe manner.

As to the actual motions, the chishi should always be moved slowly and deliberately with the weight under control at all times, never using momentum or "swing" to move from one position to another. This controlled motion aids in neuroeducating the muscles, joints, and ligaments to not only work in communication with each other, but also to react quickly and forcefully when called upon to do so. For example, photo A-3 illustrates moving the chishi to a position that resembles the middle-block (*chudan uke*). Diligent practice of this movement will make the technique faster and stronger, because the body becomes accustomed to moving against resistance in this manner, thereby becoming more efficient when the actual block has to be made.

B-1 A single, heavy chishi provides great resistance for overall body conditioning. From a solid stance, the chishi is initially held out in front of the body with the weighted end up.

B-2 Without changing the position of the hands, the chishi is moved as far as possible to the left side of the body while keeping the shoulders square.

B-3 The weight is now brought over to the right side of the body, a movement that can be performed with linear or circular motion.

B-4 Returning to the frontal position in good form is an important aspect of training with traditional Okinawan weights.

B-5 Without moving the hands, the wrists are turned in toward the body as the weight is lowered. From here, the movement is reversed, moving the chishi away from the body before returning to the starting position (B-1).

Neuroeducation is an important aspect of supplementary resistance training, since the muscles will act in accordance with the way the brain has been programmed to perform specific movements. Strength is increased by moving a heavy chishi in a slow, deliberate manner, which also builds muscle mass. Using a lighter chishi that can be moved more rapidly enhances muscular definition, and aids in teaching the body to react quickly to a given stimulus. However, proper technique must never be sacrificed for speed, and when training with the lighter chishi, the movements must still be controlled so that momentum is not used to move the weight from position to position. It is also imperative to point out that exercise devices such as the chishi are in no way intended for competitive use, where one student attempts to lift as much weight as possible to equal or surpass the amount of load being used by another student. To use the chishi in a manner other than what it is intended is to invite injury, which would destroy the entire purpose of supplementary training.

Power, speed, balance, and timing are equally important, essential factors that affect the performance of karate maneuvers; and while the practice of kata and bunkai develops the student's proficiency, supplementary training is necessary to increase the strength and velocity of a well-balanced, properly timed technique. By training with heavy and light weights, the brain becomes patterned to accept both aspects of movement, which results in an increase of both force and velocity. Balance is enhanced by the strong stances that must be maintained when working with traditional Okinawan resistance devices, which require a solid power base to stabilize the movements. Timing also benefits from the neuroeducation involved in supplementary training by teaching the body to move in a specific direction at a specific time, which directly corresponds to the techniques contained within the various kata.

Two chishi can be employed with one in each hand, which was a favorite exercise of Master Shinjo, who moved two huge weights simultaneously in semicircular fashion while maintaining a strong sumo stance (*seiko dachi*). A single, heavy chishi can work the major muscle groups in a different manner from lighter weights. One sequence would involve assuming a sumo stance and grasping the chishi handle down near the bottom at the level of the abdomen, with the weighted end pointed up. From this position, the weight is moved from side to side without relaxing the grip on the handle or changing the positioning of the hands in any way. To emphasize the gripping muscles, a heavy chishi can be moved from the same starting position as in the previous sequence by turning the wrists in toward the body to a point where the weight is facing downward. Since the hands are turned over as the weight descends, it is important to maintain a strong grip on the handle.

Two chishi can be employed to add variety to a supplementary training routine, and to work the muscles simultaneously from different angles.

The wrist action is then reversed and the weight brought away from the body to grasp the chishi from a different angle. Another use for the chishi is to grasp the handle with the hands apart, one hand at the bottom of the handle and the other up near the concrete weight. With the weight aimed forward at waist level, the practitioner then practices thrusting movements, which strengthen the muscles that are used when performing a technique that involves lunging into a forward position.

C-1 The chishi can be used for thrusting movements, with the hands spread apart on the handle. **C-2** Without moving the feet, thrust the chishi forward while maintaining good posture, with the shoulders square.

The chishi is an exercise device that can be easily made, with the only necessary materials being cement mix, various lengths of wooden dowels, nails or wire mesh, and receptacles of various sizes. Coffee cans and one-gallon paint cans serve as adequate vessels for pouring the cement, and the larger the receptacle, the heavier the weight. Wire mesh can be attached to the dowel or nails firmly driven in to bind the wood to the cement. After placing the dowel in the freshly poured cement, allow the mix to harden and then cut away the receptacle. To gauge the weight, start with the smaller coffee can size and weigh the finished chishi to determine which receptacles will be used to make progressively heavier implements. The usual thickness of the wooden dowel that is used to make the chishi is one-and-a-half to two inches, but a person with smaller hands may use dowels that are one inch or less in diameter. In any case, with very little effort a student can produce an array of chishi that runs the gamut from large to small and takes full advantage of the properties of this versatile instrument.

Other Okinawan Resistance Devices

The nigirigame, or clay jar, is another device that can be used to strengthen the grip, as well as working the lower body and helping to improve posture. One method of exercising with this implement involves gripping a nigirigame in each hand with the thumb positioned under the lip of the jar

D-1 The nigirigame is a clay jar that can be filled with sand for various weight resistances, which makes for a very effective device for improving the grip.
D-2 Keeping the shoulders down and the body square, alternately raise the nigirigame to the shoulder-level position.
E The nigirigame should be grasped with the thumb tucked under the lid, as shown.

(as demonstrated in photo E), and then performing stepping techniques similar to those in the Sanchin kata. The jars may also be lifted from knee level to shoulder level while keeping the arms straight, which stresses the shoulders and upper back, as well as the wrists and fingers. The nigirigame can be made progressively heavier by filling them with sand.

Since traditional Okinawan Goju-ryu Shobukan karate often relies on numerous grabbing and pulling techniques as a means of self-defense, a strong grip is essential to effectively carry out the movements. One implement that can be used in supplementary training is the wrist roller, which consists of a thick wooden dowel with a hole drilled in the center to accommodate a sturdy length of rope or cord. Weights are attached to the open end of the cord, which is then rolled up onto the dowel in an alternate over-and-under motion with the hands. Another simple yet effective gripping device can be made from a thick bundle of straw about six inches in length, held together with cord. As with the chishi, the thickness of the straw should be determined by the size of the user's hands. A fishing net filled with small stones worn smooth by tidal movements represents the geographical heritage of the island of Okinawa, where everyday items can be made into valuable exercise devices. This "bag of stones" is a unique implement for strengthening the fingers, and can be tossed back and forth between students, with the receiver catching the bag with the hand positioned as in photo H-2.

F-1 Wrist rollers are effective exercise devices for strengthening the forearms. Holding the handle at shoulder level while rolling the weight up involves many supporting muscles, as well as the fingers and wrists.

F-2 Heavier weights can be used when holding the wrist roller in the lower position, which is frequently used with light weights for beginners until they become accustomed to performing the movement. Both high and low starting positions are recommended for optimum results.

G A simple, thick bundle of straw held together with cord makes for an inexpensive but effective gripping implement.

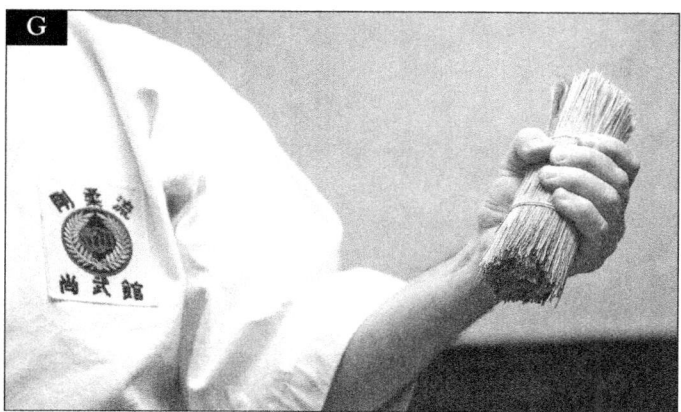

H-1 The fishing net filled with smooth stones can be tossed back and forth between students, and should be caught with the hand in the position as shown in
H-2, which simulates the grabbing techniques that are so prevalent in traditional Okinawan Goju-ryu karate.

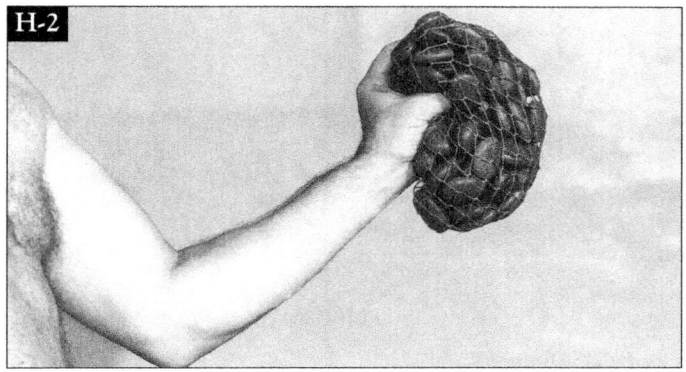

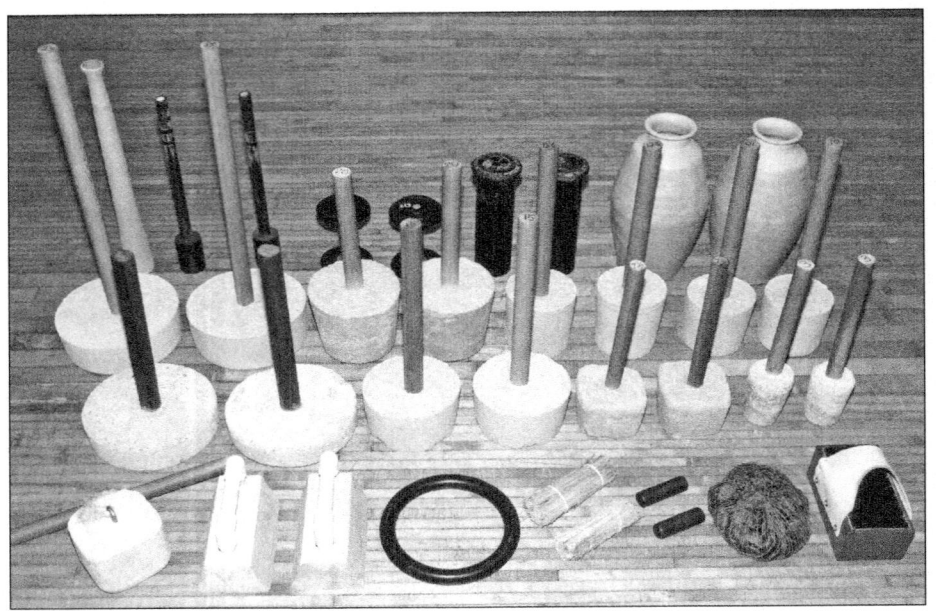

There is a large variety of traditional Okinawan weights, each of which serves a specific purpose. Pictured are different chishi, ranging in weight from twenty-five to five pounds, along with the nigirigame, wrist roller, a foot weight, and gripping devices.

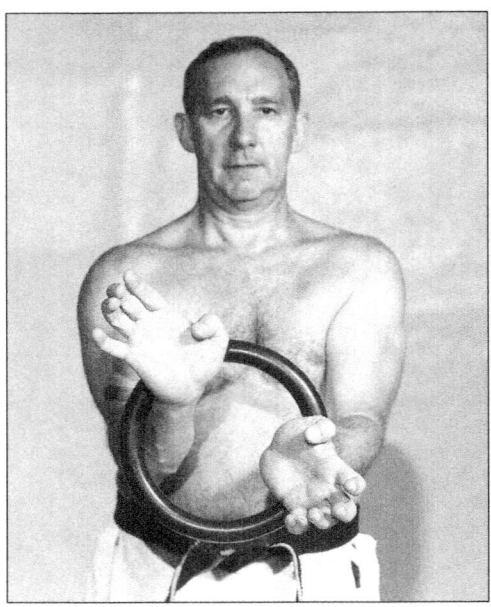

The arms can be strengthened by working with an iron ring and performing hand movements from the twelve original Goju-ryu kata.

The Old Ways May be the Best Ways

There are various other devices that can be used for supplementary resistance training, including the iron ring, foot weights, and implements that can be held in each hand while practicing striking and blocking techniques. All of these exercise tools reflect the tremendous ingenuity of a people that "made do" with whatever was on hand, and developed a system of supplementary training that enhances the performance of martial arts techniques. Though they may be a far cry from the gleaming, highly polished weight sets and machines that have become so popular today, these "old" implements work the muscles that are used in Okinawan Goju-ryu in a more direct manner, as they are intended solely for the purpose of supplementary karate training. However, it is highly recommended that students train only under the instruction of an experienced person who is qualified to teach the various movements and sequences, or severe injury could result. Those who are able to add resistance training with traditional Okinawan weights to their karate practice will realize the benefits of stronger, faster techniques, which was the original goal set forth by Master Miyagi so many years ago.

Bibliography

Alexander, G. (1991). *Okinawa: Island of karate*. Lake Worth, FL: Yamazato Publications.

American Sports Research Association (1988). *Minimizing reflex and reaction time*. Santa Monica, CA: American Sports Research Association.

Bishop, M. (1989). *Okinawan karate: Teachers, systems and secret techniques*. London: A&C Black.

Corcoran, J., and Farkas, E. (1983). *Martial arts encyclopedia: Traditions, history, people*. New York: W. H. Smith.

Flecks, S., and Kraemer, W., (1987). *Designing resistance training programs*. Champaign, IL: Human Kinetics.

Funakoshi, G. (1973). *Karate-do kyohan*. Tokyo: Kodansha International.

Funakoshi , G. (1987). *Karate-do nyumon*. Tokyo: Kodansha International.

Garhammer, G., (1987). *Strength training*. New York: Time, Inc.

Health for Life. (1985). *Secrets of advanced bodybuilders*. Los Angeles: Health For Life.

Health for Life. (1987). *Secrets of advanced bodybuilders: Supplement 1*. Los Angeles: Health For Life.

Higaonna, M. (1985). *Traditional karatedo—Fundamental techniques*. Tokyo:

Minato Research and Publishing.

Kim, R. (1974). *The weaponless warriors.* Los Angeles: Ohara Publications.

Lea and Febiger (1991). *Guidelines for exercise testing and prescription, American college of sports medicine* (4th ed). Malvern, PA: Lea and Febiger.

Luttgens, K., and Wells, K. (1982). *Kinesiology: A scientific basis of human motion* (7th ed.). Philadelphia: Saunders.

Magill, R. (1989). *Motor learning, concepts and applications* (3rd ed.). Wm. C. Brown.

McArdle, W., Katch, F., and Katch, V. (1991). *Exercise physiology* (3rd ed.). Philadelphia: Lea and Febiger.

McCarthy, P. (Trans.). (1990). *The bubishi.* Kanagawa: International Ryukyu Karate Research Society.

Nagamine, T. (1976). *The essence of Okinawan karate-do.* Rutland, VT: Charles E. Tuttle Co.

Nakaya, T. (1986). *Karate-do history and philosophy.* Carrollton, TX: JSS Publishing Co.

Nakayama, M. (1960). *Dynamic karate.* Tokyo: Kodansha International.

Oyama, M. (1965). *This is karate.* Rutland, VT: Japan Publications.

Random, M. (1984). *The martial arts.* London: Peerage Books.

Reid, H., and Croucher, M. (1983). *The fighting arts.* New York: Simon and Schuster.

Riley, D. (1984). *Strength training by the experts, 2nd edition.* West Point, NY: Leisure Press.

Thompson, C. (1989). *Manual of structural kinesiology.* St. Louis: Times Mirror/Mosby Publishing.

Time Incorporated (1988). *The body in motion: Agility and coordination.* Alexandria, VA: Time-Life Books Inc.

Time Incorporated (1987). *Staying flexible: The full range of motion.* Alexandria, VA: Time-Life Books Inc.

Toguchi, S. (1976). *Okinawan goju-ryu.* Burbank, CA: Ohara Publications.

Urban, P. (1967). *The karate dojo.* Rutland, VT: Charles E. Tuttle Co.

chapter 13

An Interview with Uehara Seikichi on Motobu-ryu Udun-di Bujutsu
by Richard B. Florence, M.A.

All photos courtesy of Richard Florence.

Introduction

So much has been written about Okinawan karate and weaponry that one might get the impression that they are the only martial arts to come out of the Ryukyu Archipelago. Reading what little history exists in English regarding Okinawa's preeminent arts, one comes across the term "te," or in the Okinawan dialect, "ti" or "di."

Generally speaking, *te*, meaning "hand," is karate's predecessor art.[1] Over time, *te* took on primarily empty-handed elements of Chinese civilian martial systems, becoming known as *karate*, from the Chinese ideographs for China's Tang Dynasty (618 CE-907)—which came to mean "China" itself due to the dynasty's cultural and political dominance—and for "hand."[2] Over time, *te* became associated with stylistic differences centering in the urban districts of Okinawa's modern-day capital of Naha. These differences were called Shuri-te, Tomari-te, and Naha-te.[3] This stylistic triad then developed into the various styles we know today, such as Goju-ryu, Shito-ryu, Shorin-ryu, and Isshin-ryu—which, in turn, have splintered into numerous further interpretations.[4]

What may interest the reader is that *te* is still taught on Okinawa. Motobu-ryu Udun-di (oki; jpn: *Goten-te*)* has remained virtually unchanged since Uehara Seikichi, the current 92-year-old headmaster, started studying it in July, 1916.[5] Motobu Udun-di was the bujutsu secretly taught to the Okinawan royal family. However, although *te* is the predecessor to karate, Motobu-ryu Udun-di is not a *te* tradition that led to karate's early development. It has a separate history and maintains its uniqueness to this day.

* jpn = Japanese; oki = Okinawan dialect

Motobu Choyu (1857-1927)

Motobu Choyu was the Udun-di instructor to the last Okinawan king, Sho Tai (1841-1901). Because of the newly implemented Haihan Chiken policy ("get rid of the province and introduce the prefecture"), "the Motobu family . . . had to go through many changes. Motobu Choyu, head of the Motobu family, was given a lot of land at the time of Haihan Chiken. He gave most of his property to his neighbors. Choyu had a big house in Shuri and 3.3 square meters of a graveyard. He gave all this land away" (Uehara, 1992, October 1: 24). Motobu then opened a dojo in Naha.

In 1924, Motobu Choyu helped form and presided over the Okinawa Tode (jpn, also *karate*; oki: *tuidi*) Research Club, which was based at Nami no Ue, Naha. The members formed the club to discuss and propagate *tode* and other Okinawan fighting arts. Among the club members were Mabuni Kenwa, Miyagi Chojun, Motobu Choki, Kyan Chotoku, Oshiro Chojo, and Yabu Kentsu. In 1929, about three years after Motobu Choyu died, the Okinawa Tode Research Club dissolved basically due to lack of interest, the former members going their own ways.

Uehara Seikichi's Early Life

Uehara Seikichi was born in Oroku, near the present-day Naha International Airport, Okinawa, on March 24, 1904. He was the fifth of seven sons. His father was a farmer and soybean-paste and soy-sauce maker.

When Seikichi was in the sixth grade, his father fell upon hard times. His father had to sell everything except for one small soy-sauce factory. The family was so poor that Seikichi could not finish junior high school and had to help the family by selling soybean-paste and sauce door-to-door.

One day in 1916, when he was about 12 years old, Uehara saw a 17-18 year old boy with his brother's wooden soybean-paste bucket. Uehara tried to get the bucket back. However, the boy beat up Uehara, knocking him out.

Uehara wanted to be strong so he could defend himself, so he went looking for a *tode* school,[6] but he was unable to find one. In those days, martial arts instructors taught at home and prospective students needed a recommendation, a practice Uehara continues to this day. Uehara did not know anyone who could give him a recommendation.

Uehara Finds a Teacher

"I figured out a way to become a student of a *tode* master," Uehara says in his book. He knew that a "Mr. X" was a *tode* master, so he followed him. Then, one day, while Mr. X was looking at a movie poster at the Teikokukan Theater in Naha, Uehara snuck up behind him and pushed him. Although Mr. X was upset, he was also curious as to why a 12-year-old boy would do such a thing. Uehara said he had heard that Mr. X was a good *tode* master and Uehara wanted to study *tode* to become strong. Mr. X took Uehara to his workout studio to study. However, all Uehara did was clean up the studio. After three months of this, Uehara lost his patience and went looking for another *tode* master.

In July, 1916, Uehara snuck up behind Motobu Choyu, who was about 65 years old and was looking at a movie poster at the Taisho Gekijo (Theater). However, "I thought I pushed him, but suddenly I had an acute pain in my wrist.... I did not know what happened."

"I do not know what you are trying to do," Motobu said. "You should not do this to people." Although he was admonishing Uehara, Choyu was not angry, he was actually smiling. "Why did you do this to me?" Choyu asked.

Uehara answered, "I hear you are the strongest bushi in Okinawa and I wanted to see if you are."

"You tested me?"

Motobu suggested Uehara attack again or do whatever he wanted to test him. Uehara tried to push Motobu in the back, but Motobu did not move at all. "I thought he had roots in the ground.... I was pushing him for about five minutes." Uehara got tired and frustrated, so "I sat down and started to cry from the bottom of my heart" and asked Choyu to teach him.

Motobu took Seikichi to Tsujimachi, near Kumemura, where Motobu lived. Motobu taught Seikichi in the morning, afternoon, and evening. The morning class was usually at Wakasa Beach;[7] the afternoon session was usually in Tsujihara Graveyard. At the evening class, which was held at what is now called the Ginowan Convention Center Beach, Seikichi would watch the other students and work on the punching and kicking he saw them do (Uehara, 1992, October 1: 74).

After six months of this, around January, 1917, Motobu asked Uehara: "'Do you really want to become strong?' And I said, yes. 'Can you do whatever

I tell you?' At that moment I realized what Choyu was trying to say. I said yes. I knew that the real austere training [shugyo] was going to start" (Uehara, 1992, October 1: 85).

Uehara Inherits a Te System

For a while, Uehara was just another student. Then the issue of succession came up. Motobu Choyu had three sons, Chomei, Chomo, and Choshun, all of whom had moved to mainland Japan and were not willing to return to Okinawa. Chomei, the eldest son, had died early in life, so Motobu had hoped that Chomo (oki; jpn: *Choshige*), the second son, would inherit the Motobudi system. However, Chomo was not interested and went to work in Wakayama Prefecture.

"Choyu was getting old and becoming desperate to leave the bujutsu of his ancestors to the next generation. Because of that, he took me, who was only 12 years old at the time, and gave me lessons. The reason he decided to teach bujutsu to an outsider who was not blood related to the family was that he needed someone to teach bujutsu to his son. At that time, Choyu had several students. Instead of teaching them this bujutsu, he chose me probably because I was young" (Uehara, 1992, October 1: 24).

In 1924, Motobu Choyu sent Uehara to Wakayama Prefecture to teach his second son, Chomo. Uehara spent six months in Wakayama. "After I taught Chomo [nicknamed, "Tiger's Tail"] Udun-di, I visited Uechi Kanbun, the founder of Uechi-ryu Karate, who was also in Wakayama. The purpose of my visit was to give him a letter from my master. After reading the letter, Kanbun asked me to stay at his place for awhile. I spent a week with him. During this week, I trained with Kanbun. During the training, Kanbun tried to take [shiru] my techniques. Before practice, Kanbun always cleaned the sand in the training area with a broom. I remember my master saying bujutsuka try to learn their opponents' movements by looking at the footprints in the sand. So I moved in such a way that Kanbun could not read my movement from the footprints in the sand. My master used to say 'never use the same technique twice when training with another person because this would lead to a danger to your life'" (Uehara, 1992, October 1: 92).

Chomo died in an air raid on Osaka during World War II, leaving Uehara the successor to Motobu Udun-di (Uehara, 1992, October 1: 28). When Uehara was 22, he felt it was time he did something with his life. So he immigrated to Manila, the Philippines, on December 24, 1926, to live with a brother who grew hemp to make rope. Motobu saw Uehara off at the port and presented the Motobu-ryu *makimono* to Uehara that day. The *makimono* was a scroll made up of poems that, in essence, is a license or certificate of proficiency.

In early 1941, Uehara was drafted into the Japanese Imperial Army in the Philippines. Uehara had made a special container to carry the Motobu makimono and always kept the container with him so that he would not lose the document. Sometime between 1941 and 1945, Uehara's unit was taking a break from a march. Answering the call of nature, Uehara left his rucksack, with the makimono case inside. While he was in the woods, an American bomb fell where he had left his rucksack, destroying it and the makimono inside it (Uehara, 1992, October 1: 99; Uehara, 1995, June 25).

While serving in the Imperial Army fighting the Filipino guerrillas, Uehara was wounded three times. Because of the nature of guerrilla warfare, Uehara's unit saw a lot of hand-to-hand combat. In one of these encounters, Uehara had killed a guerrilla with his sword, or so he thought. However, the Filipino soldier was alive, although mortally wounded. The Filipino was able to make a last effort and cut Uehara Seikichi just below his right knee with his sword. It wasn't a fatal cut and the Filipino died after making the effort. The second wound was from the shrapnel of a grenade thrown in combat, wounding Uehara in the left foot. The third was a bullet wound in the lower part of his right thigh. The bullet stayed in his thigh until his return to Okinawa (Tokyo Channel 12, 1995, September). Uehara returned to Okinawa in March, 1947, fortunately missing the devastation of the Battle for Okinawa (April-June, 1945).[8]

For many years, Uehara struggled with the idea of teaching Motobu-ryu to the public. "Choyu Sensei used to tell me, 'This bugei is an art of the Ryukyuan king, so I do not use it in front of an audience.' Because of that, I was determined not to disclose it to the public. I felt my mission ended when I taught the art to the Motobu Chomei. Because Chomei died during an Osaka air raid, to my regret, I became the only successor of Motobu Udun-di" (Uehara, 1992, October 1: 28). So gradually, "I felt strongly that I should teach this bujutsu, which was taught by my master, to the next generation. Eventually, I made a major decision to disclose to the public this secretly taught bujutsu by calling it Motobu Udun-di, or Motobu-ryu Udun-di. It was 1970" (Uehara, 1992, October 1: 103).[9] Uehara added "Udun" to distinguish the art from Motobu Choki's karate style, which he called Motobu-ryu.[10]

When using the English alphabet to write the art's name, Uehara prefers "Mutubu-ryu Udun-di" because it more accurately represents the Okinawan pronunciation.

In 1964, Uehara demonstrated Motobu-ryu Udun-di at the Okinawan Festival in Kumamoto Prefecture. In 1969, he founded the Motobu-ryu

Udun-di Kobujutsu Association, which is a member of the All-Okinawa Karate and Kobudo Combined Association and an associate member of the Japan Kobudo Association. Uehara Seikichi is also president of the Federation of Okinawan Karate and Kobudo Organizations and an advisor to the Okinawa Prefectural Karatedo Federation.

Motobu Choki

Motobu Choki (1871-1944), Motobu Chosho's third son and Motobu Choyu's youngest brother, did not inherit the family art, although he did train in it for a short time. Choki did not formally study the art primarily because he was known as a troublemaker and a fighter. At one time, he tried to learn the art by surreptitiously watching his father teach others. However, this quickly grew frustrating and he decided to train himself on the makiwara and by lifting weights. This training regimen developed great strength. He also worked hard on his leaping ability, to cover distance and avoid techniques, to such a degree that he became known as "monkey." Choki eventually took up formal instruction under Itosu Yasutsune (jpn; oki: Shishu Anko), Tokumine Pechin, and Matsumura Kosaku. Itosu expelled Choki from his dojo because of his penchant for fighting to prove himself. His relationship with Tokumine Pechin ended when Tokumine, who was also a bit of a troublemaker, was expelled from Tsuji to Yaeyama Island. Choki went to Osaka, on the mainland, in 1921, after his horse-drawn taxi business folded (Bishop, 1989: 76-77).

Uehara met Choki when Uehara was 19 years old (1923). Choki had come to Okinawa from the mainland for three months to raise funds to publish a book, *Okinawa Kempo Karatejutsu*. Bishop (1989: 77-78) recounts a story he had heard in which Choki challenged Choyu, apparently during the 1923 visit. Choyu reportedly "toyed" with Choki "as if dancing," throwing Choki about as if he were a child. Bishop notes that Choki "humbled himself and adopted many new *te* forms." However, Uehara Sensei finds this story not very plausible. He noted that in the social decorum of the Okinawan upper class, Choki would not even sit in front of his elder brother, let alone be likely to challenge him to a fight (Uehara, 1996, July 26).

Because "Choki's type of karate was a completely hard type [*goken*]," Choyu said he would teach his brother *tode* because *goken* was hard on the body (Uehara, 1992, October 1: 89). Choyu indirectly taught his younger brother for approximately three months. When Choki was in his brother's dojo, Choyu Sensei would instruct Uehara Seikichi as Choki was watching (Uehara, 1996, July 26).

With regard to that three-month period, Uehara remembers that "Every time I punched, Choki hit my arm before I could touch him. He hit me so hard he almost broke my arm" (Uehara, 1992, October 1: 89). Uehara also recalls that Choki "had such a short temper" (Uehara, 1992, October 1: 89).

Choki returned to Okinawa several times, spending extended periods of time there. By his 1936 visit, his personality had apparently undergone some mellowing, and he eventually began to train under Yabu Kentsu, one of the few men to have defeated him (McCarthy, 1987: 34). He died at his mistress' home in Tomari. During his life, Choki taught many noted karateka, including Nagamine Shoshin, Kaneshima Shinyei, Miyahira Katsuya, Konishi Yasuhiro, and Nakama Chozo (Bishop, 1989: 78).[11]

LINEAGE OF MOTOBU-RYU UDUN-DI
1) Sho Koshin Motobu Chohei (sixth son of King Sho Shitsu)
2) Inheritor's name unknown
3) Inheritor's name unknown
4) Motobu Choko
5) Motobu Chokyu
6) Inheritor's name unknown
7) Inheritor's name unknown
8) Motobu Chosho
9) Motobu Chosho (different kanji than above name)
10) Motobu Choshin
11) Motobu Choyu
    Motobu Chomo (died before carrying on the style)
12) Uehara Seikichi
    Motobu Chosei (son of Choki; has not learned the entire system)

The Style

As noted earlier, Motobu Udun-di was the bujutsu secretly taught to the Okinawan royal family. Up until Uehara, the 12th headmaster, the art was taught only from father to eldest son (of course, sometimes the art was taught to younger sons if the eldest had died).

As Uehara noted: "To completely master Motobu-ryu Udun-di, you need to start practice at an early age. Traditionally, the Motobu family started teaching the first son when he became six years old" (Uehara, 1992, October 1: 24). "It will take nearly ten years to master the austere training [*shugyo*]." "First sons were taught at a very early age to build up the body for the techniques that are special only to Udun-di. After that, they were taught real austere training" (Uehara, 1992, October 1: 26).

Regarding the art, Uehara states that he teaches "exactly what I learned from my teacher." He says that he has not added anything to the curriculum (Uehara, 1994, September 4).

Motobu-ryu Udun-di has no intrinsic-energy (*ki*) training. As Uehara explained it: "Intrinsic energy is generally called *kiko* and many people are learning it these days. It is a big mistake to think that kiko can actually work. What I mean is that nobody can knock down an opponent without touching him. If somebody thinks he can beat me by kiko, I will accept the challenge any time. It may work if the opponent is your student because you teach him every day. However, it will not work on a stranger" (Uehara, 1994, September 4).

Three Levels

Although training begins with empty-handed techniques which include kicks, the art is primarily a weaponed one, or a kobujutsu. The second level of training is learning the use of over 20 weapons, such as sai, nunchuku, tonfa, ken, spear, and long sword. Most weapons, except for polearms and staff-like ones, are used in pairs.[12]

The final level of training is *tode*, a return to weaponless combat, albeit a "higher level," which includes "techniques to subdue a weapon-wielding opponent without wounding him" (Uehara, 1995, March 11). "My master called these *tode* techniques 'the way to take hands'," using joint locks and pressure points (Uehara, 1992, October 1: 66).

The tri-level training system utilizes both hard and soft techniques and leads to martial dance (*moudi*), "the deepest aspect of Motobu Udun-di" (Uehara, 1995, March 11). It is this dance-like quality that lends Udun-di's appearance to aikido. As in aikido, the ultimate aim is to use the opponent's strength against himself. In Udun-di, excessive force and injury are avoided unless the opponent refuses to desist.

Walking

The primary focus of Motobu Udun-di is the assumption of multiple enemies, primarily in battle (Uehara, 1992, October 1: 40; 1995, March 11). Because of the necessity to be continuously on the move in a multiple-attacker scenario, "techniques are designed to be executed while walking continuously. The practitioner never stops walking, even for a moment, until the last enemy is dispatched and the conflict is brought to an end" (Uehara, 1995, March 11).

When walking, Uehara says he tries "to put the weight on my big toes and walk quickly." Stances and walking are done primarily on the balls of the feet, a practice which gives to the art a light, almost dance-like, quality.

"During the walking training, my master put firewood behind my knees so they would not bend and then I tried to walk. . . . The kicking is done while walking. . . . You do not bend your knees when kicking. You just lift up your leg to kick. Do not bend the leg you are standing on" (Uehara, 1992, October 1: 53).

Also because of the assumption of multiple attackers, Uehara said that "Motobu-ryu Udun-di is to defeat the opponent with one technique, because with multiple opponents you do not have enough time for more" (Uehara, 1995, March 11).

Motobu Hands

There are three primary forms that the hand takes: the *seiken* (common fist), the *jitti* (open hand, fingers held together and straight, the thumb parallel to the pointing finger), and the *tijukun* (fingers wrapped as if in seiken although the thumb is straight and on top of the fist, the thumb tip extending beyond the line of the fist). However, Motobu-ryu Udun-di's empty hand techniques generally depend on the thumb to strike pressure points, therefore, the jitti and tijukun "hands" are pretty much the defining forms of this aspect of the style (Uehara, 1995, June 25).

Udun-di does not promote the use of makiwara to strengthen and toughen the hands and wrists. As Uehara put it: "My teacher taught me not to use the makiwara. It was banned because punching a makiwara and a living human being are two different things. It was banned because you can develop bad punching habits from using the makiwara. Instead, my teacher allowed me to punch his stomach" (Uehara, 1995, June 25).

Udun-di does utilize ground-fighting (*neiwaza*). Uehara feels it is not generally needed and, therefore, is not stressed (Uehara, 1995, June 11).

In nearly all of Uehara's demonstrations, he wears a pair of white gloves. When asked if there was some special "religious" significance regarding them, he said: "When giving demonstrations and in practice, safety is most important. If I didn't wear gloves, I might lose my grip on a weapon. The gloves absorb the sweat, giving a secure grip" (Uehara, 1995, March 11).

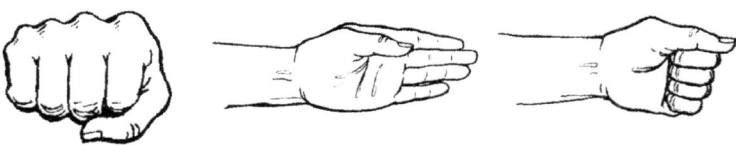

Left to right: seiken, jitti, tijukun. *Illustrations by Ray Copper.*

Kata

There is some confusion over the question of whether or not Motobu-ryu Udun-di has formal exercises (*kata*), the prearranged patterns or forms found in many Okinawan, Japanese, Chinese, and Korean martial arts. McCarthy (1987: 4) has said: "Motobu-ryu in its purest form lacks in stances and blocks and formal exercises." This idea is reinforced by the fact that Uehara himself has explicitly stated: "There are no kata or kamae in Motobu Udun-di. . . ." (Uehara, 1992, October 1: 108). However, having seen several workouts, this author can attest to the existence of Motobu-ryu Udun-di kata. Not only that, but Uehara has also stated the exact opposite of the above denial.

On September 7, 1994, Uehara told me: "Motobu Udun-di is an art that was taught only to the first sons of the royal family. This is quite different from other martial styles. Many other styles use Chinese names. They use Chinese names for kata. In our case, however, we use Okinawan dialect. I said we did not have kata; however, I meant to say that we do not have kata with Chinese names. They have been handed down from generation to generation since the old days and are called *Mutu-nu-di*. *Di* (oki; jpn: *te*) means jutsu. Our kata have Okinawan names. We have Mutu-nu-di one through five [oki: *nu*; jpn: *no*, meaning 'of']. Nowadays, we call them *Moto-te-ichi* [Motobu Hand One], *Moto-te-ni* [Motobu Hand Two], and so on so that people understand better. Mutu-nu-di means that you can use all weapons" (Uehara, 1994, September 7). Weapons-kata names are made by adding the word di to the weapon name: "*Tachi-nu-di*, *Naginata-nu-di*, and *Yai* [oki; jpn: *yari*, meaning 'spear'] *-nu-di*" (Uehara, 1992, October 1: 108).

In fact, there are only eight kata: Mutu-nu-di #1 and #2; Kasshin-di #3, #4, and #5 (which have been described as Mutu-nu-di #3, #4, and #5); Shihan Kyozai #1 and #2, which Uehara Sensei started teaching 13-15 years ago; Ti-nu-Mutu, which Uehara Sensei started teaching in 1995; and Anji-kata-nu-mai-nu-di. The three kata, the Shihan Kyozai series and Ti-nu-Mutu are only taught to shihan students and are not demonstrated to the public (Uehara, 1996, July 25).

The pinnacle kata, or "ultimate technique" is *Anji-kata-nu-mainu-di*, also referred to as *Mai-nu-di*, which Uehara did not learn. Uehara believes that the techniques found in this kata are not lost because, "strangely enough, this is the hand form [*tigata*] of the graceful classic women's dances [*onna odori*] of the Ryukyus" (Uehara, 1992, October 1: 187). Uehara Sensei does not regard Anji-kata-numai- nu-di as a kata in the strictest sense. Because of its reported closeness to Okinawan dance, he regards it the "ultimate" method of movement used in all kata that changes depending on whether or not the practitioner is empty handed or has a weapon, and what weapon the practitioner is using (Uehara, 1996, July 25).

Although stances are taught, they are not emphasized. In combat, "you have no time to think about stances or movement. You just do it without thinking" (Uehara, 1995, June 25).

EMPTY-HAND KATA

1) Mutu-nu-di #1
2) Mutu-nu-di #2
3) Kasshin-di #3
4) Kasshin-di #4
5) Kasshin-di #5
6) Shihan Kyozai #1
7) Shihan Kyozai #2
8) Ti-nu-Mutu
9) Anji-kata-nu-mai-nu-di (the Anji Dance Kata)

PRIMARY KOBUJUTSU WEAPONS

1) Rokushaku Bo (6-foot staff)
2) Goshaku Jo (5-foot staff)
3) Nicho Tanbo (two short swords)
4) Uchi Bo
5) Jo (4-foot staff)
6) Nunchaku
7) Tonfa
8) Kai (also called Eku; an oar)
9) Nicho Kama (two sickles)
10) Sai
11) Yari (spear)
12) Choto (long sword)
13) To (sword)
14) Tanto (knife)
15) Naginata

Dance

Some people have described the martial arts in general as a "dance of death," especially those martial arts that use forms (katas). Some martial arts, such as capoeira from Brazil, arnis from the Philippines, and kalaripayit from India, are noted for their direct links to dance (see Reid and Croucher, 1983: 15, 36, 37, 62; Nagaboshi, 1994: 203-206, 209; and Haines, 1968/1987: 18-19, 57). The familiar sight of Lion Dancing in Hong Kong, Taiwan, and Chinatowns across the world at Chinese New Year would not be possible if it weren't for the local gongfu schools, at least in the past, providing the bodies to make the "lion" dance (Haines, 1968/1987: 113; Nagaboshi, 1994: 425).[13]

Okinawan martial arts have a similar legacy. Mark Bishop notes that Matsumura Sokon wrote that "practitioners of court instructors' styles bear the appearance of ladies dancing" (1989: 157). Arakaki Ankichi, a noted forefather of Okinawan karate, "pointed out to his students that both karate and Ryukyuan dancing showed similarities in their movements from the viewpoint of dynamics. Karate, however, originated, as Arakaki wanted us to understand fully, from man's instinct for self-preservation, while dancing developed from man's desire to express his emotions. A karateman, Arakaki advised, would comprehend the differences and similarities between the two by studying dancing" (Nagamine, 1976/1988: 37). Funakoshi Gichin, often touted as the "father of modern karatedo," said: "It is my own observation that Okinawan folk dances make use of a number of movements that are similar to those used in karate, and the reason, I believe, is that adepts who practiced the martial arts in secret incorporated those movements into the dances in order to further confuse the authorities. Certainly anyone who carefully observes Okinawan folk dances . . . will note that they differ markedly from the more graceful dances of the other Japanese islands. Okinawan dancers, male and female, use their hands and legs far more energetically, and their entrance onto the dancing area, as well as their departure from it, are also reminiscent of the beginning and end of any karate kata" (Funakoshi, 1975: 32). Uehara Seikichi is quite certain of the strong links between Motobu-ryu Udun-di and dance.

It should be noted that, originally, court dancers were all men. In some respects, this explains why it is not too surprising to find a link between the two. "In the Ryukyus, there were officials in charge of entertaining Chinese envoys. At that time, males performed the court dance called *Okansen* where the male is dressed as a woman. On the twentieth of the first month of the Chinese lunar calendar, a dance party was held at Tsuji in Naha. One time, I went to this party dressed as a woman. I danced the Hamachidori with three women. No one in the audience noticed there was a male dancer. I still teach my students the Hamachidori as a martial dance" (Uehara, 1992, October 1: 190).

Uehara believes that "the movements of classic dance were taken from the *bu*..." (Uehara, 1992, October 1: 208) although he has not been able to find any documentation to support this.[14] "Research has yet to be done to clarify this point. However, one thing I am sure of is that bujutsu and dances, which are precious assets of the Okinawan people, developed independently" (Uehara, 1992, October 1: 209).

When comparing dance and Motobu Udun-di, Uehara points out that, "When I talk about Ryukyu dance [*buyo*], I mean women's dance only. That is because the hand movements in female dances are similar to sword techniques. The dance movements can be applied to sword fighting. You can find techniques in women's dances for use with all weapons. You cannot find such movements in ordinary karate at all" (Uehara, 1994, September 4).

For nearly two years, from September, 1974, to February, 1976, Uehara researched the relationship between martial arts and dance with Shimabukuro Mitsuhiro, chairman of the Purple Association (Murasaki no Kai), a dance association.[15] Uehara and Shimabukuro demonstrated their arts together and held several conferences to study the similarities.[16] Uehara and Shimabukuro concluded that there were numerous similarities between Motobu-ryu Udun-di and dance, including:

1) the relaxed manner of experienced practitioners
2) stances and body movements
3) the way of looking
4) hand movements[17]
5) terminology describing movement and positions[18]

– Uehara, 1994: 197

In this modern day and age, there are those who question the study of anything ancient, who look down on things that haven't been modernized, such as ancient dances, songs, ancient weapons, and even traditional martial arts that have a lineage and have changed little over time. However, studying a traditional art maintains man's links with his past. Studying such arts preserves cultural heritages that might otherwise disappear. For instance, "in the area of music and dance, in spite of the clearly discernible influence from China and Japan, Ryukyu remained most distinctly Ryukyuan. In fact, it is in the area of music, dance, and drama that the Ryukyuan language and literature have been preserved faithfully until today" (Sakihara, 1987: 209). So too does the study of traditional martial arts pass on and preserve a cultural heritage that might otherwise perish.

Sparring

Sparring is a part of training. When the students spar, they spar full contact. Because of this, they wear protective gear (*bogu*) and two layers at that for the chest. The bottom chest protector (*do*) is the padded type found most often in karate dojos. The top protector is the hard-shell kendo protector. A kendo-style helmet is often worn as well, and it is not uncommon for a trainee to come away with a dented helmet.

When I asked Uehara about competitive sparring, he answered: "Do you mean Udun-di taking part in competitions? Nowadays, karate is a competition sport. . . . However, that is competition karate and we cannot call it real *te*. Real *te* is not that easy. It is unthinkable for Udun-di students to compete in such tournaments" (1994, September 4). However, I have met at least one student of one of Uehara's master instructors (*shihan*) who competed in local tournaments with his instructor's permission while in high school.

Uehara wants his students to wear *bogu* so that they can get a realistic but safe feel for proper punching and kicking. He recommends the same for competition karate fighters and has said: "I do not recommend *sundome* [controlled techniques that stop approximately one inch from the target]. *Bogu* is necessary by all means in competition karate" (Uehara, 1994, September 4).

Udun-di is not Karate

Although it is the predecessor art of karate, *te*, at least in the form of Motobu-ryu Udun-di, bears little resemblance to modern karate. "The taijutsu of Motobu Udun-di is different from that of Okinawan karate, which was influenced by southern kempo of Fujian Province, China. There is no similarity between Motobu Udun-di weapons techniques and mainland Japan kobudo, katana, spear, and long sword. Therefore, it seems that Motobu Udun-di is a bujutsu that is peculiar to the Ryukyus. . . . However, there is the possibility that the Motobu Udun-di weapons techniques were influenced by the Chinese martial arts. There are many things unknown about the origins of Motobu Udun-di" (Uehara, 1992, October 1: 22-23).

There have been many students who trained under Uehara Seikichi, or his students, who later left to form their own organizations, such as Higa Seitoku of the Bugeikan, Toma Shian of the Seidokan, Taba Seiichi of the Renbukan, and Shiroma Seihan of Jo-ryu Mai Te Gassen Karatekai. Not all of Uehara's students have been taught Udun-di. In fact, certified dojos that say "such-and-such Motobu-ryu dojo" indicate that all the instructor has learned is the open-hand part of Udun-di. Only those who have studied both the empty-hand and weapons are allowed to say they teach Motobu-ryu Udun-di.

Left to right: Nozaki Yukikazu and Moromizato Shinzato with weapons.

A Question of Succession

Uehara "strongly recommends" that a person not make a living from martial arts. He has said: "When you fight an opponent, be ready to fill two graves, yours and your opponent's. Be ready to die [jpn: *shinken shobu*, the idea of mutual death in combat]. That is why you should not make a living from bujutsu" (Uehara, 1995, March 11). Rather, he feels "people should learn karate to maintain good health. If you are not healthy, you cannot do a good job at work. Also, you can spend the money, which you might use on medicine for happiness, to take your family out for dinner, for example. This is what I want my students to learn. Karate should be used for good health. Also, you should not use karate as a means to make money. You should have a job and learn karate in your spare time. You should never use karate as a tool for fighting. If there is an accident, you could end up in jail" (Uehara, 1994, September 4).

Kamiunten Fumiko, one of Uehara's high-ranking (*renshi*) students, who has been training in Udun-di for 13 years, further explained what Uehara is saying: "We don't use this skill as a means of earning a living. So we don't allow students to have a dojo" (Uehara, 1994, September 7).

Uehara has yet to teach anyone the entire art. He continues to show new techniques even to those students who have been with him for over 20 years. Motobu-ryu Udun-di's future is unknown at this time. Uehara does not like to even say who his best students are, let alone designate a successor. At this time, not even Uehara's master-level students (*shihan*) know who will carry on the Motobu fighting art.

There is a member of the Motobu family who may actually take over the art. "After Choki died in 1944, while I was still in the Philippines, I strongly felt I had an obligation to teach Motobu Udun-di to a blood-related member of the Motobu family. It was my great pleasure to teach Choki's son Chosei" in Osaka for ten days in the summer of 1979 (Uehara, 1992, October 1: 89). Motobu Chosei teaches karate in Osaka in his dojo, the Daidokan, and is president of the Motobu Association, an association which several of Choki's students formed because they were living in various cities in mainland Japan and wanted to preserve their teacher's ideas. Motobu Chosei's and the Motobu Association's primary influence is, of course, the kata-based karate of Motobu Choki.

Below, left to right: Anma Sensei (from the Saitama Prefecture Dojo), Shimabukuro Takashi, Ikeda Horitoshi (from the Saitama Prefecture Dojo), Uehara Hideko (Uehara Sensei's wife), Uehara Seikichi, Ishikawa Masanobu, and Nozaki Yukikazu at the International Budo University, 11 March, 1995.

Uehara Sensei with Moromizato Shinsuke (a-b), and with Nozaki Yukikazu (C-1-4).

With regard to that first training session in 1979 with Motobu Chosei, Uehara said: "In the case of Chosei, his father was a well-known Motobu... [words indistinct]. He learned mostly from his father. I have been teaching him my techniques. He has a fifth-dan in judo. He is a police officer and a department chief. He started with judo so he did not believe in Motobu Udun-di for a while at the beginning. When we had a match, he could not use his fifth-dan judo skills on me. He was not a match for me. His wife finally got embarrassed and went home. I met her at a banquet later. She told me that she was so embarrassed that she could not watch the rest of the practice. I told her that her husband's ancestors left Motobu Udun-di for us. Chosei hurt his back the next day. He fell on his buttocks many times. We were supposed to train for a week. However, he got exhausted on the third day. I was training about ten people. Anyway, they gave up training on the third day. They took me sightseeing. We went to many places" (Uehara, 1994, September 7).

Kamiunten Fumiko further explained the relationship between Motobu Chosei and Uehara: "What Choki Sensei taught was centered around kata and is quite different from Udun-di. Chosei was taught by his father. Since Choki was a well-known person, Chosei thought nobody could beat him. When Chosei met Uehara and received lessons, he found out that what he learned from his father was no match for Uehara. He realized there was a difference between his skill and Udun-di in Okinawa. He was very surprised. So Uehara Sensei taught Chosei Sensei for three months. Chosei didn't realize that Okinawan Udun-di was superior, but finally he realized this and decided to learn from Uehara. Chosei Sensei now teaches what Uehara Sensei teaches" (Uehara, 1994, September 7).

Uehara and Motobu have kept in touch since that initial training session, although they rarely have time to train intensively because they both have rather busy schedules.

Uehara does have a son, Uehara Tsuyoshi (b. 1951). However, Tsuyoshi never took up the serious study of any martial art, let alone Motobu-ryu Udun-di. Instead, he became a medical doctor. In a television documentary on Uehara Seikichi, Tsuyoshi said that he didn't take up the study of the martial arts because his father told him he should have a steady income (Tokyo Channel 12, 1995, September).

In 1989, Mark Bishop noted that "Motobu-ryu is still a fairly unknown style and more often than not misunderstood or dismissed as 'a silly version of aikido.' In actual fact the style has a depth that cannot be easily grasped by observing the odd demonstration" (1989: 154). It is still misunderstood.[19]

INTERVIEW

The following is an interview conducted on September 7, 1994, at Sunset Beach, which is very close to the U.S. Naval Hospital at Camp Lester, Okinawa.[20]

- **KF (Kamiunten Fumiko): Does *di* simply refer to bujutsu technique, or does it also mean spiritual things—for example, mental attitude or how people should enjoy life?**

Di (oki; jpn: *te*) simply means art or method (*jutsu*). However, when you say Mutu-nu-di, it means spiritual things as well. It includes everything.

- **RF (Richard Florence): Is there a philosophy, or is it a combat art?**

It teaches everything you need to know to fight in a battle: mental attitude during a war, how to fight while riding a horse, how to take advantage of wind and sunlight during a battle. It even teaches what to eat, how to eat, how to tie a headband. Everything is included. We also teach how to ride a horse without a saddle. You do not have enough time to saddle a horse in an emergency. You can tie a rope around a horse and ride it. We teach how to use swords, spear, and halberd while riding a horse. We actually ride bareback during weapon practice. In the old days, people tied a scabbard on their back when they rode a horse because you could easily draw a sword that way.

- **KF: What he is saying is that wisdom is condensed in Motobu Udun-di for the royal family to survive in case of an emergency. The primary objective is not to attack enemies first, but to escape when you are surrounded. For that purpose, Udun-di teaches how to fight efficiently. As Uehara Sensei was saying, one of the strategies is to fight your enemies by keeping your back to the sun. It also teaches such details as how to take advantage of the wind or how to escape from the enemy. After all, a leader, if he manages to survive, can build up his force and attack again in the future.**

- **RF: Shuri-te, Naha-te, and Tumari-te eventually became what we know as karate. Did contemporary karate adopt Udun-di techniques?**

I do not think so. They were completely different from contemporary karate.

- **KF: What is contemporary karate then?**

I better not comment on that because I do not want to criticize karate.

- **KF: Then, what were Naha-te, Shuri-te, and Tumari-te like in the old days?**

I do not know what they were like in the old days. I started to learn Motobu Udun-di 80 years ago. I have no knowledge of things that happened before that. I know only about what I learned from my teacher. I know nothing about other styles. Each karate style claims that their karate is the real one. However, karate styles of all students are different from each other although they learned from the same teacher. Therefore, only the teacher of each ryuha knows which tradition is the real one. In this sense, you cannot judge skills of other factions.

- **KF: Were Shuri-te and Udun-di different from each other in the beginning? Or was Udun-di a part of Shuri-te?**

There is no similarity between Udun-di and other factions. Shuri-te and Naha-te are quite different from Udun-di.

In the old days, the different factions had friendship matches to see who was better. Sparring was the only way of competing. It was the senior students who took part in this. There was no so-called kata back then. Friendly matches (*te-awase*) were arranged by teachers. They talked to each other to arrange friendly matches for their students. When they had a friendly match, a senior student put soot on his hands. People used firewood for cooking in the old days; therefore, cooking pans had soot on the bottom. A junior student put starch made from sweet potatoes on his hands. They thought it was not polite for a junior student to put soot on a senior student during a match. It was their way of showing courtesy. Soot marks on a junior's body clearly told where the elder grabbed and hit. On the other hand, starch does not adhere to a sweating body. You cannot tell where the senior student was hit unless you looked carefully. People did not wear uniform jackets during a match. You cannot tell where you got hit if you are wearing a jacket.

There was no sparring in the old days. Now, a challenge match [*kakidameshi*] is different from a friendly match [*te-awase*]. When people heard that there was a highly skilled strongman somewhere, they went to challenge him. This is *kakidameshi*. In a way, *kakidameshi* is a challenge to a person. As I said earlier, *te-awase* was arranged by teachers. Therefore, te-awase and kakidameshi are completely different things.

- **KF: People sometimes got killed during a te-awase, which was meant for competing. Nobody interfered in such a fight.**

- **RF: . . . Today, is Motobu-ryu the only te being taught?**

You have to be able to use all kinds of weapons and fight any opponent if you want your style to be called te. . . . [Passage omitted because the translator did not understand what Uehara says here.] When somebody said "kassente"

Left to right: Shimbukuro Takashi, Uehara Seikichi, Moromizato Shinsuke, and Amuro Tomoyoshi at sunset at sunset beach, 7 September, 1994.

in the old days, he meant fight. Anybody could challenge him. In the old days, each village had a tug-of-war festival each year. Kassen-te was held at the festival. It was like a death match. People could actually get killed. You no longer can have that kind of match these days. *Te* actually means fight. It does not mean kata. It was a completely free-style fight. When you say something *-te*, you have to be ready to accept challenges from anybody. Otherwise, you cannot use the word *te*. Udun-di is the only faction of *te* being taught today.

- **RF: What ranking system does Uehara Sensei use?**

Well, I started giving dans and kyus. After all, such a ranking system is necessary when you teach students. Dans came from judo. Okinawan *te* did not have such a system.

- **RF: Are there any foreigners training in Motobu-ryu?**

We have one Moroccan. He lives in Salamanca, Spain, and comes to Okinawa once every two or three years. He stays for about a month when he comes. He is the only foreign student.[21]

- **KF: Why do you have so few foreign students?**

There are too many techniques to learn. Also, other styles emphasize kata. However, our students have to learn actual fighting skills while learning kata at the same time. It takes a long time to master our skill. A person from another country cannot stay here and study under me for a long enough time; that is probably why I have so few foreign students. Also, they should start at a young age.

I do not want my students, who might have learned only kata, to say that they know all about Udun-di. They have to master all the techniques of using weapons. After they master the weapons techniques, they go back to the beginning of their training. Therefore, many students just quit. I used to have many students. However, many quit because they knew that they would be at the top if they moved to other styles. Some of them have quit Udun-di and started their own dojo. I expelled some students who did something bad.

Anyhow, I award ranks to my students only when I finish teaching them true techniques. The master-level students (shihan), who will be my successors, are in the stage of learning the true techniques. I am anxious to find out what level the master-level students would be ranked in other styles. The techniques they learn have to be practical and you just cannot master such techniques in six months or a year. It will take you at least five years to master them all even if you devote yourself entirely to learning Udun-di.

It took me ten years, from age 12 to 22, to learn all the techniques. I had three practice sessions—in the morning, afternoon, and evening—every day. It would have taken me 30 years to learn if I had only one practice session a day. I began learning Udun-di at the age of 12. I lived with Sensei. I had to be at the dojo by a quarter to five in the morning. It became my habit and I still get up around 4 a.m.

So, it is not easy for students who are from other countries to learn everything in a short time. They can learn kata. However, it is not easy to learn actual techniques. Also, you can teach students different techniques depending on their age.

In a way, Udun-di was developed for actual fighting or battle. We try to end a match without harming opponents. You cannot do that unless you are stronger than your opponent by far. I teach master-level students early on Sundays. Each student has a different personality so that I have to teach them differently. You have to teach ten different ways if you have ten students. During practice, they use all sorts of weapons. They are not empty handed. A small wrong move can become a fatal mistake. You could get hurt very seriously or even killed. Therefore, you have to be very careful. If you are familiar with using a weapon your opponent has, you can tell his weak points. If you have never seen the weapon your opponents has, then you would not know how he will move or attack you. So you have to be able to use all kinds of weapons.

My teacher used to say that you ought to be ashamed of your poor skill if you hurt your student during practice. If you are inexperienced, you will hurt others. This is what I was taught. I never hurt my students during practice.

Today, I had a full one-hour training. I am trying to complete training the master-level students as soon as possible so that I can retire....

• **RF: Are there any Okinawan Udun-di master-level instructors overseas? Do any of your students have dojos in another country?**
There is a person who has a dojo in another country who claims to teach Udun-di, but I did not certify him; nor was he my student. Some people in the U.S. are teaching what they call *tode*. However, it is not real *tode*.

• **RF: What does Uehara Sensei think about the current state of affairs of modern martial arts? Is it good, strong, or is it falling by the wayside? What does he think about the overall quality of martial arts? Some people think that the martial arts have become weak, bastardized, have lost their vision, and are no longer effective.**
Contemporary karate is different from that of the old days. That is because students, even if they are under the same teacher, learn differently. Teachers themselves may teach differently as they grow older. Therefore, we cannot say what the karate people know now is exactly the same as that of the old days. However, it does not mean it is bad. I am a firm believer in making new kata befit a new era. I have been telling my students to make many useful new kata if they want. . . .

- **RF: Thank you very much.**

Please feel free to come visit us again. We will be here on this beach on Sunday mornings.

Special Acknowledgement

This chapter could not have been written without the invaluable help of Arasaki Toshihiro who spent many hours translating Uehara's written and spoken words.

Notes

[1] In Japanese and Okinawan, words are often Romanized differently when appearing alone and when in combination with other words or sounds. For instance, *ti* and *te* use the initial "t" sound when appearing alone; however, when appearing as the second or later syllable of a word, they sound more like *di* and *de*, respectively.

[2] Nagaboshi Tomio (adopted name of Englishman Terence Dukes; 1994: 456) believes that the major influence on any indigenous Okinawan martial arts was Chinese Buddhist monks and traders. The Okinawa Board of Education (1995: 2) places the major impetus for the Okinawan development of a civilian martial art on the need for sailors to defend themselves against pirates. The flourishing trade with China and Japan fostered a large population of sailors in the Naha area.

[3] Today, Shuri and Tomari are districts of Naha. Before Okinawa became a prefecture in 1879, Shuri was the royal district housing the king's castle; Tomari was the port district; and Naha was the business and residential district. There were, and are, other, lesser-known districts of Naha.

[4] Tomari-te is said to have been much like Naha-te. However, there are no contemporary karate styles that claim direct or primary influence from Tomari-te. Other Okinawan styles, such as Uechi-ryu and Kojo-ryu, owe very little to *te* as their founders lived and studied for extended periods in China, primarily in Fujian Province.

[5] "Udun-di" is the Okinawan dialect (Hogen), from the Shuri area, rendering of the term "Goten-te" in Romanized Japanese, meaning "palace hand." Although it can be spelled as Mark Bishop (1987) renders it, "Udun-ti," Uehara pronounces it *udun-di*. Kerr (1958/1980; xxvii) notes that the Shuri dialect is considered standard and that there are many local variants "so marked as to render speech mutually unintelligible within a relatively small

district or area. A distance of two or three miles brings notable variation." See also Sakihara (1987: ix).

6 In his autobiography, *Bu no Mai*, Uehara uses the "Tang hand" kanji, which can be pronounced *tuidi*, *tode*, or *karate*.

7 Uehara continues the practice of beach training. As of June, 1995, he teaches Sunday mornings at Nakagusuku Castle and Wednesday and Friday evenings at Sunset Beach.

8 The Japanese Imperial Army sent nearly 80,000 Okinawans to the mainland island of Kyushu and another 60,000 from southern Okinawa to the northern part by 1944. Sanchez (1993: 11) reports that in the battle, 80,000 to 140,000 Okinawans were killed; 100,000 Japanese were killed; and 10,755 Japanese were captured. Kerr puts the figures at 62,000 Okinawans and over 90,000 Japanese killed (1958/1980: 5). Yoshida (1995: 3) says that "one of every four Okinawans died during World War II.... Together with Okinawans who died of hunger and malaria just before and after the war, an estimated 150,000 of the then 600,000 Okinawans lost their lives...."

9 Bishop (1989: 154) and Uechi (1977: 772) say 1947; Nakaya (1986: 40) says 1961.

10 An *udun* (oki; jpn: *goten*) was a plot of land and a house or building on that land that belonged to the *oji* (royalty) or *anji* (sons of the king's uncles and brothers) classes and came to describe the social class that was given these plots by the king. There were 38 uduns in the Sho Shin-O period (Uehara, 1992, October 1:17). There were approximately 72 royal or noble families throughout history and the noble and gentry families numbered nearly one-third of the total population (Kerr, 1958/1980: 188).

11 For more on the life of Motobu Choki, see Kim, 1974: 79-83.

12 Reportedly, King Sho Shin-O outlawed the private ownership and stockpiling of weapons, the first of two such prohibitions (the second enacted in 1609 by the Satsuma clan). However, there is some confusion regarding this matter. McCarthy (1994: 21) states this act came into effect when King Sho Shin-O ratified the "Act of 11 Distinctions" in 1507. On the other hand, Sakihara states that the statement in question was found on a monument erected in 1479 and called the "11 Great Achievements of the Age." Sakihara translates the relevant section of achievement four as "brocade and embroidered silk are used for garments and gold and silver are used for utensils. Swords and bows and arrows exclusively are accumulated as weapons in the protection of the country" (Sakihara, 1987: 165). Sakihara explains that, "In 1926 Iha Fuyu misread the passage therein to mean 'this country used the armor for utensils, and assumed that the king had confiscated all arms which were then made into practical tools such as farm

implements. Thus originated the fallacy of a disarmed, peace-loving Ryukyu..." (Sakihara, 1987: 199).

[13] Taking this analogy to its extreme, there is even a system of aerobics using martial arts called Martial Dance, developed by Chaz Wilson. For a very interesting discourse on the religio-psychological origins of dance as they pertain to martial-arts forms, see Nagaboshi (1994: 166 passim).

[14] On the other hand, Haines (1968/1987: 72) feels that it is very likely that Okinawan dance is the "precursor to karate."

[15] King Sho Shin instituted a system of colored headbands to distinguish the different classes; later on, hats replaced the headbands. Royalty (*oji*) and local lords (*anji*) wore purple, territorial lords (*keimochi*; jpn: *shizoku*) wore yellow or red, and the commoners (*niya*; jpn: *heimin*) wore blue or green (Shinzato et al., 1972/1991: 106).

[16] For an English translation of the November 25, 1974, *Naha Okinawa Times* article on the Uehara-Shimabukuro research and the pamphlet from the August 20, 1976, Motobu-ryu Murasaki no Kai conference written by Miyagi Takao, see Hargrove (1986). As far as I have been able to determine, this is the only English translation available, which is unfortunate because it is very poorly translated and edited, a shortcoming of the whole book. Apparently, whoever translated the items was either mainland Japanese or learned mainland Japanese and was unfamiliar with Okinawan names and terms.

[17] Bishop (1989: 157) feels that these "correspond exactly with *ti* [*te*] techniques."

[18] Bishop (1989: 157) says "the phraseology used... is the same (for example, 'hold your arms as if water will run off them,' or 'feel as if the top of your head is suspended by a fine thread.'"

[19] In talking with various people at the March 10-13, 1995, Budo Seminar in Katsuura, Japan, including some koryu-trained practitioners who had seen Uehara demonstrate his art before, I heard quite a bit of skepticism. After his demonstration at the seminar, which included some *tode*, Uehara opened the floor to seminar participants. This event was one of the most, if not the most, popular parts of the four-day seminar. No one argued the effectiveness of the 91-year-old instructor's joint-locking and pressure-point abilities.

[20] The interview is edited for redundancies and for length. Participants were Uehara Seikichi; Richard Florence; Kamiunten Fumiko, a renshi student of Uehara, the secretary of the Motobu-ryu Udun-di Kobujutsu Association, and a frequent translator for Uehara; and Arasaki Toshihiro, who translated the Japanese into English.

[21] Bonlahfa Mimoun, seventh-dan Seidokan Karate under Toma Shian, a student of Uehara. There is also an American martial-arts student, Robert Bryner of Los Angeles, who comes to Okinawa periodically to train with Uehara. Since this interview, at least one other American has been studying with Uehara.

References

Alexander, G. (n.d.). *Okinawa: Island of karate*. Lake Worth, FL: Yamazato Publications.

Bishop, M. (1989). *Okinawan karate: Teachers, styles and secret techniques*. London: A&C Black.

Draeger, D. F. (1974/1983). *The martial arts and ways of Japan: Volume III–Modern bujutsu and budo*. New York: Weatherhill.

Funakoshi, G. (1975). *Karate-do: My way of life*. Tokyo: Kodansha.

Funakoshi, G. (1988). *Karate-do nyumon: The master introductory text*. Tokyo: Kodansha International.

Haines, B. (1968/1987). *Karate's history and traditions*. Rutland, VT: Charles E. Tuttle.

Hargrove, F. (1986). *The 100 year history of Shorin-ryu karate*. Hampton: Frank Hargrove.

Jenkins, W. (1951). *Okinawa: Isle of smiles*. New York: Bookman.

Kerr, G. (1958/1980). *Okinawa: The history of an island people*. Rutland, VT: Charles E. Tuttle Co.

Kim, R. (1974). *The weaponless warriors: An informal history of Okinawan karate*. Burbank, CA: Ohara Publications.

McCarthy, P. (1987). *Classical kata of Okinawan karate*. Burbank, CA: Ohara Publications.

McCarthy, P. (1994). *The bubishi*. Yokohama: International Ryukyu Karate Research Society.

Nagaboshi, T. (1994). *The Bodhisattva warriors: The origin, inner philosophy, history and symbolism of the Buddhist martial art within India and China*. York Beach, ME: Samuel Weiser, Inc.

Nagamine, S. (1976/1988). *The essence of Okinawan karate-do (Shorin ryu)*. Rutland, VT: Charles E. Tuttle Co.

Nakaya, T. (1986). *Karate-do: History and philosophy*. Carrollton: JSS Publishing Co.

NHK Television, Channel 12. (1995, September). *Human drama documentary: An expert in Okinawan budo: a 91-year-old youth*. Tokyo: NHK.

Okinawa Prefecture Board of Education. (1995). *Okinawa karate "kobudo" graph*. Naha: Okinawa Prefecture Board of Education.

Reid, H., and Croucher, M. (1983). *The fighting arts: Great masters of the martial arts.* New York: Simon and Schuster.

Reischauer, E. (1977/1990). *The Japanese today: Change and continuity.* Rutland, VT: Charles E. Tuttle Co.

Sakihara, M. (1987). *A brief history of early Okinawa based on the Omoro Soshi.* Tokyo: Honpo Shoseki Press.

Sanchez, A. (1993). *Okinawa: Past and present.* Los Angeles, CA: EMS Glenny.

Shinzato, K., Tomoaki, T., and Shotoku, K. (1972/1991). *Okinawa-ken no rekishi* [History of Okinawa prefecture]. Tokyo: Yamazato Publishing Co.

Uechi, K. (1977) *Karatedo.* Naha: Uechi Ryu Karatedo.

Uehara, S. (1992, October 1). *Bu no mai: Ryukyu oke hiden bujutsu: Motobu-ryu Udun-di* [Dance of martial arts: Secretly taught arts of the Okinawan king's family: Motobu-ryu Udun-di]. Tokyo: BAB Japan Printing Bureau.

Uehara, S. (1995, March 11). Lecture at the seventh international seminar of budo culture: The technique and inner teachings of Motobu udundi, moudi, secret martial art of the Ryukyu kingdom royal family. Katsuura: Nippon Budokan Foundation.

Uehara, S. (1994, September 4). Personal interview.

Uehara, S. (1995, June 25). Personal interview.

Uehara, S. (1996, July 25). Personal interview.

Yoshida, R. (1995, October 31). "Okinawans still victimized: War's legacy fans anti-military sentiment." Tokyo: Japan Times.

Karate Techniques:
Applied Physiology and Biomechanics
by Ronald Freund, M.D.

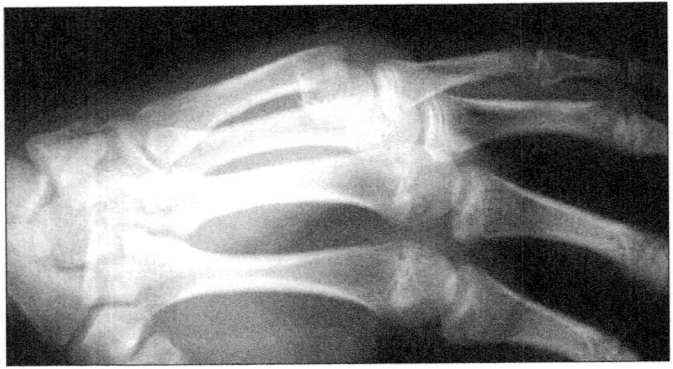

Figure A: X-ray of a hand with an injury commonly known as the "boxer's fracture."

The proper form for the execution of fundamental karate techniques is recognizable by all karateka, regardless of their style. Although the form is understood, the rationale underlying the form is generally not. When certain techniques are subjected to analysis of the relevant biomechanics or physiology, the inherent wisdom that is uncovered is significant. Whether by chance or by design, the practical advantages were recognized by the earliest practitioners of karate and propagated through subsequent centuries. Adherence to the principles of proper form can reduce the risk of injury and enhance the speed and power of a particular technique. The basis for this assertion is grounded in an understanding of the physical principles which apply to the technique.

Fractures which occur as a result of punching are commonly encountered in an orthopaedic practice. The fracture pattern usually consists of a distal metaphyseal fracture of the fifth metacarpal (a fracture close to the knuckle). This injury is so frequent that the sobriquet "boxer's fracture" is usually applied (Fig. A). Fighting produces some 16% of these injuries (McElfish, 1983: 383), while the rest are the result of punching an inanimate object. This injury pattern, however, is much less frequent among professional fighters wearing boxing gloves (McCown, 1959: 98). Fractures of the metacarpal head from punching, although more severe, are rare (Hastings, 1984: 503).

In a properly executed karate punch, the impact is borne on the heads of the second and third metacarpals. Axial loading of the metacarpals is transmitted through the carpometacarpal joints to the carpus and forearm and is thereby dissipated (Fig. B). Fractures of the second metacarpal have a relatively low incidence overall. Vigorous punching of makiwara does not appear as a cause of karate fractures (Crosby, 1985: 42). Indeed, fractures typically occur while sparring (Crosby, 1985: 41; Kelly, 1980: 103). The fractures which occur under these circumstances are the result of accidental impact or blocking kicks (Kelly, 1980: 104).

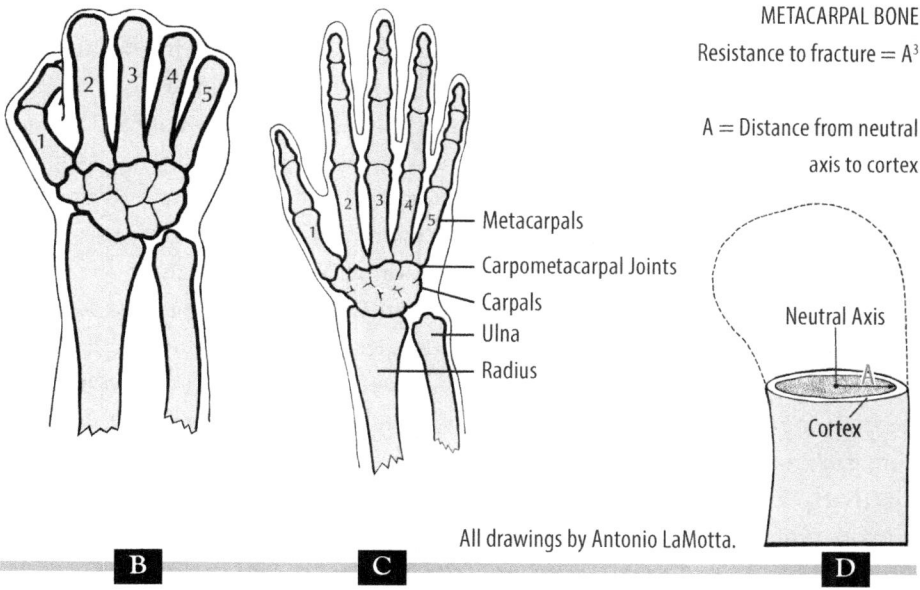

METACARPAL BONE
Resistance to fracture = A^3

A = Distance from neutral axis to cortex

All drawings by Antonio LaMotta.

Why, then, if the karate punch is delivered correctly, is fracture so unlikely? The answer can be found in analysis of the biomechanics involved. The second metacarpal is typically larger in diameter at the metaphysis, producing a greater area moment of inertia, and larger in overall length than the fifth metacarpal (Fig. C). These features result in enhanced capability to withstand both impact and tension loading of the bone cortex (hard outer layer of bone). As bone bends progressively, the yield strength of the cortex is exceeded, and fracture occurs through the tension side of the cortex. Resistance of the cortex to bending (Fig. D), and thereby to fracture, occurs roughly as the cube of its distance from the neutral axis (Radin, 1979: 47). For this reason, significant differences in strength are present between metacarpals of differing diameter, supporting the use of the second metacarpal as a focus for delivering a punch.

The second carpometacarpal (CMC) joint is more constrained than the fifth CMC joint, allowing only a few degrees of motion in the sagittal plane (front to back). The fifth CMC joint is more mobile. As such, at impact the fifth metacarpal goes into flexion, changing its alignment from the neutral axis, increasing the bending moment at the dorsal cortex. In addition, the fifth metacarpal is anatomically more curved in a palmar direction (toward the palm) than the second metacarpal. Since cortical bone fails under tension, a metapyseal fracture is more likely to occur in the fifth than in the second metacarpal.

Analysis of the physiology involved in the delivery of a classical karate punch also reveals hidden truth in the technique. Both straight and reverse punches are delivered in a "corkscrew" manner, beginning with the forearm in supination (palm up), and ending in pronation (palm down) at impact. The hand is kept relaxed and the fist is tightened only when contact is made with the target. Both of these components of a karate punch increase its speed. The punching movement involves flexion of the shoulder and extension of the elbow. This extension is produced primarily by the triceps muscle. If antagonist muscles are contracting simultaneously, the force and speed of extension will be diminished. Reciprocal inhibition is the process wherein muscles which oppose a certain action (antagonist muscles) are inhibited in their ability to contract when the action occurs. Rotation from supination to pronation, as in a karate punch, produces reflex reciprocal inhibition of the forearm's main supinator, the biceps muscle, which also acts as an elbow flexor. Similarly, by holding the hand relaxed until impact, the digital and wrist flexors remain relaxed. Since these muscles originate above the elbow, they act as secondary elbow flexors, and can impair the extension force of the triceps, thus retarding the acceleration of a punch. Kinetic energy is more dependent upon the speed than on the mass of the weapon (kinetic energy = mass/2 x velocity2). Increases in speed, therefore, significantly enhance the effectiveness of a delivered punch. A faster punch is obviously also more apt to make contact with its target since blocking it is more difficult.

Wrist posture is emphasized during karate training. The wrist is held in neutral flexion/extension when a punch is delivered. If the wrist is allowed to slip into flexion or extension at impact, injury can occur. The kinematics of load transmission across the wrist have been studied and elucidated. Axial load is primarily distributed on the radial (thumb) side of the wrist, through the scaphoid bone, one of the smaller bones (carpals) in the wrist, to the radius, the larger of the two forearm bones (Viegas, 1989: 461). Overload can result in the production of a fractured scaphoid bone and/or instability between two of the small carpal bones (Blatt, 1988: 251). The most stable position for the wrist to sustain axial load is with the wrist in neutral flexion/extension, which corresponds to the proper classical form.

Stable joint position can reduce the potential for injury. It can also enhance the effectiveness of a technique by creating a more rigid weapon with which to transfer the energy of a strike. An excellent example of this premise can be found when considering the ankle joint. The correct form for a side kick places the foot in slight dorsiflexion and inversion. The talus is the bone which makes contact with the lower end of the two lower leg bones. The talus is wider anteriorly than posteriorly and becomes more stable in this position as the talus is supported more snugly by the medial and lateral malleoli, which form the outsides of the ankle joint (Fig. E). In addition, the subtalar and tarsal joints, the joints below the ankle which form the midfoot region, become locked with the ankle inverted, further transforming the foot/ankle composite into a more rigid, less compliant weapon. The result is less energy loss as a result of joint motion and more energy delivered to the target.

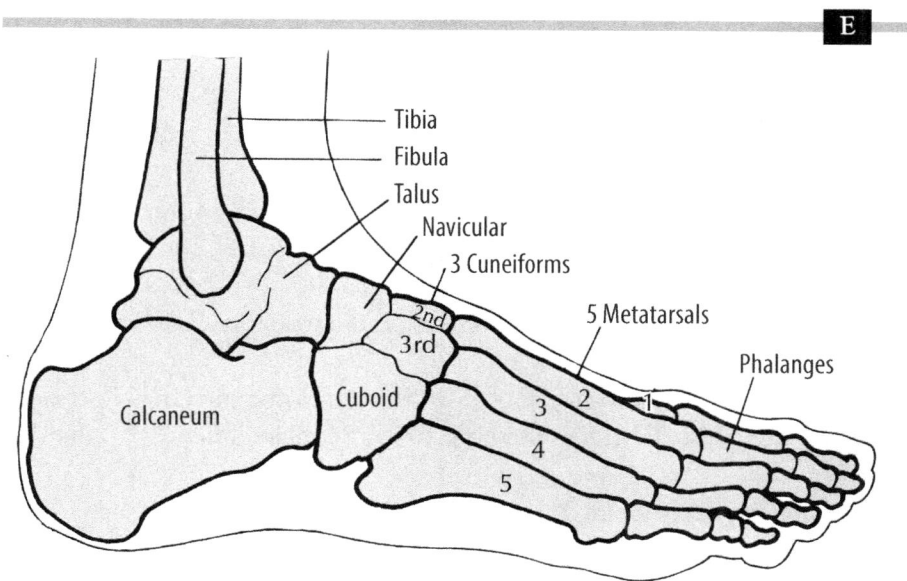

A final biomechanical consideration, perhaps less important on a practical basis, regards the *hara*, or center. The philosophical import of the *hara*, as the location of the soul, is outside the scope of this chapter. Karateka are taught that their center is a point upon which the knot of the sash (*obi*) properly should rest, corresponding loosely to a site approximately two inches below the navel. The *hara* is the center of movement and stability. In fact, this area corresponds anatomically to a point just in front of the second sacral vertebra, the human center of gravity when standing.

The virtue inherent in what is considered proper form is considerable. Analysis of a form with respect to its underlying biomechanical and physiologic properties yields an understanding of those advantages proper form can provide. Yet such analysis fails to provide insight regarding the development of the techniques. Our martial forebears taught techniques that were able to maximize their effectiveness while reducing the risk of self-injury, remarkable enough when one considers that their era preceded our understanding of the involved mechanics and physiology. Whether by instinct or by careful observation and refinement, these early teachers were able to empirically develop their techniques to the highest level of effectiveness. Their pragmatism is evident in the apparent simplicity of the basic forms, yet simplicity belies the conclusive value for students of karate. The more critically we examine the essentials of karate, the more we can appreciate the rich legacy we endeavor to learn.

References

Crosby, A. (1985). The hands of karate experts—clinical and radiological findings. *British Journal of Sports Medicine*, 19: 41.

Hastings, H., and Carroll, C. (1984). Treatment of closed fractures of the metacarpophalangeal and interphalangeal joints. *Hand Clinics*, 4: 503-527.

Kelly, D., et al. (1980). Index metacarpal fracture in karate. *The Physician and Sports Medicine*, 8(3): 103-106.

Mayfield, J. (1988). Pathogenesis of wrist ligament instability. In D. Lichtman (Ed.), *The Wrist and its disorders*. (pp. 53-57). Philadelphia: W.B. Saunders Co.

McCown, I. (1959). Boxing injuries. *American Journal of Surgery*, 98.

Mcelfish, E., and Dobyns, J. (1985). Intra-articular metacarpal head fractures. *Journal of Hand Surgery*, 8: 383.

Radin, I., et al. (1979). Mechanics of fracture and fracture fixation. In *Practical Biomechanics*. New York: John Wiley and Sons.

Voegas, S., et al. (1989). The effects of various load paths and different loads on the load transfer characteristics of the wrist. *Journal of Hand Surgery*, 14A: 458-465.

chapter 15

The Distinguishing Traits of Mas Oyama & Kyokushin Karate
by Michael J. Lorden

Mas Oyama performing Kanku kata at Niagara Falls, during his last visit to the USA. *Photo courtesy of Michael Monaco.*

Oyama and His Destiny

There is a tradition within Japanese culture of bestowing nicknames upon famous individuals. One such nickname bestowed upon one of the world's most famous karate masters, Mas Oyama, was "The Godhand." Westerners not familiar with Japanese culture and tradition may find this reference inappropriate or somewhat over-dramatic. However, by 1955, even Western journalists were referring to Mas Oyama as "The Godhand." This was due, in part, to witnessing Oyama's incredible feats of breaking (*tameshiwari*) and fighting during exhibitions given in the United States and South America.

Oyama Masutatsu is often called Mas Oyama, but was born Choi Yong-i on July 27, 1923, in South Korea. At the age of nine, he began studying southern Chinese kenpo under a Mr. Yi. An avid reader, Oyama was affected deeply after reading the biography of Otto von Bismark, Prussian chancellor of the German empire. With great aspirations, Oyama felt his destiny was in Japan and left Korea at the age of thirteen. For the next two years, Oyama continued his martial arts training while working at various jobs. In 1938, Oyama wanted to serve the country he now called home and joined the Yamanashi Youth Air Force Academy. In September 1938, Oyama became a karate student of Funakoshi Gichin at Takushoku University.

Oyama always spoke highly of Funakoshi and referred to him as his true karate teacher. He would remark on Funakoshi's gentle yet overwhelming presence. Oyama also said that, of the many things he learned from Funakoshi, kata was the most important.

By the age of eighteen, Oyama had earned the rank of *nidan* (second-level black belt) rank. Oyama was very much a patriot at this time in his life and volunteered for special military duty. However, his quest to serve his country in this even greater capacity was short lived. The announcement that Japan had surrendered ended Oyama's military career and subsequently placed great stress on his life. Oyama's recourse was to train even harder in the martial arts. At the young age of twenty, Oyama was awarded his *yondan* (fourth-level black belt) in karate from Funakoshi. Oyama wanted more from his martial arts training and began training under the guidance of Goju-ryu instructor, So Nei-chu. So was Korean and a man of strong will and spiritual convictions. It was So who inspired Oyama to make karate his life-long dedication, propelling him to face his own challenges and develop his own achievements and victories. At the same time he began training with So, Oyama earnestly took up the practice of judo as well. After four years of training, he received his yondan ranking in judo also.

Older, side-view photo of Mas Oyama and a more recent one of him in *anza* (informal seated) position in front of class at the Kyokushin Headquarters, Tokyo. *Photos courtesy of the International Karate Organization.*

Mas Oyama performing *nukite* (spearhand) and *osai-uke* (oppressed block). *Photo courtesy of the International Karate Organization.*

In 1946, taking with him only cooking utensils and books, Mas Oyama began an arduous training regimen atop Mt. Minobu in Chiba Prefecture. For eighteen months, while isolated in the mountains, Oyama tested himself against nature's elements with such scenarios as training and meditating under icy waterfalls; performing countless jumps over bushes and boulders; and using trees and rocks as makiwara to condition his hands, feet, and legs. In addition, he performed kata a minimum of one hundred times each day as well as thousands of repetitions of basic techniques (*kihon*), continuously pushing himself to the limits of human endurance.

Oyama returned to Tokyo from the mountains in 1947. The first post-World War II karate tournament was being held in Japan at the time. Oyama competed in this All-Japan Karate Tournament held at the Maruyama Kaikan in Kyoto and emerged victorious. An intense young man at twenty-four years of age but still not satisfied with his achievement, Oyama returned to the mountains for another year of grueling fourteen-hour training days. He still felt something was lacking in his martial arts and that he had not truly reached his full potential. After this final isolation and training period, Oyama returned to civilization ready to apply all that he had learned.

Seeking to test the effectiveness of his karate, Oyama set out to match his strength against full-grown bulls. During the next few years, Oyama would battle a total of fifty-two bulls, all selected for the slaughterhouse. He would slice the horns from them, including one at a public demonstration in Chicago, and killed four with single punches. During one such battle in Mexico, Oyama was gored and nearly died from his wounds. He was hospitalized for six months. Oyama faced several other bulls later but eventually stopped after receiving complaints from animal rights supporters. Mas Oyama's battles against bulls became legendary in the martial arts community. Even today, if someone does not recognize the Kyokushin name or is not familiar with the style, he always seem to know of Oyama and his fights with the bulls.

One would think, after pitting one's strength against bulls or pushing oneself to the maximum of physical endurance during isolation in the mountains that this would be an adequate test for an individual. But, not for Oyama. He wanted to test the practical application of his karate. He believed that it was essential to train with an opponent with contact, in the same manner as boxers. In 1952, he accepted an invitation to come to the United States in a challenge to face other fighters. For one year, Oyama accepted 270 challenges. He fought boxers, wrestlers, bouncers, and anyone who issued a challenge. He was undefeated, with the majority of matches being won with a single punch. Oyama was now being referred to as The Godhand by everyone. In Japan, his power was summarized in the slogan: "One strike, certain death!"

Interior view of the Kyokushin Headquarters in Tokyo, Japan.
Photo by Rummel Wagner.

Oyama opened his first dojo in 1954. Many of Oyama's first students were from other styles of karate who came for the full-contact training (*jissen*). Due to the intensity and severity of the training, the dropout rate was very high. For the next three years, Oyama persisted and succeeded in building his student enrollment to seven hundred. He then moved to a larger facility not far from where he would eventually build his world headquarters.

Mas Oyama in a lowered fighting posture.
Photo courtesy of the International Karate Organization.

In 1964, construction was completed and Oyama officially opened his headquarters in Tokyo's Ikebukuro section. He also adopted the name *Kyokushin* (Ultimate Truth) for his style. Oyama would preside over his worldwide organization from this location for the next thirty years until his death. Under his leadership, Oyama built Kyokushin into the largest karate organization in the world, with a membership exceeding fifteen million in more than 120 countries. He traveled extensively throughout the world promoting Kyokushin, personally instructing the various countries' branch chiefs and giving demonstrations to royalty and heads of state as well as organizations such as the FBI. His last trip to the United States was in 1992 when he attended one of the Kyokushinkai's many annual events, the American International Karate Championships, hosted by Shihan Michael Monaco in Rochester, New York.

Oyama authored several books on karate including: *What is Karate?* (which sold over 500,000 copies), *This Is Karate, Advanced Karate*, and the *Kyokushin Way*. Several films and videos have been done on Oyama, the man, his training, and his tournaments. In Japan, there was also a comic book series about him.

While in his prime, founder (*sosai*) Mas Oyama was considered by many to be the strongest karate man alive. He defeated three hundred top karateka in full-contact fighting that continued over two days. This record is unbroken and has never even been attempted by another. It is said that throughout the years a karate master makes up for any loss of strength with perfect timing and perception. This theory definitely held true for Oyama, for even at the age of seventy he was virtually unbeatable.

Throughout his martial arts career, Oyama faced countless opponents and challenges and was victorious in all. On April 26, 1994, Mas Oyama died in Tokyo at the age of seventy of lung cancer, originally thought to be pneumonia.

Kyokushin – Pursuing The Ultimate Truth

To Oyama, facing death each time he battled a bull, accepting all fighting challenges, or isolating himself high atop a mountain for extended durations of rigorous training were ways to test his karate. Facing and overcoming all of these obstacles not only gave him a greater perspective and appreciation of life and his karate, but provided a thorough introspection. This introspection would yield some provocative insights. The following are a few of Oyama's thoughts:

- The karate master who has attained the inner truth is stronger than the master of all other martial arts because he has no need to rely on such weapons as swords or pistols (Oyama, 1973: 307).
- A man whose sixth sense is dull, whatever he may choose to do, will never succeed (Oyama, 1973: 307).
- Inner truth comes about through a fostering of the sixth sense depending on the accumulation of direct experience through the basic five senses (Oyama, 1973: 307).
- Karate's true value lies in its effect on the training of the physical abilities and on its meaning as a spiritual discipline. This is the very reason for... karate and all other martial arts (Oyama, 1973: 319).
- To win, a man must first overcome himself. Without self-knowledge karate leads to nothing but frustration. With self-knowledge, you will learn to understand and value other people (Oyama, 1973: 319).

Oyama being interviewed during the All-Japan Championships.
Photo courtesy of the International Karate Organization.

Oyama's battles and challenges were tests that provided answers about his spiritual commitment and about himself. These answers were fitting to his new-found style, Kyokushin—"the ultimate truth."

Kyokushin is based on two proverbs: "Three years the grip, three years the stance, three years the punch" and "One becomes a beginner after one thousand days of practice and an expert after ten thousand days of practice" (Oyama, 1973: 137). Oyama's belief that karate is for a lifetime means it takes a lifetime to truly learn it. Patience and perseverance are necessary for progress in Kyokushin. One does not take up karate as a means to an end. It is a lifetime progression and if done correctly, one day the student realizes he has arrived at the desired destination without being cognizant of the actual journey.

After witnessing a Kyokushin tournament or demonstration, those unfamiliar with the style may be led to believe that there is nothing more to Kyokushin than fighting (*kumite*) and breaking. To others, because of the full-contact fighting without protective gear, it may appear brutal. Both of these presumptions could not be further from the truth.

Training in Kyokushin is intense and demanding. This is a hallmark of its founder and also one of the reasons Kyokushin is referred to in Japan as "the strongest karate." Kyokushin's intense, strenuous training is not designed to weed out the weak or to build out-of-control egos and bullies. To the contrary.

The purpose of Kyokushin karate training is to make the body strong and powerful. By building a strong body through an intense physical conditioning process, a student encounters his toughest opponent—himself. Facing oneself in this environment, a person becomes aware of his physical limitations and capabilities. To pursue beyond these limitations or increase these capabilities, one must be willing to push a little harder. By pushing a little harder, one not only becomes stronger physically, but also mentally.

Because of what he has come to realize about his own physical capabilities through his own training, the Kyokushin teacher (*sensei*) understands that students require constant motivation to try a little harder. Ask any student if he trains as hard, as intensely, or as long on his own as he does in the dojo. The answer will always be the same, no. For the most part, people give in to themselves too easily or give up too quickly. Accepting failure or taking the easy way out has become the norm rather than the exception. One trains oneself in two ways: pushing the "body" just up to its limits and training the "mind" in such aspects as temperament and values. When the body and mind are strong, one becomes balanced, obtaining a sense of harmony along with a strong spirit. This is being true to oneself. This is the ultimate goal of Kyokushin training.

Tameshiwari.
The author performing tameshiwari (breaking) of a baseball bat with his bare shin.
B. Kasper and P. O'Neil holding. *Photo by Rummel Wagner.*

Kyokushin's training is also intense because it is a martial art. Why do most people begin training in a martial art? Oyama also used a questionnaire for his students. One of the first questions was: "Why do you want to study karate and what do you wish to gain from its practice?" To this day, the answers have usually been the same: to get in good physical shape, learn self-defense, and acquire discipline. The answers are also the same from parents who enroll their children.

Karate evolved from the earlier fighting disciplines of China as a practical means of defense. As these various systems traveled from country to country throughout the Orient, they took on characteristics of the various countries, as well as their inhabitants. Modifications to these systems were made to meet the needs of their practitioners. However, what did not change was the discipline, dedication, and physical conditioning that were conducive to self-defense and fighting.

Mas Oyama trained in various forms of the martial arts. He felt that karate was moving too far away from its parent art, kenpo, in that the circle and point movement was being replaced by straight line and sharp angles. Oyama took techniques from other martial arts that he believed were the best each style had to offer. He developed his technical repertoire in conjunction with developing his personal character. This combination and Oyama's emphasis on intense training practices enabled him to create a strong karate style with practical fighting applicability. Along with this, he remained steadfast to the principal of discipline, believing in oneself, and the requirement of physical conditioning if one was to reach his full potential as well as achieve the benefits that karate offered. Oyama also maintained that karate was not something that you occasionally trained at or participated in, but that it was for a lifetime. He was of the belief that one lived by the ways of karate. By this he meant one should use the discipline, respect, and perseverance learned in karate to enhance and help him through his day-to-day living. This is "karate-do," or "the way of karate." Karate is much more than going through the motions of kicking and punching. Mas Oyama always referred to Kyokushin as Budo karate, in which one adhered to a strict code of ethical and moral conduct. He was also adamant that karate began and ended with courtesy.

Kyokushin Etiquette & Training Methods

A typical training session at a Kyokushin dojo begins with the student, upon entering the dojo, calling out in a strong voice, "*Osu.*" Osu is a form of respectful greeting and also a reminder to have patience and perseverance in your training. After changing into his uniform (*dogi*), the student enters the training area and begins to warm-up. At the appropriate time, the senior student will call out, "Line up." All students then quickly line up side by side in straight rows facing the front and the sensei. On the command, "*Sensei ni rei,*" all students bow to the teacher. The students are then given the command, "*Seiza,*" and all take the formal kneeling position. The command "*Mokuso*" is given and everyone closes their eyes for a brief moment of meditation. The meditation time before class is used to clear any outside thoughts from your day-to-day life and prepare yourself for training. On the command, "*Mokuso yame,*" everyone opens their eyes. Commands are then given by the senior student to bow to a photograph of founder Oyama, bow to the teacher, bow to the seniors, and bow to each other. Bowing is done by placing the fists of both hands on the floor in front of you and bowing until the head is just off the floor. The instructor then gives the command "*Geiko hajime*" (begin training), followed by "*Tatte kudasai*" (please stand).

Here and next page, the author's students performing flexibility exercises at start of class. *Photos courtesy of M. Lorden.*

The instructor then begins to take the students through a warm-up session. This includes a complete manipulation (loosening) of all joints, beginning at the feet and proceeding up to the head. It is important, while going through this routine, that one maintains a systematic procedure from toes to head. After completing the joints warm-up, the instructor then takes the students through a series of flexibility (stretching) exercises for the muscles. Stretching not only aids in loosening the muscles for execution of techniques during training, it reduces the chance of injury during training and normal day-to-day activities. After the stretching routine, two to three sets of push-ups and sit-ups are performed before beginning basics training.

Practicing Basics in Stationary Stances

Basics are performed from stationary stances. For upper extremity techniques that utilize the hands and arms, the hour-glass stance (*sanchin dachi*) is primarily used. In the sanchin stance, the feet are approximately shoulder width apart, knees slightly bent one to two fists distance apart, feet turned in at an approximate forty-five degree angle, with one foot slightly in front of the other. This stance allows for proper rotation of the hips during execution of the techniques. The bend in the knees, along with the forty-five degree angle of the feet, applies pressure to the muscles of the legs that aids in strengthening the legs and lower torso. The sanchin stance also helps develop a strong base or foundation for the proper execution of other techniques and movements. Without a strong foundation, techniques will lack power and focus.

The second stance that is used for techniques involving the hands and arms is the straddle stance (*kiba dachi*). The kiba dachi is generally referred to as the horse stance in many karate styles. This is a wide stance with the feet about two shoulder widths apart, knees over the ankles, and hips and weight lowered. As with the sanchin stance, the straddle stance helps build and strengthen the hips and lower extremities. *Geri waza* (kicking techniques) follow and are performed from the *fudo dachi* (preparatory stance).

In the *fudo* stance, one takes up a position with the feet straight and shoulder width apart. The hands are either holding the belt (*obi*), assisting in building balance, or up at head level with the elbows pointing toward the floor. This raised hand position reinforces in the student the need to protect his head during fighting. The basics training will last from twenty to thirty minutes. There are no stops during this time. Each basic technique (blocks, strikes, thrusts, kicks) is done for thirty repetitions. There are thirty-six separate techniques, each performed for thirty repetitions. This is a total of 1,080 repetitions. In addition to developing proper execution of techniques, power, focus, and stamina, basics training is an excellent aerobic workout and is performed at each training session. Before moving on to the next set of drills, students will do sets of push-ups and sit-ups.

Practicing Basics in Moving Stances

After completion of the basics, students move into positions for moving training (*ido geiko*). For this drill, the forward-leaning stance (*zenkutsu dachi*) is used. In the forward-leaning stance, the lead leg's knee is bent and centered over the ankle. The back foot is shoulder width apart, approximately two body widths in length to the rear of the front foot, with the knee locked. The weight distribution ratio is 70% on the front leg and 30% on the back. The students will perform each basic technique as in the basics training described earlier, only this time while moving and maintaining the forward-leaning stance. Each technique will be done for two sets. A set consists of five forward movements, each time executing the prescribed technique; a turn followed by a block; and the five forward movements and techniques executed again; followed once more by the turn and block. This sequence is repeated again to conclude the two sets. After moving training, students run several laps around the dojo keeping their hands up alongside their heads, again in a position to protect their heads. While running, the senior student will call out, "*ichi, ni*" (one, two); then students execute right and left punches and sound off with "*san, shi*" (three, four). After the running, students line up and perform *nogare* breathing. Nogare is a form of slow, controlled deep breathing used during fighting and for recouping air loss during strenuous exertion. After nogare, students line up for *kata* (formal exercise) training.

Practicing Kata and Combinations of Techniques

The following katas are practiced in Kyokushin karate:

Taikyoku I-III	Sanchin	Seienchin
Pinan I-V	Tensho	Kanku
Soku-dai I-III	Yantsu	Garyu
Gekisai-dai	Tsuki No Kata	Seipai
Gekisai-sho	Saifa	Sushiho

There are also weapons kata for the bo, nunchuku, and tonfa. In addition, senior students (brown and black belts) must learn the kata in *ura*. "Ura" means that each move is preceded with a 360 degree backward turn. Kata training consists of students being assembled in separate groups according to rank in various parts of the dojo. Each group receives instruction in a particular kata from a senior. After instruction with the seniors for the prescribed time, all colored-belt students line up together and proceed through their katas. As the katas progress in order of requirement for rank, students not of the rank for the next kata, remove themselves and sit in seiza and watch as the others continue. This process continues until only the more advanced students remain and conclude their required kata. Kata training may be followed with additional sets of push-ups and sit-ups or with additional laps around the dojo while punching before proceeding to the next phase of training.

Sanchin Kata. Note the perspiration on
F. Aguilar's uniform. *Photo by Rummel Wagner.*

Renraku

Renraku, literally "connection," usually follows in the training. Renraku is basically a series of techniques (generally four or five) performed in various combinations. These combinations of techniques are performed like the earlier described *ido geiko* techniques: forward for a series of movements, turn, and repeat. Renraku can be performed from a variety of stances; however, the stance most widely used is the fighting stance (*kumite dachi*), sometimes referred to as *hidari* or *migi hanmi* (left- or right-angled body).

Kumite dachi resembles a boxer's stance with the feet approximately shoulder width apart and approximately shoulder width in length. Heels are slightly raised (the thickness of a sheet of paper) off the floor. Weight distribution of the stance is 50% on each foot. In Kyokushin for fighting, this stance is preferred to the more low, fixed, formal stances. Although the more formal stances in karate, such as *zenkutsu dachi, kiba dachi, fudo dachi,* and *sanchin dachi,* allow for techniques to be delivered with more power, they are restrictive for actual fighting and self-defense. With the *kumite dachi* or *hidari-migi hanmi,* what little power is lost in the delivery of the techniques is made up for in the mobility that is afforded.

As mentioned earlier, during renraku, the students assume a stance resembling a boxer's posture. From here, they can slide forward, backward or side to side, maintaining the same feet position while delivering their techniques. They can also advance with their techniques and alternate either their right or left foot from rear to front. Again, numerous combinations of kicks, strikes, blocks and thrusts are performed. Once a student has adequate knowledge and performance of basic techniques, the assortment of combinations is endless.

Makiwara training. Tom Casella and the author (background) using a traditional wrapped-straw makiwara. *Photo by Rummel Wagner.*

Renraku is performed at various speeds and intensity, but always with follow-through of the techniques. If a student is taught to always stop his technique short of target, he will also stop his technique when actually fighting or in a self-defense situation. If you never train to make contact, you will not make contact under stressful conditions. Also, if you never receive contact during your training, the body has no reference for how to react to being hit. Therefore, the body is not adequately conditioned to receive a punch or kick, which may not only result in an injury, but may also produce psychological disturbances, such as panic. Remember, karate was intended for self-defense. If you train unrealistically, you will not be able to react successfully to a real-life encounter.

Use of Training Aids

Another facet of Kyokushin's training is the extensive use of training aids, such as foam-padded shields, makiwara, and suspended heavy bags. Kyokushin students spend countless hours utilizing these training aids. Each individual technique and various combinations of those techniques in their repertoire is executed over and over again utilizing the devices.

There are also drills in which several students, each holding a striking pad/shield, form a circle. The students forming the circle hold their respective devices at a predetermined position and height. The student selected to strike the pads enters the center of the circle formed by the students and moves from pad to pad when told to switch by the instructor. At each station, the student, as hard as he can, executes several repetitions of the technique or combinations appropriate to that station. When given the order, he races without pause to the next station and again, as hard as he can, executes that technique or combination. This drill not only develops power and focus, but also builds stamina while allowing the student smooth transition from technique to technique.

The makiwara and heavy bag are both essential tools in Kyokushin training. Both strengthen and condition the body while again enabling power and focus to be developed. A typical suspended bag in a Kyokushin dojo exceeds 150 pounds and is over six feet long. The bag is hung so the bottom is inches off the floor while the top is above the student's head. This allows for full use of all techniques delivered, either high or low, against an opponent. Students wishing to participate in jissen-kumite tournaments, in which full-contact is allowed without pads, train exhaustively on the heavy bag. There is a saying in Kyokushin: "For every minute of jissen-kumite, you must train three thousand minutes" (Oyama, 1975).

Kumite and Sparring Practices

Kumite (fighting) training is done at every training session in the Kyokushin dojo in one way or another. All participating students wear cloth-padded shin and instep guards. Kumite training is a gradual, building process. Newer and lower-ranked students are paired with more advanced and experienced students. Each experienced or higher-ranked student is fully aware that he is not there to intimidate or beat up the less experienced student. He understands that it is a learning process and that he is there to teach and help the other student. Various forms of fighting drills with little to no contact are initially performed. These may include, but are not limited to the following: one student using hands only while the other student can only block; one student using only kicks while the other only uses hand techniques; both students limited to only using their hands or feet; and free-style, in which both students use both hands and feet and try all their techniques. The fighting progression is slow with contact increasing gradually over the months as the student progresses and becomes stronger. As students progress in rank and experience, they are paired with someone of similar rank and experience and again fight at the intensity of their level. When paired with each other, the more senior students will fight at a higher-intensity level, but always with the understanding that it is not an all-out war. All children in the dojo wear protective headgear as well as the shin and instep guards during fighting training. As the children grow older and advance to the adult classes, which are separate from the children's, they begin to train without the head protection. Following fighting training, students go through several conditioning exercises before class ends.

Jissen-kumite. The author testing J. Regan and J. Martinez in full-contact, no-pads fighting. *Photo by Rummel Wagner.*

Ending of a Regular Class

The class' final conditioning exercises are performed with a partner. Students go through a routine of push-ups, sit-ups, leg raises, lifts, and hand-stands, all with the aid of a partner. Sit-ups are done with the students seated on the floor, facing each other. Interlocking their legs at the ankles, keeping their knees bent, the students recline to a position not to exceed forty-five degrees, then come forward until their chests touch their knees. The sit-ups are done in unison for several repetitions.

With the assistance of R. Glover, the author practices leg strengthening exercise for knock-down fighting.

Push-ups are performed with one student acting as a base, while the other uses the base student and does incline push-ups. This requires that the student acting as the base take up a position on his hands and knees. The second student then places his ankles on the back of the base student at the shoulders. It is important that the student doing the push-ups keeps his ankles in the shoulder area of the base student. The student then performs three to five sets at twenty repetitions. Two students alternate positions between sets of push-ups. All push-ups are performed on the knuckles of the fists. When all the partners' exercises are completed, students line up for the closing of the class.

Students line up in rows facing the instructor as they did for the opening of the class. On command, all bow to the teacher and then, on command from the senior, everyone kneels. The senior will then announce "*dojo kun*" (training hall oath), then says the oath out loud. The dojo kun consists of seven parts. The senior stops after each part and all students recite out loud the portion that the senior just finished until all seven parts are completed. Following the oath, the senior gives the command, "*Mokuso*," for a brief period of meditation. This is done to clear the mind and prepare to go back to activities outside the dojo. After a brief period, the command "*Mokuso yame*," is given and all stop meditating and open their eyes. The same commands that were given at the start of class, for bowing to the founder, instructor, seniors, and all, are given at this time in the same order. The instructor then gives the command "*Geiko yame*" (training ends), followed by "*Tatte kudasai*," (stand, please). All students stand, bow one final time to the instructor, and then proceed forward to shake hands one by one with the instructor. When shaking hands with the instructor, both hands are presented and the student sounds off with "*Osu*." Students line up in formal stance until dismissed from training. For those students wishing to compete in full-contact tournaments without protective gear, there are separate training sessions designed specifically for that.

Special Training for Competition

Knock-down training sessions differ from regular dojo training in that the practice of basics and kata is eliminated. The focus of knock-down training is on endurance, conditioning, strength, and fighting applications. The length of these sessions is generally the same as for regular dojo training, which are one and a half to two hours. Hundreds of push-ups and sit-ups are commonplace. Heavy-bag work is timed, using three minute rounds, with thirty seconds rest between rounds. This continues for a minimum of ten rounds.

Various other selected exercises designed for strength and endurance are also performed. One such exercise is the assisted, one-legged hop. This exercise requires one student to place one of his feet upon the shoulder of the other student. While the supporting student holds the other's leg, the student doing the exercise bounces lightly on the ball of his foot. The holding student then slowly turns and moves the bouncing student around the dojo. This exercise is usually done for about five minutes for each leg. The students then change positions and the exercise continues for the other.

Another common drill consists of the students delivering hundreds of low roundhouse kicks (*gedan mawashi geri*) to a large sand-filled canvas bag that is suspended from a rack just off the floor. The contact point on the leg when delivering the kick is the shin, while the target during fighting is the inside or outside portion of the opponent's leg.

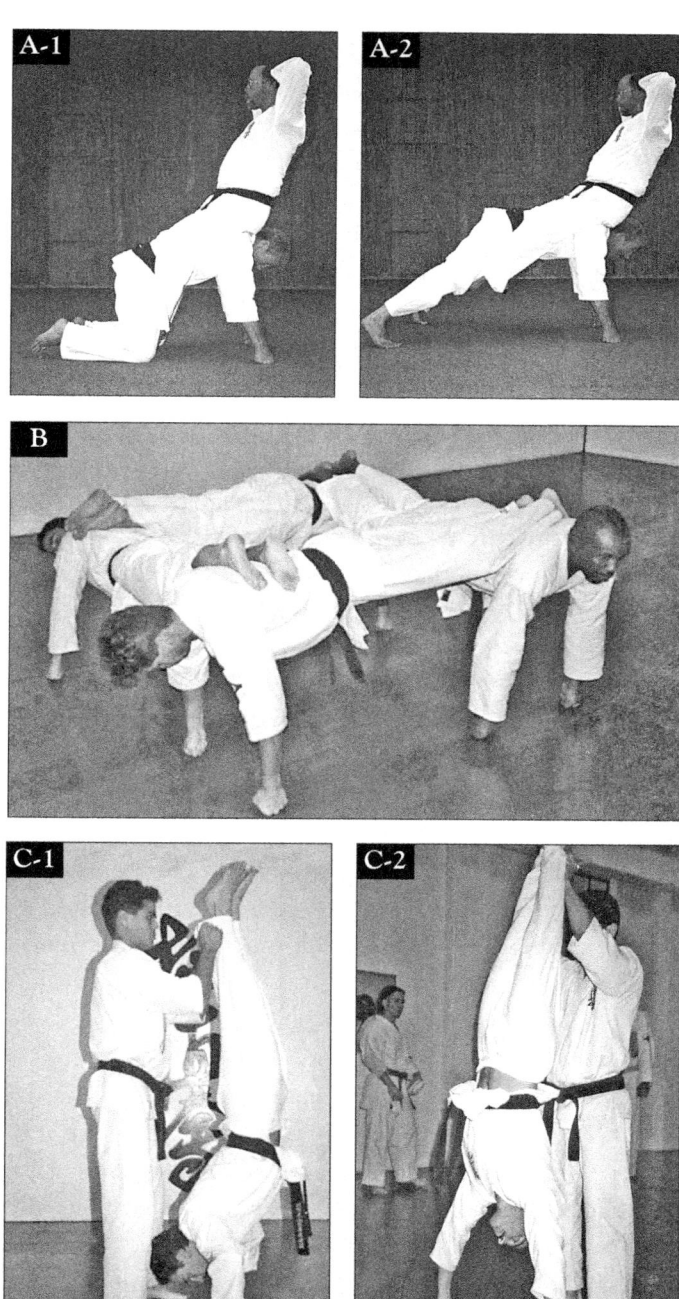

A-1-2: R. Glover with the author: A variation on push-ups.

B: F. Aguilar, B. Kasper, J. Martinez, and C. Whitney doing four-man push-ups.

C-1-2: J. Martinez and T. Casella practicing hand-stands for strength.

Several rounds of full-contact fighting are also done during these sessions with one student wearing protective equipment that covers his head, arms, chest, and legs. Specially designed pants are sold in Japan for this type of training, but are very expensive. Ice hockey pants with internal padding work just as well and are less expensive. Several rounds of less intense contact are then done without the equipment.

The students then undergo several more minutes of conditioning exercises for stamina and strength. For this part of the training, I like to use a form of circuit training. The students begin running around the inside perimeter of the dojo. When they have run for one minute, they are given a specific exercise (push-up, sit-up, walk-stretch, etc.) to perform, doing as many repetitions as they can for thirty seconds. After the thirty seconds, they run again. This continues for twenty minutes, with the student running for one minute, exercising for thirty seconds, and so on. The last part of training consists of a cool-down period.

Students undergo full-contact, knock-down training, in addition to attending regular classes, for a minimum of one year before they are allowed to compete in knock-down competition. In addition, students wanting to compete in knock-down fighting normally have attended two years of regular Kyokushin training before beginning knock-down training. Competition in Kyokushin full-contact tournaments is generally reserved for students at brown- and black-belt ranks. Although dissuaded by their instructors, there are some students of lower rank who request to compete in these events. However, like their brown- and black-belt counterparts, they too must successfully undergo the separate sessions of full-contact, knock-down training before entering jissen, full-contact competition.

Jissen Knock-down Competition

The rules are quite simple for Kyokushin full-contact, knock-down competition: no punching to the face, no kicking to the groin, and no holding. Other than that, everything else is allowed. One point (*ippon*) is awarded and a competitor declared the winner in this three-minute match when one opponent stops the other, either by a knockout or a technique that disables him, thus preventing him from continuing. A competitor may also gain a full-point victory after receiving two half-points (*waza-ari*). A waza-ari is awarded when one opponent knocks down the other with a strong technique, but the fallen opponent is able to resume fighting within ten seconds. If the competitor receiving the half-point is able to knock down his opponent a second time and receives a second waza-ari, he is declared the winner.

Kyokushin Jissen Kumite *Photos by M. Monaco.*

In the event that the three-minute time limit expires and one opponent has a half-point to his credit, he is declared the winner. In the event neither competitor scores a knock down during the three minutes, a decision is made by the four corner judges. At the command of the center judge, each corner judge holds aloft either a white or red flag, corresponding to the color ribbon tied to the belt of the competitor, that the judge feels dominated the fight. In the event of a tie, a three-minute extension is given after which a decision is again requested. If there is a tie once more, a second three-minute extension is given and the competitors fight once more, after which, if there is still a tie according to the judges, the match is decided by *tameshiwari*.

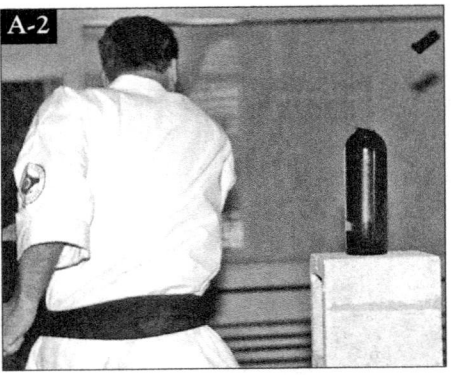

A-1-2) Author performing a bottle cut. Note that the base remains standing.

B) J. Regan and others holding steadily while F. Anguilar performs a *yoko-geri* (side kick) to three one-inch boards.

C) J. Martinez performs tameshiwari with punch.

D) B. Kasper performs tameshiwari with an elbow strike. *Photos by Rummel Wagner.*

Prior to fighting, all competitors must perform tameshiwari. They must break a minimum of three boards with three different techniques: *seiken* (forefist), *shuto* (knifehand), and *sokuto* (knifefoot). Any competitor may elect to attempt to break more than the required three boards. If a competitor elects to try more than three boards and fails, he is not given a second chance at the additional boards, but must attempt the three boards only. If he fails to break the three boards, he is out of the competition and does not move on to the fighting portion. In the event of a tie after the three extensions, each fighter is weighed. The fighter who is lighter than the other by ten pounds and who broke a greater number of boards is the winner. If both fighters are within ten pounds of each other, the student who broke the greater number of boards is the winner. If both fighters are within ten pounds of each other and both broke the same number of boards, then a third three-minute extension is given and they fight once again. Generally, there are three weight divisions within a Kyokushin knock-down tournament: heavy, middle, and light. The exception to this is the World Tournament, held once every four years at which there are no weight divisions. There are very few karate events that require competitors to engage in tameshiwari before fighting, like Kyokushin does.

E) The author strikes J. Martinez
with a two-by-two-inch board
while he is doing the Sanchin kata.

Photo by Rummel Wagner.

The author strikes B. Kasper with a two-by-two-inch board while he is doing the Sanchin kata. *Photo by Rummel Wagner.*

Tameshiwari

Tameshiwari is a strong part of Kyokushin training. Although it is used in a carnival-like fashion by some karate practitioners, tameshiwari is an important way of testing sprit and basic technique. However important, by itself, tameshiwari is not karate. When a karate student faces the challenge of tameshiwari, he faces it alone. The student must have an understanding of the material to be broken and in a Zen-like way become one with it. Gradually increasing in hardness of material (wood, cement, bricks, ice, etc.) and in numbers of a selected material, tameshiwari is one of the many requirements for advancement in rank for all adult Kyokushin students.

Grading

Promotion tests for advancement in *kyu* rank, the color belts before black belt, are given four times per year in a Kyokushin dojo. Students may be eligible for three promotions during the year, but rarely does a student progress at that rate. The higher the rank a student attains, the longer the time between tests. On the average, it will take a student attending class three times per week five to six years to reach black-belt. *Yudansha* (black-belt) promotions are only offered once a year.

Each test consists of two parts: written and practical. The written phase of the test includes: multiple choice, fill-in-the-blank, and matching questions; Japanese vocabulary; and identification of the various techniques and stances through depiction in photographs. The practical portion of the test consists of the students performing all the required techniques for that specific rank individually and as a group. Students also demonstrate kata, self-defense techniques, *ido geiko*, and *renraku* individually as well as in a group. Students attempting grading also engage in fighting matches. The duration of the bouts, the number of bouts, as well as the intensity of the exchange are determined by the rank they are attempting to achieve.

In addition to the written and practical phases of the testing procedure, those candidates attempting to attain black-belt must also submit a paper on a Kyokushin-related topic selected by the instructor.

The order of colored belts for the kyu rank within Kyokushin is: white, blue, yellow, green, brown. Each color is designated with an appropriate numerical rank. As the student progresses in kyu rank, the number decreases. Therefore, a newer student of white-belt rank will be tenth or ninth kyu whereas a brown-belt student will be either second or first kyu.

Black-belt ranking is in the reverse order. First-level black-belts are awarded the *shodan* (beginner level). Subsequent ranks in an ascending order are awarded as the black-belt student progresses.

Rank is not awarded at random in Kyokushin and it is not taken lightly. In addition to attending the regularly offered training sessions at the dojo, students wishing to advance must also participate in special clinics, annual winter and summer camps, and special events, such as the twenty-four hour, continuous training seminar. Kyokushin students understand that if you must train extensively for knock-down fighting, you must train even more intensely and extensively for promotion.

Oyama's Influence and Inspiration

Mas Oyama incorporated full-contact, no-pads fighting in karate. He believed that one could not fully test the effectiveness of his techniques without actual contact, like what a boxer learns in his training. It is common knowledge that many of Oyama's first students were from other styles of karate that did not practice full-contact fighting. Many of these students trained with Oyama only for the experience of this form of fighting while still practicing their other styles. Upon returning to training in their original dojo, they soon learned that they were far superior in fighting to their dojo counterparts. Many of these students found themselves being reprimanded for their aggressive fighting by their instructors. Some were asked to leave their dojo while others became disheartened and left on their own. In both instances, many resumed their karate training with Oyama. These students leaving and joining Oyama caused tension between Oyama and instructors of the other styles. Some of these instructors felt insulted and sent groups of their students to the Oyama dojo to seek revenge. To this day in Japan at the Kyokushin headquarters, you will find two students positioned at the door as a precaution against such attempts.

Oyama performing *shuto gamen-uchi* (knifehand strike).
Photo courtesy of the International Karate Organization.

Mas Oyama produced numerous great fighters and instructors during his career. Some of these individuals, for reasons of their own, went on to form their own successful organizations. Each one employs the jissen way of full-contact fighting as well as the intense form of training they learned from Oyama. They all have different names for their styles and organizations, but in reality what they teach is Kyokushin karate.

Since the passing of Mas Oyama in April 1994, the Kyokushin organization that he devoted his life to building has been in turmoil. There are two separate factions calling themselves International Karate Organization (IKO) Kyokushin Kaikan. This is the name Mas Oyama called his organization. The two factions in Japan vying for the right to the IKO Kyokushinkai are currently engaged in a legal battle. At this time, the courts have ruled in favor of the Oyama family and Nishida Yukio. The contesting party appealed the decision and lost the appeal also. There is another and final appeal currently underway. According to reports from Japan, the likelihood of this appeal overturning the previous decision is unlikely. If this is true and the courts find in favor of the Oyama and Nishida, the IKO will once again be united under Oyama control.

In Mas Oyama's earlier years, in his twenties, when he first journeyed to the mountains and fought the bulls, he focused on and was concerned with only increasing and testing his body's strength, pushing it to the limits. However, as Oyama aged, he began to consider the more evasive meanings in life, looking inside himself, considering the spirit and not just the flesh. He concluded that strength alone does not define karate or a man:

"just as human life that lacks a true philosophy is not worthy of the name, so a karate that is not built on truth, though it may possess strength, is not real karate."

– Oyama, 1958: foreword

Kyokushin is real karate. It was built on the truths of its founder Mas Oyama—The Godhand.

Acknowledgement
A special thanks to the people who helped make this chapter possible: F. Aguilar, T. Casella, R. Glover, B. Kasper, J. Martinez, M. Monaco, P. O'Neil, J. Regan, R. Wagner, C. Whitley, the International Karate Organization (IKO), and to all students at the Kyokushin Karate Schools in Hollywood and Orlando, Florida, and in Colorado Springs, Colorado.

References
Ligo, N. (1994). *Budo karate illustrated*. Davidson, NC: Self Published.
Oyama, M. (1958). *What is karate?* Tokyo: Shuppansha Publications.
Oyama, M. (1973). *This is karate*. Tokyo: Japan Publications.
Oyama, M. (1975). Quoted from speech made at First World Tournament.
Oyama, M. (1979). *Advanced karate*. Tokyo: Japan Publications.
Oyama, M. (1979). *The Kyokushin way*. Tokyo: Japan Publications.

Without Spirit Budo is But an Empty Shell
by Jon Bluming

All photographs courtesy of J. Bluming.

Introduction

There are many stories told about Kyokushin Kaikan karate pioneer Jon Bluming and his teacher Oyama Masutatsu (Mas Oyama), not all of which are true. Here Bluming, who was for many years Oyama's senior European student, gives his candid version of the way things were. Richard Bowen, Grahm Noble, Robert W. Smith, and Joseph R. Svinth contributed to the completion of this chapter.

Beginnings

I was born in Amsterdam, Holland, in February 1933. When I was sixteen, I joined the Dutch Marines. In November 1950, I was sent to Korea, where I served with the Van Heutz Battalion until September 1951. The Van Heutz Battalion was attached to the 38th Regiment of the US Second Division, and today it has a Dutch Medal of Honor in its regimental colors. We fought in some terrible places, and I was wounded twice during that tour. Being young and stupid, I volunteered for a second tour in July 1952. I was wounded a third time while defending Outpost Erie in October 1952. I remained in Korea until September 1953.

Judo

While recuperating in Tokyo's Annex Hospital in April 1951, I saw Mifune Kyuzo giving a judo demonstration. I have always been intrigued and obsessed with ways of defending myself at ranges extending from a few feet to intimate contact on the ground. And what Mifune did was so spectacular that I knew I had to do it too. So, after getting out of the Marines in January 1954, I started studying judo in Amsterdam. I earned by 1st dan on December 19, 1954. Earning dan rank in just eleven months is unusual, but hardly unique. Professor Yamashita Yoshikazu, judo's first 10th dan, earned his 1st dan in just three months and his 4th dan in only two years.

In the spring of 1955, I became captain of the Dutch Tung Jen judo team. In the summer of 1956, I became the first Dutchman the Kodokan promoted to 2nd dan. A year later, the Tung Jen team won a European title, and I made the winning ippon. About the same time, I broke a toe on my right foot and, in a contest, I still threw seventy-five judoka ranked from 4th kyu to 3rd dan in just twenty-six minutes. My teacher Hirano, promoted me to 3rd dan and told me I needed to go to Japan to train. So I did. Along the way, I started a judo club in Halifax, Nova Scotia, and studied a bit with Mits Kimura in San Francisco.

Throwing Y. Oda, 5th dan, who was the Kyoto Police Champion, with *harai goshi* (hip sweep). Donn Draeger took this photograph during the summer of 1960.

Training at the Kodokan

Upon arriving in Japan in February 1959, I immediately enrolled at the Kodokan. There I met Donn F. Draeger and Bill Backhus, both of whom were to be my friends for life. In November 1959, I was made a member of the Kenshusei. This was a program for judoka expected to be future champions and teachers. The Kenshusei's regular instructors included Daigo Toshiro, Kawamura Teizo, and Osawa Yoshimi. Members also got to attend special seminars given by teachers like Mifune Kyuzo and Samura Kaichiro. The competition was fierce, and during a promotional tournament in December 1959, I defeated the All-Korea champion using a left *osotogari* (large outer reap). As a result, the Korean Yudo Association awarded me 4th dan. However I was still only a 3rd dan at the Kodokan. I didn't earn 4th dan there until the summer of 1960.

1) Throwing T. Seino, 5th dan, with *uchimata* (inner-thigh reaping throw).
2) Last lesson from the Kodokan's last 10th dan, the late Kotani Sumiyuki.

Shotokan

In March 1959, I started studying karate at the Shotokan headquarters. To my disgust, the Shotokan's instructors wouldn't let me do randori or kumite. Their excuse was that their fighting was too dangerous. The truth was that they recognized that it would have looked bad for their black belts to be beaten by a white belt. This isn't bragging. Read C.W. Nicol's book, *Moving Zen* (1975). Even as a beginner, Nicol could beat many Shotokan karateka without much trouble, unless he agreed to fight their way.

Shotokan's problem is that it hasn't changed in fifty years. Training still consists of going through the same three steps forward and then turn around, with the only variations being in the fist and foot techniques. This isn't very realistic. Neither is the absence of grappling techniques. On the ground, Shotokan karateka are babies.

Shotokan also puts too much emphasis on kata. Back when people trained to defend themselves from knives and swords, kata was necessary because learning to deflect a sword with your bare hands is dangerous. Today people use guns rather than knives and, as nobody can block bullets, you need to spend your training time doing randori if you want to be a fighter. Maybe it's different when you get real old. Donn Draeger once told Bill Backhus and me that randori is something you do when you are young and kata is something you do when you get old. But neither Donn nor I ever got that old. While Donn was an expert on judo kata, he loved randori more. And in ground wrestling he could beat the pants off anybody. Including me.

Bluming with Donn Draeger on a bridge
in Nikko, Japan, summer, 1961.

Worst of all, Shotokan players learn to stop their strikes just short of the target. If they get into a fight that isn't scored by a computer they won't do any damage, as all their training has taught them to pull their punches. One way of overcoming this problem is by hitting things. I still hit the brick wall of the gym thirty times between each set during my weight-lifting. I concentrate on striking with the knuckle of the index finger, as that keeps it molded for the real thing. After all, you never know when you're going to need it. People should start by punching bags or makiwara, because you can't punch very hard with broken knuckles or arthritic fingers.

Still, if people are happy doing something that doesn't hurt me, who am I to tell them that they are wrong? Obata Isao and Nakayama Masatoshi subsequently became my very good friends, and all I'm saying is that Shotokan karate wasn't right for me.

Kyokushinkai

Seeing I wasn't happy at the Shotokan, in April 1959, Donn Draeger introduced me to Mas Oyama. Oyama loved having a fighter aboard and did not care in those days if a *gaijin* (foreigner) beat up his black belts. Bill Backhus went with me and we became Oyama's first foreign students.

We started in a little urine-smelling dojo behind Rikkyo University in Tokyo—it smelled that way because of the open toilets of the apartment building above the dojo. The dojo was no bigger than an ordinary living room in the average Dutch family home and it never had many members. If you look at old photographs, you never see more than maybe twenty-five students in it.

The dropout rate was high mainly because Oyama allowed semicontact fighting. Many were called but few could take it. There aren't many people in the world who really want to learn how to fight or do the hard work needed to get somewhere. Instead, most people would rather dabble in a dojo. Even if they just do kata, they don't do it until they bleed, they just dabble. It wasn't any different back then, either.

I was beating up most of Oyama's black belts after just a couple weeks of training. This was not really that surprising. Besides being used to the pain (there is always pain when training with Japanese national judo champions!), these were little fellows and I was a heavyweight with the speed of a middle-weight. Using weights, Donn Draeger was building me up from 79 kilos (174 pounds) to 102 kilos (224 pounds). He had a terrific weightlifting program that added strength to my natural speed and understanding of the fighting sports. May the gods bless him, for I loved that man.

During my almost three years studying karate with Oyama, I always wore a white belt. Before I left for Holland in November 1961, he promoted me to 2nd dan and gave me a teaching and branch chief certificate. When Oyama promoted me to 6th dan on January 15, 1965, some people said that nobody could legitimately advance from 2nd dan to 6th dan so quickly. Donn Draeger wasn't shy, so he asked Oyama about it. Oyama's answer was published in *Muscular Development* in December 1966:

> Bluming is a dedicated karate expert with an aggressive style. He can punch and kick with the best of them. His high rank is unusual for a foreigner, but justified by tradition. In days of old, the strongest, most effective fighters were given the highest recognitions. Bluming today, internationally-speaking, is the strongest in my opinion. If any karate man will dispute his rank, let him face Bluming in a match. If he defeats Bluming, I will strip Bluming of his rank, and I myself stop karate.

Oyama was not worried that I was going to lose, either. As I recall, another article reported that he was offering something like $100,000 to anyone who could beat me. Nobody responded, not even the big mouths whose pictures filled the pages of *Black Belt*.

Troubles in Europe

Other people had just as much faith in my abilities. For example, Joop Reuvecamp, the sports editor of the Amsterdam newspaper *Het Parool*, sent Olympic judo champion Anton Geesink a registered letter saying that I had agreed to fight him anywhere under any rules he wanted. After that, Geesink received five more official challenges sent via the Amateur Judo Union, the Dutch Sports Federation, and even the TV talk show hostess Mies Bouwman (the last challenge, in 1962, would have raised money for handicapped people). Geesink responded to none of them except to say that his judo association wouldn't allow the contest. This was not true. The papers all carried interviews with Dutch Judo Federation leaders and they said they would not stop Geesink from meeting anyone in a judo match. Only after I challenged him to an open bout in a boxing ring did he say that he would not fight me because I could break bricks and kick through concrete blocks.

I had trained with Geesink in Japan. When he came to the Kodokan in February 1961, we were filmed and you can see him on the right side of the dojo and me on the left. I always had deep respect for his judo skills. I tried hard to be friends with him, too, but as a person he often wasn't very nice, especially in money matters. As a result, most of his students and friends eventually left him. Most of the people who sided with him then are my friends now.

When I returned to Holland in November 1961, I was supposed to participate in the world judo championships in Paris. Because of all the politics involved, most of which had to do with other people making money, I was kept from competing. When I complained, people told me that I should stop complaining because complaining was destructive. Eventually I stopped, of course, but thinking about it still makes me mad. I worked so hard and since I couldn't compete, so much of that effort was wasted.

Ineligible to compete because of organization politics, I started coaching. My most famous student was Willem Ruska, who won two Olympic and three world championships. I worked with Ruska from December 1961, when he was just a 3rd kyu, until May 1964, by which time he was a 2nd dan. Then I kicked him out of my dojo. The reason for my action was mentioned in a letter I wrote to Donn Draeger. Donn was outraged and showed the letter to Kano Risei, who was the head of the Japan Judo Federation and the Kodokan. As a result, Ruska wasn't allowed to train at the Kodokan anymore. Maybe Donn shouldn't have shown the letter to Kano, but it happened and Ruska has been mad at me ever since.

The funny part though, is that after leaving me, Ruska started training with Geesink. They had a falling out a couple years later and today Ruska says worse thing about Geesink than he does of me!

In 1963, I started my own dojo, the Budokai, in Amsterdam where I taught judo and karate. While judo is a sport, anything goes in my karate classes. I don't mean that you try to intentionally hurt your training partners, but that you become an all-round fighting machine using only the tools given you at birth. While the sissies and con men say otherwise, what they teach is not karate. That is only something they call karate so that they can line their pockets. In my karate classes, you learn to hit, kick, defend, throw, and wrestle. With gloves and headgear, you can really blast away and still not change the other fellow's face so that his mother doesn't recognize him. As for the hard low kicks, you train your shins to be as hard as your fists, then learn to block using your knees and legs. Pain is present in any sport and, at least in ours, you also learn how to defend yourself.

When I showed my system to Oyama in 1966, he was shocked. While I'm the first to admit that what I do isn't perfect, I haven't met anyone who has anything better. Oyama evidently agreed, as his biggest worry was that someone would find out.

Oyama Masutatsu Stories

In the past, I've avoided discussing the "famous" Kyokushin Kaikan karate business. I needed some time to think about saying anything now, too, as I wanted to be strictly honest toward the memory of my old friend and teacher, Mas Oyama. He did a lot for me, introducing me to the karate world and giving me a new purpose in life. This changed my life completely for the best. For me, Oyama was like a father I never had. In the old days, he showed me all the things you need to be a teacher and helped me through some rough times. On the other hand, I am tired of all the phonies who did not go the straight way.

Bluming training with future Olympic champion
Inokuma Isao in 1961. The two men remain friends today.

So, let me tell it like it was.

Published accounts describing Oyama preparing for the big karate championships in 1947 are very funny. Especially the Americans, who fought the Japanese in World War II, should know that. MacArthur was the big honcho in Japan from August 1945, until the Korean War, and he declared right away that there was to be no more budo in Japan until he declared otherwise. He even rounded up all the samurai swords he could lay his hands on and had them dropped in Tokyo Bay. They would be worth hundreds of millions of dollars today. He was not messing around and nobody dared disobey his rules.

Around 1948, judo started again at the old Kodokan on Suidobashi. Karate was done mainly by the Shotokan, where sparring matches were not allowed until the late 1950s, and by the Goju-Kai and Wado-ryu, where the sparring was so soft that a split lip or a nose bleed would throw the officials into a state of shock. So while there might have been some professional boxing clubs where fighting was done on a knockout basis, a karate championship in Kyoto done on such a basis was absolutely out of the question.

When hearing stories about the old days, remember that the Japanese are great storytellers. If the story is good, they don't check to see if it is true. Even today, I meet people who heard from their fathers or grandfathers about the roughhousing I supposedly did in my younger days. It doesn't amaze me anymore and I am tired of telling people that the stories are impossible because if you hit somebody, you were hauled into a police station, charged, and sent to jail or kicked out of the country. I admit I had a few fights, but always with witnesses saying that I did not start it.

As for Oyama's alleged 270 American bouts, remember that he was in the States as a professional wrestler. Since when are professional wrestling matches on the level? All Oyama ever told me about those days was that Americans were crazy, that their wrestling was phony and prearranged, and that as fighters, they were weak. My guess is that most of what he did was just break bricks and things between matches. If he had ever fought any of the American professional wrestlers, really fought them, I think he would have beaten most of them easily.

The story about Oyama fighting bulls is not true. He never met a real bull, for he never visited Spain. I also doubt that he was gored, for he never told me about it and he used to tell me everything. Kurosaki Kenji was there and he told me what happened. They went early in the morning to a stockyard in Tateyama Prefecture. Workmen prepared a fat old ox for Oyama by hitting one of its horns with a hammer so that it was quite loose. Oyama did not kill the ox, he only knocked off the loose horn.

Oyama showed Bill Backhus and I the 16mm "bull fighting" movie in 1959. I told Oyama never to show this film in Europe because it looked too phony and everyone would laugh at him. As far as I know, nobody saw that movie again.

Even Oyama's famous world championship of the 1970s were a joke. By then, foreigners were not allowed to win. To prevent it, Oyama had all the gaijin fight each other first, and of course pitted the best against each other. Because everyone wanted to win, the injuries were terrible. Meanwhile, he put the leading Japanese against low quality Japanese from his own school, who knew their place and of course didn't try too hard. So they had it easy.

Occasionally, in the finals, the referee would give a good foreign fighter a decision over a Japanese fighter. Oyama would stand up all red in the face. Then he'd call the referee over to his table and chew him out and reverse his decision. This was against all the rules of sportsmanship. Read Nakamura Tadashi's book or go talk to him in New York. It is very emotional and very sad.

Oyama was a strong man in his young days, but I never saw him fight anybody, not even in his own dojo. So his "countless encounters" and "challenges" were all before my time. Kurosaki Kenji tells me that they were all before his time, too, and that goes back to 1952, when they both trained at Yamaguchi Gogen's dojo in Tokyo. So I think maybe he never fought in his life.

But he was a great teacher who trained many good fighters and his books were very popular. When I read his first book, *What Is Karate?* (1957), I was really impressed. I was in his second book (*This Is Karate*, 1965) and had the opportunity to look into the way he did things.

Breaking Tricks

The thing that amazed me most was "the monkey business" (Oyama's own words) involved in the breaking tricks. I didn't know about this when I did my first breaking demonstration in Holland. Since I had read in Oyama's book, *What Is Karate?*, about somebody breaking twenty-five roofing tiles at once, I simply brought some tiles I had found along the road. I thought that twenty-five sounded like a lot, for these things were heavy and felt strong. So I only put eight on top of each other and gave it my best. I made it but nearly broke my wrist. Of course I wondered how that kid managed twenty-five.

Well, I found out while working on the book, *This Is Karate*. I went to the pile of tiles they had prepared for punishment and picked up the top tile. It felt like paper, it was so light, and on its underside was a baked-in line along the length of the tile. So the middle of the tile was maybe a millimeter thick. No wonder a 110-pound chicken could go through twenty-five of them!

The bricks were no different. They were specially baked and if someone leaned on them they would crumble. His wood was also very lightweight. As for that famous bottle trick, first you prepare the bottle by rolling a sharp stone around the bottle's neck. That way when you hit it, it breaks along the carved line.

Kurosaki Kenji was the only one who really impressed me with his breaking tricks. Using his head, he broke two red bricks from British television. The nasty cracking sound horrified everybody watching. I was a good breaker, too, but I paid the price for my mistakes. Which brings me to the ice-breaking trick. When you break ice blocks, be careful. If you aren't, you'll hit the edge of the ice with your wrist rather than your *shuto* (knife-hand) and break your wrist instead of the ice. This happened to me in 1975. During a demonstration, Loek Hollander had arranged for each of us to break several big blocks of ice. What I did not know until years later is that he had arranged for workmen to cut his blocks almost in half using diamond strings and then refreeze them so that nobody would notice the cuts. On the other hand, my blocks were solid. Anyway, Loek broke his three blocks so easily that I forgot the rule about the wrist and immediately broke the little bone under my wrist. I was so angry that right away I hit again and went through the ice anyway. I was in a plaster cast for the next six weeks.

Bluming at his peak: 1961 summer Olympic training at the Kodokan.

The Budokai

As I said before, in 1963 I opened my own budo club called the Budokai. Kurosaka Kenji came over in 1966, about the time Oyama started calling himself "the Godhand." Even the Japanese press laughs at that one. In 1990, we changed the club's name to Kyokushin Budokai and, in 1966, some friends and I renamed it the International Budokaikan. Today it has many associated clubs and some real good fighters.

In the Budokai we teach no kata, only fighting. Excepting Donn Draeger, I've never known a kata champion who could beat by grandmother in randori if she had her umbrella. To keep injuries down, we provide students with a lot of coaching and supervision. But, as the Japanese method of slapping people into line doesn't work in Europe, we don't make anyone do anything he doesn't want to do. Therefore, the standards are only as high as the individual makes them. Which can be very high, as the teams we send to full-contact tournaments usually win. For instance, in Tokyo in 1993, Chris Dolmen, our only 9th dan, became the first world champion in "free fighting." From 1994 to 1997, Budokai teams won the Japanese All-Round Karate Championships in Tokyo. As a result, the Japanese no longer allow us to compete.

Unfortunately, there isn't much money in teaching budo this way. Today I'm retired, but to earn a living when I was younger, I took a fifteen percent partnership in a casino. The work kept me very busy, especially at night. I acted in seven movies, too, but the movies pay poorly in Holland so eventually I quit. Between the workload and the political squalor within the European Kyokushin Kaikan, in 1971, I told Oyama that I was too busy to lead the organization and to give the job to Loek Hollander. Oyama was really upset. He pleaded with me, but I wanted to stop. Finally he gave in and Hollander got the job. Hollander then went and filled his pockets and killed the Kyokushin Kaikan. I now think that giving up the leadership to Hollander was the stupidest thing I ever did in my entire life.

In 1976, some buddies and I were in Korea getting decorated for our service during the war. Afterwards, my wife and I went to Tokyo where I visited the Kyokushinkai honbu dojo for the first time in years.

On the street in front were guards. The place looked like a yakuza headquarters—and for all I know, it is. Although he called himself "the Godhand," everybody else called Oyama "Mr. Ten Percent." This was due to his relations with various politicians and businessmen, including one *Time* magazine called the Godfather of Japan. In the "young lions" of Mas Oyama's Kyokushin Karate Headquarters (1985), Necef Artan tells how Oyama's students spent four hours a day going through Tokyo "asking shopkeepers to display posters in their windows." Such activities would be protected rackets in Europe or America. But in Japan, politics and the yakuza are like a hand and a glove on a very cold day and one never does business without the other.

Anyway, I went in the door and up the stairs to Oyama's office. Although Oyama wasn't there, the old memories came back and I got all choked up. The young black belts posted as guards obviously didn't recognize me, even though my picture was hanging on the wall. One went to stop me, so I gave him my best cold look and told him in Japanese who I was and added that if he touched me he would be a cripple instantly. The poor kid nearly had a heart attack, as Oyama had told them all kinds of stories about me. When I left, some of the kids touched my arm or shoulder and said they were honored.

I talked to Oyama on the phone later the same day and afterward we ate dinner at an expensive Kobe beef restaurant. When Oyama went to wash his hands, his wife told me that he wanted me back with the Kyokushin Kaikan. So when he returned, we talked and I told him I would try again if he would first get rid of Loek Hollander. He wouldn't and that was that.

The last time I saw Oyama alive was in 1983. I was visiting Korea and a Korean general asked me what I did for work. When I told him, he said that he had a friend visiting from Japan who was a famous karate teacher named Oyama. Surprised, I told him my story. The general laughed and said, "Now I know why your name was familiar—you're Bluming, the Beast from Amsterdam!"

Then he called Oyama and arranged for us to meet. The old man was really glad to see me and we had a good talk. He said he would send me a first class airline ticket so that I could come to Tokyo the following year. He even agreed to get rid of Loek Hollander. But in November 1983, I got a letter from the Kyokushin Kaikan saying that it did not want me back, and that I should look after my own business. It seems that Loek Hollander had told Oyama at a world conference that I was a gangster and had held up a bank with a drawn pistol. Now I admit that I was a partner in a casino, but that's hardly the same as being a gangster. What's more, if I were robbing banks with drawn pistols, then I wouldn't have been selected to serve as an honorary bodyguard for Dutch Prince Bernhard in 1986, 1991, and 1996. But anyway, Oyama believed Hollander's story, as have a lot of other people.

Bluming (far right) acting as bodyguard for the Dutch royal family in 1961. The blond man in front of Bluming is Crown Prince Alexander. The man with the white flower in his lapel is Prince Bernhard.

Shortly before his death, Oyama discovered that I'd been right and Loek Hallander had been wrong. That's why today you'll find no articles about Loek Hollander or a picture with his name under it in any of the Japanese budo magazines: Oyama forbade it. To make things right, Oyama even sent Maeda Akira, 7th dan, to Holland in the autumn of 1993. In April 1994, I was scheduled to go to Tokyo to talk to Oyama when I received a fax saying that he had just died of cancer. I cried and cried. I was so sad, angry, and frustrated.

During the following months, I had several meetings with the new Kyokushin Kaikan leaders. Loek Hallander was still there and he and his cronies still struck me as more interested in money than in budo. Meanwhile, the Japanese walked and talked like the hottest things on earth—and still couldn't put together a team that could win against shoot-boxing, which in my eyes is a very weak kind of freestyle fighting. So that was the end of that.

As for Mas Oyama, in the teaching of the Buddha it is written, "Can a student be angry with his teacher?" The more devoted the student, the more privileges he has! But those privileges do not include lies. To a stranger I might sound bitter but I am not. Mas Oyama turned my life around, all for the best. He had a good heart and was an excellent teacher. As for everything else, I wish the politics in the various judo and karate organizations would have been less. I wish I'd been born a better diplomat, as maybe that would have helped. I wish Oyama hadn't died, as his death means I can't talk to him anymore, or tell him the love I still have for him because of the old days. I wish the Japanese weren't so nationalistic and conceited, and that they would have given Donn Draeger the credit he deserved as a teacher, coach, fighter, and writer. What makes me saddest, though, is to have to admit that so much of what passes for budo is really nothing more than monkey business.

When I was promoted to 10th dan, everyone stood there waiting for me to write a poem. This was my poem:

Without kokoro [spirit], budo is but an empty shell.

index

active breaking, 142-144, 146
aikido, 14, 20, 25, 123, 176, 187
air compression theory, 93
All-Japan Karatedo Association, 141
All-Okinawan Goju-Kai, 84-85, 237
All-Okinawa Karate and Kobudo
    Combined Association, 174
All Okinawan Karatedo Federation, 84
Aragaki, Ryuko, 78, 152-153
Arakaki, Ankichi, 180
archery (*kyudo*), 18, 20, 25, 194 note 12
artifacts, 1-2, 4-5
Backhus, Bill, 232-234, 238
basic karate fist (*seiken*), 58, 144, 177, 225
Battle of Sekigahara, 18
boat oar (*kai, ekku, iyeku*), 7, 102, 179
bola (*suruchin*), 5, 9, 102
Book of Five Rings (Go Rin No Sho), 19
"brass knuckles" (*tekko*), 102
breath/spirit harmonizing, 93-94, 144
Bryner, Robert, 196 note 21
Bubishi, 1, 5, 24, 82
Bugeikan, 183
bushido, 15, 17-19, 23-24, 28, 31-33, 40
challenge match (*kakidameshi*), 189
Chinese hand (*tode*), 15-16, 23, 69,
    170-171, 174, 176, 192, 194 note 6, 195
Chinese kempo, 2-3, 78-79, 82, 183
Chibana, Choshin, 71, 83-84
Confucianism, 18, 21, 66-67, 69
cross-power theory, 90-91, 93, 97
Dai Nippon Butokukai (Greater Japan
    Martial Arts Association), 82-84
Dai Nippon Butokukai Karate Jukkyoshi
    (Greater Japan Martial Arts Karate
    Teachers' Association), 83

Daoism, 21
dojo ethics (*dojo kun*), 25, 35, 219-220
Draeger, Donn, 20, 231-236, 240, 243
European Kyokushin Kaikan, 241
Evans, Gerald, 13
Exhibit Hall of Okinawan Karate, 1-12
Fang, Chiliang, 79
Federation of Okinawan Karate and
    Kobudo Organizations, 174
fencing (*kendo*), 19, 25, 83, 182
focus (*kime*), 147
folklore, 2-3
foot fist (*sokusen*), 59-61
fracture, 46-47, 198-200
full-contact training (*jissen*), 207-209,
    217-218, 220, 222-223, 227-228, 240
Fujian Province, 23, 78-79, 183, 193 note 4
Funakoshi, Gichin, 15-17, 24-27, 31-32, 34,
    37-38, 71, 180, 203-204
Funakoshi's twenty guiding principles
    (*shoto niju kun*), 26, 34-35
Fushinomiya, Prince, 68
Garyu kata, 215
Geesink, Anton, 135-136
Gekisai-dai kata, 215
Gekisai-Ichi kata, 80, 82
Gekisai-Ni kata, 80, 82
Gekisai-sho kata, 215
Goju-ryu, 3, 11, 54, 72, 76-86, 151-154,
    156, 164-167, 169, 204
Goju-ryu Shinkokai, 83
Gojushiho kata, 95
Gokenki, 79
gripping jars (*nigirigame, kami*), 78, 85, 152,
    163-164, 166
ground-fighting, 177

Hakutsuru Ken (White Crane), 79
Hanashiro, Chomo, 63, 68, 71, 83, 172, 175
hand conditioning container (*sunabako*), 10
Higa, Seiko, 80, 83-84
Higa, Seitoku, 183
Higashionna (Higaonna), Kanryo, 67, 77-81, 85-86, 152
Hirohito, Crown Prince, 25, 81
hoe (*kuwa*), 102
Hokama, Tetsuhiro, 2-6, 8, 10-12
Hollander, Loek, 239, 241-242
iaido, 25
Ikeda, Horitoshi, 185
injury, 30-31, 45-47, 50, 126, 130, 144, 148, 150, 155, 161, 167, 176, 198, 200-202, 213, 217
International Budokaikan, 240
International Karate and Kobudo Federation, 84
International Karate Organization, 228
International Karate Organization (IKO) Kyokushinkaikan, 228-229
International Koei-Kan Karatedo Federation, 141, 143
iron clogs (*geta*), 10
Ishikawa, Masanobu, 185
Isshin-ryu, 133, 169
Itosu, Ankoh (Yasutsune), 24, 64-65, 67-70, 75 note 2, 174
Itosu's Ten Lessons, 69-70
Itto-ryu, 129
Japan Kobudo Association, 174
Jigen-ryu, 64
Jo-ryu Mai Te Gassen Karatekai, 183, 193 note 4
Jundokan, 84
Kamiunten, Fumiko, 185, 187-190, 195 note 20
Kaneshima, Shinyei, 175
Kanku kata, 203, 215

Kano, Jigoro, 25, 29, 38, 81-82, 152-153, 236
Karate-Do Preservation Society, 83
Kassen-te, 190
Kim, Richard, 63, 74
Kimura, Mits, 231
Kinjo, Hiroshi, 63-65, 68, 71-72, 74-75
Kinjo, Takashi, 62
Kiyoda, Juhatsu, 65
Kojo-ryu, 193 note 4
Kodokan, 25, 231-232, 235-237, 240
Konishi, Yasuhiro, 175
Kurosaki, Kenji, 238-239
Kururunfa kata, 80
Kusanku kata, 136-138
Kuwae, Ryosei, 64, 67
Kyan, Chotoku, 71, 170
Kyokushin, 203, 206-211, 215-218, 222-223, 225-228, 230, 234-236, 240-243
Lee, Bruce, 6
long staff (*bo*), 3, 5, 7-9, 68, 75, 82, 102, 153, 179, 215
Mabuni, Kenwa, 71, 170
Maeda, Akira, 272
mai-nu-di, 178-179
manji sai, 102-103
martial sport, 14-15, 20, 23, 27, 35, 37, 40-41, 53, 55, 64, 74, 80, 117, 182, 234, 236, 238
Nakayama, Masatoshi, 24, 26-28, 234
Maeshiro, Choryo, 71
Matayoshi, Shinko, 102
Matayoshi, Shinpo, 8, 102
martial dance (*moudi*), 7, 176, 178, 180-182, 195 notes 13 and 14, 179
Matsumura, Bushi, 64
Matsumura, Sokon, 7-8, 24, 180
Matsumura, Kosaku, 174
Matsumura's Precepts on Bu, 66-67
Meibukan, 84
Mifune, Kyuzo, 231-232

Mimoun, Bonlahfa, 196 note 21
Miyagi, Chojun, 71-72, 76-86, 151-156, 167, 170
Miyahira, Katsuya, 175
Miyazato, Eiichi, 76, 80
Monaco, Michael, 207
Moromizato, Shinsuke, 186, 190
Moromizato, Shinzato, 183
Motobu Association, 185
Motobu, Choki, 83, 170, 173-175, 185, 187
Motobu, Choyu, 170-175
Motobu-ryu, 169-170, 172-173, 175-178, 181, 183, 185, 187, 189-190
Motobu-ryu Udun-di Kobujutsu Association, 195 note 20
Munenori, Yagyu, 14, 119
Nagamine, Shoshin, 175
Naha-te, 3, 77-82, 85, 152, 169, 188-189, 193 note 4
Naihanchi Shodan, 95, 98-100
Nakama, Chozo, 175
Nakasone, Genwa, 68, 71
Nashimoto, Prince Moriwasa, 83
Nishiuchi, Mikio, 52, 102-103, 110-111
Nishiyama, Hidetaka, 26, 34
Nozaki, Yukikazu, 183, 185-186
nunchaku, 5-6, 102, 179
Obata, Isao, 234
Okazaki, Teruyuki, 26, 34
Okinawan dance (*odori*), 7, 178
Okinawan Goju-ryu Kenshi-kai, 3
Okinawan Goju-ryu Shobukan Association, 85, 153, 164
Okinawa Prefectural Karatedo Federation, 174
Okinawa Tode Research Club, 170
Okinawan weapons, 2-3, 5-9, 69, 101-103, 105-106, 115, 169, 176, 178, 181-183, 188-189, 191
one-knuckle punch (*shohken-zuki*), 56-59

Onishi, Eizo, 141-142
Oshiro, Chojo, 63-64, 68, 170
Oyama, Mas (Masutatsu), 203-211, 227-230, 234-243
passive breaking, 143-145, 148
pechin officials, 75 note 3, 174
Pinan I-V katas, 215
police, 79, 82-84, 103-104, 187, 231, 238
precepts of shuhari, 72-73
protective gear (*bogu*), 182-183, 209, 220
punching post (makiwara), 44-50, 58, 61, 69, 78, 144, 148-149, 152, 174, 177, 199, 205, 216-217, 234
Pwang Gai Noon-ryu, 52-55, 58-59, 61-62
ranking, 30, 80-81, 83-84, 190, 227
Renbukan, 183
respiration theory, 91-94
Rikkyo University, 234
Ritsumeikan University, 82-83
rocks in a net (*ishibukro*), 10, 164-165
Ryu Ryu Ko, 78-79
sai, 5, 9, 101-115, 176, 179
Saifa kata, 80, 215
Sakugawa, Kanga, 3, 8
samurai sword (*katana*), 32, 183
Sanchin kata, 11, 53-54, 78, 80-81, 85, 133, 143, 152-153, 164, 215, 225-226
Sanseiru kata, 80
school clothing (*gi*), 29, 221
Seidokan, 183, 196
Seienchin kata, 80, 215
Seipai kata, 80, 215
Seisan kata, 80
self-development, 14, 16-17, 19, 35, 37-40
shield (*timbei*), 102
Shikiyanaka, Chinen, 68
Shimabukuro, Takashi, 185
Shinjo, Masanobu, 84-86, 153-154
Shinpan, Shiroma (Gusukuma), 71, 83
Shinto, 18, 21

Shinzato, Jinan, 82-84
Shisochin kata, 80
Shiroma, Seihan, 183
Shito-ryu, 71, 169
Sho Shin-O, King, 194 notes 10 and 12
Shorikan, 84
Shorin-ryu, 8, 95, 98, 169
Shotokan, 15, 25-26, 233-234, 237
Shuri-te, 3, 82, 98, 169, 188-189
sickles (*kama*), 102, 179
social relationships, 13-14, 19, 27-30, 174, 194 note 10
Soku-dai I-III katas, 215
stone lever weight (*chishi*), 10, 152, 157-164, 166
stone padlocks (*sushi*), 10
stone weight (*sashiishi*), 11
Supairenpei kata, 80-81
Sushiho kata, 215
swordsmanship (*kenjutsu*), 19, 64, 118, 126, 129, 142
Taba, Seiichi, 183
Takushoku University Karate Club, 26, 203
tameshiwari (breaking), 32, 141-150, 203, 210, 223-226
Tanaka, Masahiko, 13
Taikyoku I-III katas, 215
te, 2-3, 5, 15-16, 23-24, 32, 169-170, 172, 174, 178, 182-183, 188-190, 193 note 1
Tensho (turning palm) kata, 80, 215
tetchu, 102
theory of opposites, 89-90
three-sectional staff (*san-setsu-kon*), 102
Toguchi, Seikichi, 76, 80, 83, 85
Tokugawa, Ieyesu, 18
Tokumine, Pechin, 174
Toma, Shian, 183, 196 note 21
Tomari-te, 3, 82, 169, 193 note 4
tonfa (also pronounced *tuifa, tungua*, or *tunkua*, 102, 176, 179, 215

Tsuki No Kata, 215
tunfa (*tunkwa*), 5, 8
Uechi, Kanbun, 62, 172
Uechi, Kanei, 62
Uechi-ryu, 62, 172, 194 note 4
Uehara, Hideko, 185
Uehara, Seikichi, 169-175, 181, 183, 185
Uehara, Tsuyoshi, 187
Ueshiba, Morihei, 14
Wado-ryu, 237
weightlifting, 149, 234
weapons ban, 3, 23, 102
weapons use (*kobujutsu*), 3, 174, 176, 179, 195 note 20
White Crane (Hakutsuru Ken), 79-80
World War II, 82, 205
wrist roller *(makiage kiga)*, 10
Yabu, Kentsu, 71, 75 note 1, 83, 170, 175
Yagi, Meitoku, 76, 80-81, 85
Yaguchi, Yutaka, 41
Yamaguchi, Gogen, 80-81, 239
Yamane no Chinen Sanda, 75 note 2
Yamashita, Yoshikazu, 231
Yamate-ryu, 123
Yantsu kata, 215
Yasuhito, Chichibu, Prince, 81
Yogi, Jitsuei, 80
Zen Buddhism, 14-17, 19-23, 26, 28, 33-37, 39-40, 69, 73, 92, 119
Zen Nihon Kendo Renmei, 102

Printed in Great Britain
by Amazon

63149898R00141